COOPERATIVE LEARNING

COOPERATIVE LEARNING
Critical Thinking and Collaboration Across the Curriculum

Second Edition

By

DENNIS ADAMS

MARY HAMM

With the Collaboration of

Martha Drobnak and Althier Lazar

CHARLES C THOMAS • PUBLISHER
Springfield • Illinois • U.S.A.

Published and Distributed Throughout the World by

CHARLES C THOMAS • PUBLISHER
2600 South First Street
Springfield, Illinois 62794-9265

© *1996 by* CHARLES C THOMAS • PUBLISHER

ISBN 0-398-06587-X (cloth)
ISBN 0-398-06588-8 (paper)

Library of Congress Catalog Card Number: 95-48390

Printed in the United States of America
SC-R-3

Library of Congress Cataloging-in-Publication Data

Adams, Dennis M.
   Cooperative learning : critical thinking and collaboration across
the curriculum / by Dennis M. Adams, Mary Hamm, with the collaboration
of Martha Drobnak and Althier Lazar. — 2nd ed.
     p.   cm.
   Includes bibliographical references and index.
   ISBN 0-398-06587-X. — ISBN 0-398-06588-8 (pbk.)
   1. Team learning approach in education.   2. Group work in
education.   3. Critical thinking.   I. Hamm, Mary.   II. Title.
LB1032.A33   1996
371.3'95—dc20
                                                 95-48390
                                                    CIP

PREFACE

This book is designed to help teachers plan collaborative learning experiences in a way that makes a difference in the lives of their students. We take a close look at the issues, trends, and practical teaching concerns that surround cooperative learning and put forward specific content area lessons for teachers who would like to become more familiar with active team learning in the classroom. Although the concepts are applicable across all grade levels, the activities are most appropriate for elementary and middle school learners. Major themes include collaborative approaches to "old basics" of reading, writing, and mathematics. We also explore the possibilities for cooperative learning in the "new basics" of science, the arts, and technology. In addition there is a chapter on assessment and another on the inclusion of special needs students.

The book builds on the research while trying to avoid an academic journal approach that breaks the narrative up with countless references and text that is not interesting to a general audience. Every effort is made to make reading inviting for teachers, parents, administrators, workshop leaders, curriculum developers, and evaluators. Our major goal is to help preservice and inservice teachers learn how to teach important concepts through cooperative learning. As a teacher you should not hesitate to select out, copy activities, and adapt ideas and suggestions that you feel are most helpful for your students. The text is arranged so that you may enter any of the areas covered and quickly pull out specific ideas for your classroom.

Our approach to cooperative learning has been developed over a decade of work with teacher training courses and in-service workshops with teachers interested in active collaborative possibilities for restructuring classrooms and reinvigorating the curriculum. This book incorporates that practical background and examines cooperative groups in light of new subject matter standards and national goals. On a national level, *Goals 2000* has been in operation for only a couple of years. Although it is taking hold across the country, there has been some discussion in Congress of removing federal incentives for encouraging the states to fashion world class standards. A 1995 study by the American Federation of Teachers, *Making Standards Matter,* points out that federal budget cutting will hurt the chance to reform our educational system and raise the achievement of all of our students. However, the same report points out that with or without national support, 49 of the 50 states are already revising their own standards in a way that does not contradict national goals or new curriculum standards. At the very least, there is "a broad consensus that standards do matter and are the foundation for improving student achievement."

Although the focus here is on cooperative learning as a strategy for asic academic achievement, we recognize the potential for influencing civic competency and fostering a democratic way of life. Social studies stands as an important subject on its own field of study in its own right; however, concerns often associated with the subject should permeate all the basic subject areas. As Thomas Jefferson suggested, "the main purpose of education is to prepare productive citizens in a democracy." As things stand today, far too many students are leaving school without being literate enough to be productive and without an understanding of the rights and responsibility of citizenship.

This book is designed to enhance instruction by connecting cooperative learning to thought-provoking academic activities. Rather than deal with every issue related to cooperative learning, the emphasis is on selected concepts and teaching strategies for the core subject areas. By jointly searching for information, knowledge, and understanding, we believe that students can actively learn together as they think about and experience their subjects. To develop students who can collaboratively and creatively link content area subjects requires teachers who can do the same. The quality of top teachers has always been one of *invitation;* inviting students to join them in reaching out to an interpretive horizon of possibility.

Using collaborative learning activities means structuring student interaction in small mixed-ability groups, encouraging mutual interdependence, and providing for individual accountability. In this atmosphere of mutual helpfulness, students are supposed to talk to one another as they try to resolve issues through face-to-face discussion. By taking part in cooperative experiences, students are encouraged to learn by assimilating their ideas and creating new knowledge through interaction with others. The teacher organizes the classroom, teaches social skills, encourages critical thinking, and responds to emerging insights.

Interest in collaborative models is growing rapidly as reliable research evidence increasingly points to cooperative learning as promising practice for improving social skills and academic instruction. Even the Associated Press contributed to the trend by sending out a story to newspapers around the country that referred to cooperative learning as "the wave of the future" in education. There is little question about the power of cooperative learning and the potential of learning teams for helping create a community of learners. The biggest argument over its use seems to be coming from proponents who favor different methods of implementation.

CONTENTS

COOPERATIVE LEARNING

Chapter 1

CLASSROOM/SCHOOL COLLABORATION:
The Shared Responsibility of Cooperative Learning

What children can do together today, they can do alone tomorrow.
— Vygotsky

Cooperative learning involves working together to accomplish shared goals that are beneficial to individuals and the group. Students are able to learn together *and* perform alone within an environment that allows them to actively construct knowledge. In the cooperative classroom (or school), communal responsibility and civic engagement are not viewed as optional extras. When everyone is involved, cooperation can become part of the fabric of schooling at every level.

Building team-based organizational structures in the classroom can make it easier for teachers to reach out to *their* peers and ensure that colleagues are successful. More than other innovations, cooperative learning can change school climate by encouraging cooperation, cohesion, and teamwork. Teachers who are new to the technique can learn a great deal from peers who have preceded them. The whole process can even contribute to collegial teams and help establish a true learning community for teachers. Whether or not collaboration reaches beyond the classroom, teachers can use many cooperative learning methods with their classes.

A common element in successful classes and successful schools is a shared sense of community and a socially integrating sense of purpose. Shared common interests and common ground make for better civil discussions than a school or community culture that places an absolute value on individual choice and unconditional rights. Schools, like the community in general, need common spaces where people meet and share a life in common. When there is no limit on individual self-realization, public spaces decay and civic culture is weakened. As teachers develop their skills with cooperative learning, they can foster quality common spaces and encourage civic conversation across group lines.

When it comes to individual classrooms, teachers are beginning to

3

proces

recognize that cooperative learning is more than having students cooperate in a group activity or project. Cooperative groups employ a set of strategies to encourage having students to cooperate while learning in a variety of settings and disciplines—at different grade levels. The process involves: promoting positive interdependence by dividing the workload, providing joint rewards, holding individuals accountable, and getting students actively involved in helping each other master the topic being studied.

Cooperative learning is one of the success stories of educational reform. It has solid teacher support and a favorable research base. Researchers have also commented on how cooperative learning improves problem-solving skills and attitudes towards learning (Tobin, K. G., 1990). More and more teachers are incorporating the concept of group work (with individual accountability) into their classrooms. It is also becoming common to see suggestions for active learning teams in new content standards and classroom designs.

Collaboration and Connecting Standards to the Classroom

Underlying the more general "opportunity to learn" and "delivery" standards of *Goals 2000* legislation is the concept of students working together to gain a powerful understanding of how strands of content can be integrated and synthesized. Unlike some earlier innovations, cooperative learning has shown real staying power and has been incorporated into *content standards* that spell out the knowledge and skills that students should have and *performance standards* that suggest actual performance levels that students should reach.

Cooperative learning has permeated the standards projects and teacher training from the preservice to the inservice level. The NCTM mathematics standards, for example, fall into four broad categories: problem solving, communication, reasoning, and mathematical connections. All of the categories leave space for collaboration. In addition, cooperative learning is one of several approaches and methods that have been consistently supported by the research across the curriculum (Davidson, 1990). As teachers learn when and how to structure instruction cooperatively, the process transforms itself from a hot new method into a routine part of instruction. Whether it's the school, the community, or the nation, there is nothing more powerful than an idea whose time has come. And, when it comes to education, cooperative learning is one of those ideas.

As with other parts of the curriculum, cooperative learning must be fashioned with a sensitivity to how students develop interpersonal skills that lend themselves to connecting content areas. By working in pairs or

The National Education Goals in Brief

By the year 2000:

- **All Children Ready to Learn**

- **90 percent Graduation Rate**

- **All Children Competent in Core Subjects**

- **First in the World in Math and Science**

- **Every Adult Literate and Able to Compete in the Work Force**

- **Safe, Disciplined, Drug-free Schools**

- **Professional Development for Educators**

- **Increased Parental Involvement in Learning**

mixed-ability small groups to help each other learn, students learn academic content while taking more responsibility for their own learning. There is a growing consensus that active team learning can enrich the curriculum.

Increasingly, group work revolves around inquiry, problem-solving, literature, poetry, journal writing, art projects, drama, and song compo-

to minority [handwritten margin note]

sition. Within new learning environments, collaboration can help produce instruction that enhances critical thinking across many domains. Cooperative learning can also help integrate minority children and students with special needs into the regular classroom. In her unpublished research, Mary McArdle reports that as students show more willingness to interact and reward others there is more lasting cross-cultural friendship and more acceptance of students with disabilities.

Encouraging Student Work Teams

Getting started with cooperative learning means defining student and teacher responsibilities. One of the first steps is usually preparing students to work together. Another beginning concern is organizing the classroom so that it is easier for students to develop and practice group process skills. Cooperative learning will not take place with students sitting in rows facing the teacher. Desks must be pushed together in small groups or replaced with small tables to facilitate group interaction. Resource and hands-on materials must be made readily accessible. Collaboration will not occur in a classroom which requires students to raise their hands to talk or move out of their desks. Responsible behavior needs to be developed and encouraged. Authoritarian approaches to discipline will not work if we are expecting students to be responsible for their own learning and behavior.

basic assumption [handwritten margin note]

Changing the classroom organization so that students are eye-to-eye and knee-to-knee probably requires change in the physical structure. This may mean adding work tables or pushing chairs together to form comfortable work spaces that are conducive to open communication. Other changes involve the noise level in the room. Sharing and working together even in controlled environments will be louder than an environment where students work silently from textbooks. Teachers need to learn to evaluate whether noise is constructive.

When the initial activity or problem-solving is over, students need to spend time reflecting on the group work. A basic question at the end: *What worked well and how might the process be improved?* This kind of frequent group processing can improve future effectiveness. Evaluating cooperative learning necessitates a variety of procedures. Learning outcomes will undoubtedly continue to be measured by such instruments as standardized tests, quizzes, and written exams. In addition, cooperative learning demands subjective measures. Students and teachers need to be involved in evaluating learning products and the learning climate. The learning climate involves such things as self-esteem, individual and group achievement, discipline, cooperation, values, expression, and learning together.

Effective interpersonal skills are not just for a cooperative learning activity; they also benefit students in later educational pursuits and when they enter the work force. In organizing two-, three-, four-, or five-member cooperative groups it is best to try and organize as heterogeneously as possible. We suggest not going beyond five students in a group. If you are forming a partnership (two students), you might consider having everyone put down the four people that they would most like to work with, turn their choices in, and the teacher picks the partners with the secret list in hand. (Everyone usually gets at least their number four choice.) Even a small group can mix children by gender, race, ethnic background, and academic ability.

Peer tutoring is a good way to introduce new vocabulary and new concepts and small group settings improve student concept acquisition for everyone. Many culturally diverse learners show extra gains in cognitive growth, self-esteem, and a changed attitude towards learning (Cohen, E.G., Lotan, R., and Catanzarite, L., 1990). Social interactions are fundamental to negotiating meaning and building a personal rendition of knowledge.

A wide range of culturally diverse learners seem to find cooperative learning activities more satisfying and useful than individual learning activities. They report a preference for groups or extended family settings as primary learning environments (Fields, S., 1988). Fields also suggests that cooperative learning fosters social skills, positive peer relationships, and higher levels of self-esteem in all students. As learning teams discuss science and mathematics, children can construct meaning by jointly working on solutions to problems, raising original problems, and exchanging ideas. In the process, subject matter can come alive as student teams connect the concepts being studied to their everyday experiences.

It is important to involve students in establishing rules for active group work. Rules should be kept simple and might include the following:

Everyone is responsible for his or her own work.
Productive talk is desired.
Each person is responsible for his or her own behavior.
Try to learn from others within your small group.
Everyone must be willing to help anyone who asks.
Ask the teacher for help if no one in the group can answer the question.

Group roles and individual responsibilities also need to be clearly defined and arranged so that each group members contribution is unique and essential. If the learning activities require materials, students may be required to take responsibility for assembling and storing them. The operative pronoun is "we" instead of "me."

Cooperative learning works best when all of the following elements are in place:

- **positive interdependence**
- **face-to-face interaction**
- **individual accountability**
- **personal responsibility for reaching group goals**
- **frequent practice with small-group interpersonal skills**
- **regular group processing and reflection**

Positive interdependence can develop when students recognize that they can reach their personal learning goals only when everyone in the group reaches their goals.

Face-to-face interaction involves student discussion, reasoned decision-making, and acting on suggestions that help each group member achieve individual and group goals.

Individual accountability means making sure that individuals take personal responsibility for doing a fair share of the group work. Individual tests may be given, personal portfolios developed, and teachers can observe students doing the task at hand or teaching what they have learned to someone else.

Interpersonal skills are needed for small group work where children need to know and respect one another. As teamwork skills develop, students are more likely to support each other and resolve conflicts constructively.

Group processing involves the small group reflecting on how well they worked together, what individual actions were helpful, and what might be done to improve the teamwork in the future. The combination of student and teacher processing is a way to put the focus on positive feedback and improve individual effectiveness in contributing to the achievement of group goals.

With these five essential elements in place, teachers can effectively make sure that students work cooperatively with classmates in a manner that helps small-group members get better together.

The Teacher Makes the Difference

Being a safe, pleasant place with new computers and plenty of instructional materials may all be important to the successful school.

However, for children to learn more, nothing counts as much as inspired and inspiring teachers. With cooperative learning, teachers have a powerful tool for teaching and learning. These structures and activities are not expected to replace all other teaching strategies. The intent is put into place a powerful alternative to devoting most of the school day to individualistic, competitive learning. In using these techniques, teachers are on safe ground conceptually, theoretically, and empirically. The research *and* teacher reports on cooperative learning have been consistently positive. Two heads, it seems, are often better than one when it comes to learning academic content.

[margin handwriting: basic intent of coop]

In a cooperative learning classroom, teachers need to provide time for students to grapple with problems, try out strategies, discuss, experiment, explore and evaluate. Having students *talk* about key concepts is as new to some teachers as having students work in *small cooperative groups*. National standards in the basic content areas encourage a break with tradition by encouraging teachers to put students in small groups where they can argue about key concepts and work on problems as a team. The primary focus is on the student's own investigations, discussions, and group projects. The teacher's role shifts to one analogous to that of a team coach or a manager with expertise in the area. Whatever approach a teacher takes to implementing cooperative learning in the classroom, there are certain shared characteristics. Students are given opportunities to integrate their learning through group discussion, discovery experiences, practice, and other group activities. In addition, any approach to cooperative learning usually incorporates group goals, individual accountability, and an equal opportunity for all group members to achieve success.

Teachers need to model attitudes and present themselves as problem solvers and models of inquiry. One way to do this is by letting students know that everyone is an active learner, and no one knows all the answers. Teachers also need to exhibit an interest in finding solutions to problems, show confidence in trying various strategies, and risk being wrong. It is more important to emphasize the aspect of *working on the problem* than getting "the answer." Near the end of an investigation, the teacher can develop more class unity by pointing out how each small group research effort contributes to the class goal of understanding and solving problems or exploring a topic. By creating a safe environment, where students are encouraged and affirmed, teachers can push the boundaries of the curriculum into new spaces.

The Social Nature of Learning

Cooperative learning builds on the idea that much of learning is social. Working in teams provides students with opportunities to talk and participate actively in classroom life. The teacher acts as a pilot, selecting meaningful topics for discussion, mapping out opportunities for collaboration, and observing the interaction of working groups. Students then work together to make connections between new ideas discussed in class and prior knowledge. As students are encouraged to jointly interpret and negotiate meaning, learning comes alive. Constructing meaningful explanations means giving students regular opportunities to talk, read, write, and solve problems together. Groups need time to share, clarify, suggest, and expand concepts. Starting with a student's own experiences and background knowledge, the process can move to one of a shared group idea or to a more elegant individual expression.

Unstructured interaction between peers relies heavily on shared experiences for understanding. Informal conversation with friends is often expressive, with feelings, beliefs, and opinions freely stated. The structure of such conversations can serve as a starting point for coming to terms with new ideas. Through informal conversation learners shape ideas, modify them by listening to others, question, plan, express doubt, and construct meaning. In the process, they feel free to express uncertainty and experiment with new language.

Talking to their peers about subject matter can enhance the learning process. Small group discussion also provides constant feedback within a supportive environment that allows individuals to become more at ease with sharing thoughts with others. This kind of expression can also help group members examine, compare and affix personal meaning to shared concepts or beliefs. By having a response group, students can place ideas into a personal and collective context. Through collective and individual work, ideas take shape and become more alive.

Whether teachers use cooperative learning to build respect for other points of view, supporting group members, offering constructive criticism, or learning academic material, *there's no better way to jump-start a stalled class.*

Cooperative Learning vs Individualized, Competitive Learning

Elementary school teachers have always used groups. But these groups were usually based on "ability," or some kind of skill hierarchy, like choosing teams. Individualized learning was different—and it had its usefulness. In traditional arrangements, each student worked at his or her own pace and was expected to be left alone by other students. It was sometimes possible for children to self-select appropriate material and pace themselves to complete a work assignment. With this approach the individual took on the responsibility for completing the task, sometimes evaluating progress and the quality of the effort. Individualized learning also forces students who are naturally social to work in isolation, struggling to piece together fragments of information. A large amount of the teacher's time is spent in correcting, testing, and record keeping. With individualized learning, the goal or task objective was usually perceived as most important, with each student expected to achieve the objective. The teacher was the major source for assistance and reinforcement. The trouble with such solitary learning is that it filled in only part of the learning picture and missed the power of collaboration.

Another aspect of traditional learning was competition. Students monitored the progress of their competitors, and compared ability, skills, and knowledge with peers. Instructional activities tended to focus on skill practice, knowledge recall, and review. The assignments were clear, with rules for competing specified. The teacher was the major resource and often directed the competitive activity. A competitive atmosphere often induced anxiety, fear of failure, and ultimately withdrawal for many students.

Cooperative group learning takes a different approach. It builds on what we know about how students construct knowledge, promoting active learning in a way not possible with competitive or with individualized learning. In a cooperative classroom, the teacher organizes major parts of the curriculum around tasks, problems, and projects that students can work through in small mixed ability groups. Lessons are designed around active learning teams so that students can combine energies as they reach toward a common goal. If someone else does well, you do well. Social skills, like interpersonal communication, group interaction, and conflict resolution are developed as the cooperative learning process goes along.

Teachers can use cooperative learning with confidence that it has a solid research base *and* a history of successful classroom use. Dozens of

research studies and many more teacher reports confirm, among other things, the positive impact of cooperative groups on academic achievement, critical thinking, and the transfer of what has been learned to new situations (Johnson, D.W. and R. Johnson, 1994).

The research also suggests that cooperative learning:

- *Motivates Students*
  Groups of students talking and working together on a problem or project experience the fun and the sharing of ideas and information.
- *Increases Academic Performance and retention*
  Studies show that classroom interaction with peers causes students — especially those from diverse cultural and linguistic backgrounds — to make significant academic gains, compared with students in traditional settings.
- *Encourages Active Learning*
  Extensive research has shown that students learn more when they're actively engaged in discovery and problem solving.
- *Helps with the Creative Generation of New Ideas*
- *Increases Respect for Diversity*
  Students who work together in mixed ability groups are more likely to select mixed racial and ethnic acquaintances and friendships. When students cooperate to reach a common goal they learn to appreciate and respect each other.
- *Promotes Literacy and Language Skills*
  Team study offers students many chances to use language and improve speaking skills. This is particularly important for second language students.
- *Helps Prepare Students for Today's Society.*
  Group approaches to solving problems, combining energies with others and working to get along are valued skills in the world of work, community, and leisure.
- *Improves Teacher Effectiveness*
  By actively engaging students in the learning process teachers also make important discoveries about their students' learning. As students take some of the responsibility for some of the teaching, the power of the teacher can be multiplied (Slavin, 1983; 1989, Sharon, 1980, Abraham & Campbell, 1984; Levine & Trachtman, 1988).

Like any method or approach to teaching, there are times when things may not go as well as you would like. But overall cooperative learning has proven itself to be quite effective. Its popularity is increasing because teachers can tell that it works.

Promoting Active Learning and Helpfulness

Whether it's finding out about new concepts, solving problems, or questioning factual information, a collaborative approach has shown that it helps develop academic skills. At the same time, it taps students' social nature to build self-esteem and social understanding (Moore Johnson, 1990). Collaborative skills are more important than ever in today's academic setting, workplace, and civic culture.

Talking about problem solving with others has been shown to spark an alertness of mind not achieved in passive listening. When students talk and reason together to complete a task or solve a problem, they become more involved in thinking and communicating (Carnegie Foundation for the Advancement of Teaching, 1988). Successful cooperative learning promotes interaction through face to face communications and links individuals to group success. Students are supported, encouraged, and given feedback as they critically analyze problems and issues. Group members are held responsible individually and collectively. Everyone has a responsibility to finish all assignments, master instructional objectives, and ensure that all group colleagues do the same.

As individuals work with a small group of supportive classmates, children develop a sense of community and caring. Cooperative learning communities develop many social skills: communication, confidence in their ability, respect for others, and a sense of value ("I've got something to offer"). In a cooperative classroom, students are frequently engaged in interpersonal skills such as shared decision making, managing conflict situations, and maintaining good working relationships among group members. When a lesson is over, a group typically takes time to reflect on how well they did as a group—and what could be done better. All of these skills will be crucial in the workplace of tomorrow.

Cooperative learning thrives in an atmosphere of mutual helpfulness where students know about what's happening—and why. Part of creating the right environment means having the teacher define objectives, talk about the benefits of cooperative learning, explain expectations, and explain behaviors such as brainstorming, peer teaching, constructive criticism, and confidence building.

For the students, it's more than having something meaningful to work on. They need to learn how to be good at listening, communicating, and using constructive criticism. Learning to engage in productive conversation, helping others without simply telling them the answer, and giving constructive criticism is all part of the process.

Professional Support Groups Work for Teachers

Teaching is a dynamic act that creates and realizes decision-making power over what happens in the classroom. A professional work environment supports responsible, autonomous problem solvers. The new wave of school reform moves organizational structures from top-down management to teacher empowerment. Professional power must go hand-in-hand with responsibility.

As a student of teaching, teachers cannot put in their class time and skip the homework. Assessing and coaching colleagues is now part of the job description. Professional development and peer coaching work best when they are based on the concept of cooperative learning. A small support group of colleagues, bound by an ethic of caring, can go over the work done by individual teachers, offer constructive criticism, and give suggestions. Professional development and support is for *everyone.* Schools are offering counseling from outstanding teachers and remedial intervention programs to teachers who are having trouble.

The actual hands-on, minds-on interaction with peers raises awareness and instills confidence in a way that reading or hearing about a new teaching strategy cannot. After some initial experiences with cooperative learning, the rough edges can be smoothed with additional reading, practice, and on-site peer mentoring. Teacher workshops and university classes can help—especially when teachers try activities, share experiences, and give and receive assistance within a collegial structure that supports collaboration. As peers help with planning, implementation, and feedback, both students and teachers experience the various processes of cooperative learning and come to more fully understand the power of the technique (Moore, Johnson, 1990).

Collegial Collaboration: Peer Coaching in A Supportive Environment

Peer coaching is a model that can provide opportunities for teachers or students to assist and receive assistance from peers. Team members provide feedback, plan projects, help implement teaching suggestions, offer support, and give constructive criticism. Collegial cooperation serves as a caring support group that helps individuals over rough spots. It offers the possibility for groups to reflect, check perceptions, share frustrations and successes. As members of the group grow to respect one another, they form caring relationships. By sharing personal interpretations they collectively weave messages in ways that reach the mind and the heart.

When a teacher is a part of a support team that encourages others to be openly exploratory and inquiring, he or she has opportunities to affirm their understanding and share their insights and ways of thinking with others. The give and take among group members of a peer coaching team is constructively critical at times. Good coaches are honest about their peer's work. Peer coaches need to work together, share their ideas with other members of the collaborative team. Team leaders learn how to promote positive learning transactions in the classroom. As active problem solvers and analytical thinkers they strive to see all parts of a problem and the ways peers are thinking. As a team they delve deeply into inquiry and possible solutions to problems.

In peer coaching dialogue involves the interplay between feeling and thinking. Built on trust, and the ethic of caring, dialogue becomes an integral tool of learning. The purpose of dialogue is to "come into contact with ideas, to understand, and work cooperatively (Nodding, 1984, p. 186). Caring teachers think of themselves as facilitators of learning, not just knowledge imparters. In this role they open doors to complex interaction among each student's past experiences, personal purposes, and subject matter requirements. By connecting topics to students' lives, schools can develop a vital link to those realities.

Individual and Group Accountability Are Keys to Collaboration

Like any instructional strategy, implementing cooperative learning principles requires multiple objectives and approaches to reach the best a student has to offer. Cooperative group interaction can start by having students help each other in solving problems and completing academic tasks. The next step is to combine this idea with positive interdependence between group members and individual accountability. Group interdependence means that each individual plays a unique role. The team loses if they don't put out individual effort; they win or lose together. Whatever the outcome, students learn to think and act within multiple contexts.

Accountability ensures that everyone is contributing to a common goal. Individual accountability gives teachers a way of checking the role that each student is playing in the group's work. Individual accountability is accomplished through:

1. Group rewards that are based on individual performance, (for example totaling scores on individual quizzes)
2. Having students make individual presentations on a group project or do unique tasks in their group which contribute to group presentation. (For example, one group member reports on the homes of the Navaho Indians, one reports on foods, another on rituals, etc.)
3. Providing incentives for students to work together to learn new material, but being *tested* individually.

Group accountability is also essential. If students are discussing last night's basketball game instead of working on mathematics, they aren't going to get much mathematical knowledge from their group discussion. Teachers must clearly define the task and closely monitor groups to ensure they are on task. When children expect positive interaction they naturally share ideas and materials, and become accountable for their own knowledge. All group members are expected to contribute to the group effort. By dividing the tasks among them to capitalize on on a wide range of strengths. Individuals receive support for risk taking and other group members are perceived to be the major source for assistance, support, and reinforcement.

Being willing to learn from failure, becoming more attuned to resources, and working beyond personal limits were the attitudes that teachers frequently mentioned as affecting success with cooperative learning (Slavin et al., 1985). When teachers and students are encouraged to work collaboratively, there is a positive effect on the overall school environment (Connelly & Clandinin, 1992).

Organizing an Interactive Learning Environment

Cooperative learning will not take place with students sitting in rows facing the teacher. Desks must be pushed together in small groups (two or more) or students can sit at small tables to facilitate group interaction. Groups of three or four usually work better than groups of six or seven. Resource and hands-on materials must be made readily accessible. Collaboration will not occur in a classroom which requires students to raise their hands to talk or move out of their desks. Instead of waiting with their hands up, they ask the student next to them. A basic rule of the game is that they have to ask at least two students before asking the teacher for help when they don't understand something or get stuck on a problem.

Other changes involve the noise level in the room. Sharing and working together, even in well-controlled environments, will be louder than an environment where students work silently from textbooks. Putting old carpets and other sound absorbing things in the room helps. Still, teachers need to tolerate higher noise levels and learn to evaluate whether or not it's constructive.

Evaluating cooperative learning requires a variety of procedures. In spite of new evaluative techniques, some learning outcomes will probably continue to be measured by instruments like standardized tests, quizzes, and written exams. Fortunately, new performance-based tests that have open-ended questions and problem-solving functions are starting to be used. The collaborative classroom also makes use of these tests and other measures like portfolios, and holistic scoring. (These approaches will all be explained in the assessment chapter.) Students need to be involved in evaluating learning products, the classroom climate, and individual skill development. Self-evaluation and peer evaluation have been added to teacher assessment in cooperative learning. Otherwise, the teacher can be trapped under an avalanche of minutia. One of the goals is to help teachers do a better job by *not* taking work home every night.

As interactive learning environments are organized, everyone involved learns to shape questions, interpret data, and make connections between subjects. Students can learn to take responsibility for their own learning and assist others in their small group. Task-oriented work groups can combine student initiative with social responsibility. This allows those with more information to stimulate the students with less—and vice versa. The same thing is true when it comes to teaching thinking processes like comprehension, decision making, and problem solving.

Cooperative groups can provide the structure for personal learning agendas and the joint application of critical thinking skills. By working together, students can distinguish hypotheses from verified information and recognize reasoning based on misconceptions. In cooperative groups, everyone is an active player in classroom activities. Topical projects, writing assignments, problem-solving, or journal reaction papers are just a few examples of activities that require active group planning, negotiating, and the collaborative distribution of work.

As groups to try to reach a consensus, they can create an analysis grid or management plan whereby comparisons and contrasts can be made as well as students' speculations about outcomes. Within the tension of discussing different points of view (even heated discussion) learning takes place.

Another Effective Way to Structure Cooperative Groups

Johnson et al. (1984) suggest these steps for teachers interested in implementing small-group interactive learning:

1. Designate content and cooperative group objectives.
2. Specify the size of the group (typically from two to six depending on the nature of the task and the time available).
3. Split students into groups (you may assign students or allow students to form their own group).
4. Prepare the room for cooperative learning so that the teacher is accessible to all groups and so that group members can sit close enough to communicate effectively and not disturb another group.
5. Design a way to distribute instructional materials (this can be accomplished in a variety of ways; you may wish to give only one set of materials to each group or give each group member different materials so as to force task differentiation).
6. Designate roles such as summarizer-checker, facilitator, recorder, runner, encourager, and observer.
7. Make clear the directions of the task.
8. Apply strategies such as positive goal interdependence, peer encouragement, and support for learning (the group may be asked to produce a single product or put in place an assessment system where rewards are based on individual scores and on the average for the group as a whole).
9. Arrange intergroup cooperation.
10. Review the success criteria by explaining the guidelines, boundaries, and roles.
11. Determine desired behaviors (taking turns, using personal names, listening carefully to each other, encouraging everyone to participate).
12. Monitor students (circulate to listen and observe groups; note problems).
13. Give assistance when asked.

14. Step in where groups are having problems in collaborating successfully.
15. Present closure to the lesson.
16. Assess the quality of students' learning.
17. Have students evaluate how well the group functioned together.
18. Provide and encourage feedback. Discuss how they could improve.

Shared Responsibility, Group Roles, and Respecting Differences

Collaborative group structures involve shared responsibilities. This means that a variety of tasks must be performed by group members. Each member (or pair) in the group assumes the charge of making sure that all group members work toward a group goal or objective. When students are new to cooperative learning, teachers may wish to assign certain roles to group participants. Many teachers divide the roles in the following way:

1. Facilitator
   • organizes the group's work
   • makes certain students understand the group's job
   • takes the group's questions and concerns to the teacher *after* the group attempts a solution and tries alternatives.
2. Checker
   • checks with group members to make sure that everyone understands their task
   • checks to be sure that everyone agrees with the group response and can explain it.
3. Reader
   • reads the problem or directions to the group
4. Recorder
   • writes the groups response or data collection on a group response sheet or log.
5. Encourager
   • offers support and encouragement to group members.
   • Keeps others feeling good about working together (Johnson & Johnson, 1975).

If there are four students in a group you can combine facilitator and checker or reader roles. If it's a group of three: checker, reader, and recorder . . . the other roles are shared. Even teachers who work a lot with cooperative groups don't always assign roles. Students who are used to the process can naturally share the roles.

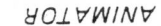

[All students assume responsibility for promoting and maintaining positive attitudes and a positive group spirit.] This doesn't mean using the "team spirit" to suppress dissent or intimidate individuals. In fact, those with an undeveloped sense of self (personal efficacy or self-esteem) have a more difficult time sharing deeply with others. Differences of opinion and conflicting views can actually result in constructive conflict and provide an important source of learning.

An Example of Assigning Roles in a Cooperative Learning/Poetry Lesson

Work in groups of 3.

1) *Checker/Facilitator*—organizes the group's work and makes sure everyone understands the group's task.
2) *Reader*—reads poem (can practice first), also reads any directions to the group.
3) *Recorder*—tells the large group how the small group answered the question.

A Sample Activity

As a group of three, assign responsibility for each role and answer the questions below. **Work cooperatively:** everyone be able to explain the group's response. The recorder will let the class know what the group came up with.

1. What are the emotions/attitudes expressed by the poem?
2. What are your reactions (feelings and thoughts) to the poem?
3. What are the three key words in the poem?
4. What is the poem saying?

Still I Rise – Maya Angelou

Just like the moons and the suns
with certainty of tides
Just like hopes springing high
Still I'll rise
Out of history's shame
I rise
I'm a black ocean leaping and wide
Welling and swelling I bear the tide
Leaving behind the nights of terror and fear
I rise
Into the daybreak that's wondrously clear
I rise
Bringing the gifts that my ancestors gave
I am the dream and the hope of the slave
I rise
I rise
I rise

[Written on the 50th anniversary
of the United Nations]

Another Sample of a Cooperative Group Activity

Lost in the Desert Activity

The situation: Your small group of students has become lost in the desert. You are at least 25 miles from a highway or nearest town. Your group only has some 15 items with them or things that they could find at an abandoned mining camp. Your task is to rank order these items according to their importance to your survival, starting with "1" the most important, to "15" the least important.

The Items [The experts ranking is to the right of the item.]

- parachute 5
- magnetic compass 11
- bottle of salt tablets 15
- one quart of water per person 3
- 2 quarts of 180 proof vodka 14
- flashlight 4
- plastic raincoat 7

- three pairs of sunglasses 9
- jackknife 6
- a map of the area 12
- 1 compress kit 10
- one top coat per person 2
- 45 caliber pistol 8
- cosmetic mirror 1

- a book entitled *Edible Animals of the Desert* 13

Experts Reasoning

1. Cosmetic mirror—in sunlight the mirror can concentrate 5 to 7 million candle power of light. The reflected sunbeam can even be seen beyond the horizon.
2. Top Coat—slows down dehydration—you need to keep *covered*.
3. Water—You could probably survive 3 days with just the first two items listed above. Although 1 quart of water would not significantly extend the survival time, it briefly holds off the effects of dehydration. Don't ration, drink when thirsty.
4. Flashlight—quick reliable night signaling device.
5. Parachute—can serve both as a shelter and a signaling device.
6. Jackknife—useful for digging, making a solar still (by placing a raincoat over the hole, placing a small stone inside, a cone will form, the temperature differential will extract some moisture to drip down into the flashlight container buried in the center of the hole.
7. Raincoat—useful for making the still above.
8. Pistol—sound signaling device, but lapses in rationality could make it lethal.
9. Sunglasses—helpful however the dark side of the parachute shelter would eliminate the visual problem.
10. Compress kit with gauze—Could be used for wrapping your arms, head, ankles, face. Blood becomes thicker under desert conditions—bleeding is not as big a problem.
11. Compass—little use.
12. Air map—may be used for starting a fire or as a head cover. The danger is that it could cause you to try to hike out.
13. Book—although the book may contain useful information, it would be difficult to adjust your eyes to reading. Eating is not a problem in this situation.

14. Vodka—quickly increases dehydration.
15. Salt tablets—modern medicines have shown these to be useless.

After your group has ranked the items in order of importance make a group sketch of how you would use them and what you are going to do. Once this is complete, the teacher gives the answers as seen by desert survival experts and students compare the difference between what their group says and what the expert said. Add up the difference on each item for a total score. Anything in the twenty range is really excellent . . . a score in the high forties and you are buzzard bait.

Structuring Group Task Behaviors

Organizing a group plan of action is an important part of shared responsibility and shared leadership. Learning how to search out, share, and receive information to continue progress on a group task are important skills in working collaboratively. Students also need to learn how to summarize and clarify that information so as to move the group in the direction of completing their task or goal. Sometimes it may be necessary to test the consensus of a group—how many members agree that a particular direction is advisable or that a particular conclusion is accurate. Other task behaviors include:

- getting the group started
- staying on task
- getting the group back to work
- taking turns
- asking questions
- following directions
- staying in the group space
- keeping track of time
- helping without giving the answer

The idea is to play to each other's strengths and support each other's weaknesses.

Teaching and learning in a cooperative environment means considering ways to encourage ourselves and others to learn. It doesn't mean that everyone has to agree about everything. Square holes make for square pegs. Collaboration doesn't equal conformity. In spite of the traditional Japanese maxim to the contrary, "the nail that sticks up" *shouldn't* be "hammered down." Rather, it is important to become comfortable with the differing opinions of others whose dimensions can't be calibrated or arbitrarily controlled. The important thing is civility, respect for group members, and being able to work together to accomplish group goals.

Group Support Systems

In addition to helping the group reach its goal and get the job done, a group member also has the responsibility to show support and empathy for other group members and their feelings. Agreement *isn't* required, support *is*. It is also important for everyone to have an opportunity to express ideas, to reflect on the process, and to analyze the feelings and ideas that other group members express.

There is a complex emotional geometry that connects individuals to one another in a group. When group interactions become tense, a release of that tension is needed; *humor* is a good way to ease members' frustrations. As Plato said, "the gods love a good joke." On a tough day so does everyone else. Support or maintenance behaviors that help keep things on an enjoyable keel:

1. *Compromising* — coming to an agreement by meeting half way, "giving in" to other group members when necessary.
2. *Empathizing and encouraging* — showing understanding and helping others feel a part of the group.
3. *Gate keeping* — giving everyone a chance to speak in the group, checking to see that no one is overlooked.
4. *Liberating tension* — creating harmony in the group.
5. *Expressing group feelings* — helping the group to examine how it is feeling and operating.

Teachers can help by:

- using names
- responding to ideas
- showing appreciation
- paraphrasing
- encouraging others to talk
- using eye contact
- not letting things get too heated
- criticizing an idea, not a person

As the group members learn to focus energy on the learning task, they also learn to identify with the group process. This helps members grow and develop by compromising, creating harmony, coaching, sharing, and encouraging are learned behaviors. When group responsibility and support behaviors are in balance, group members can work collaboratively to achieve important group objectives. When the group task is over, it is helpful for groups to evaluate effectiveness and make suggestions for improvement. This provides feedback and insights into the collaborative process.

Resolving Conflict and Solving Problems

The ability to solve problems and smoothly resolve conflict in the group are important tasks of cooperation and collaboration. Group members need strategies for negotiating and problem solving to successfully defuse conflict and create harmony. Some conflict strategies include:

1. *Withdrawal* — the individual withdraws from interaction, recognizing that the goal and the interaction are not important enough for excessive conflict.
2. *Forcing* — the task is more important than the relationship; members use all their energy to get the task done.
3. *Smoothing* — the relationship is more important than the task. Individuals want to be liked and accepted — and they work at it.
4. *Compromising* — the task and the relationship are both important, but there is a lack of time. Both members gain something and lose something, but meet the deadline.
5. *Confrontation* — Task and relationship are equally important, the conflict is defined as a problem solving situation and not personalities.

Problem solving is a useful group strategy to assist in conflict resolution. This systematic five-step process of constructively addressing conflicts involves:

1. Defining the problem and its causes.
2. Generating alternative solutions to the problem.
3. Examining advantages and disadvantages to each alternative.
4. Deciding upon and implementing the most desirable solution.
5. Evaluating whether the solutions solve the problem.

Group members must define exactly what the problem is. On occasion, this can be difficult, but it is worth the effort. Once the problem is defined, group members can then suggest alternative solutions and explore the consequences of each of those alternatives. The group members then make a decision to *try* an alternative and to review the results within a stipulated period of time.

It can also be important to teach *confrontation skills* and techniques for *successful resolution.* Some of these suggestions include teaching students to:

1. Describe behavior, do not evaluate, label, accuse or insult.
2. Define the conflict as a mutual problem. Rather than a win-lose situation, it's win-win.
3. Use "I" statements.
4. Communicate what you think and feel.
5. Be critical of ideas, not people, affirm other's competence.
6. Give everyone a chance to be heard.
7. Follow the guidelines for rational argument.
8. Make sure there is enough time for discussion.
9. Take the other person's perspective.

Negotiating is also a learning part of problem resolution. It involves mutual discussion and arrangement of the terms of an agreement. The process of learning to "read" another's behavior for clues as to a problem solution is crucial in being able to guess what will appeal to another person and how to make a deal in which each participant's preferences or needs are considered.

Complementing the task and *support* behaviors are such communication skills like *active listening.* This means both attending to and responding to group and individual efforts. Active listening allows all group members to be fully in tune with each other while allowing for conversation overlaps. Acknowledging the content, feelings, or meaning of what another person is communicating lends itself to goodwill and deeper understanding. When everyone is given a chance to express their ideas, it assures that all members of the group participate. This process makes group members secure in the knowledge that they are contributing to the group.

Constructing Cooperative Learning Environments

Once upon a time, a second grade teacher might have three groups: the bluebirds, the blackbirds, and the gorillas. Once you were in the high, medium, or low group, you were likely to stay there. In some

conclusion

schools, entire classes are "ability grouped"—sidestepping the effort to mix minority or special needs students with others at the school. Cooperative learning offers a promising way out of the ability grouping maze.

A multidimensional collaborative classroom will make learning more accessible to more students, more valuable, and more interesting. Simply putting students in heterogeneous classes and teaching the same old curriculum isn't good enough. Other aspects of instructional practice must also be meaningfully changed—deepened, extended, and strengthened. As schools focus on the depth and quality of thoughtful work, classes will be far more useful for students and teachers. Teachers need methods, materials, and time to plan, before they can make untracked classes work up to their potential. To move toward untracking the curriculum requires patience, cooperation, thorough planning, and professional development.

basic assumption

In a cooperative classroom, the teacher organizes major parts of the curriculum around tasks, problems, and projects that students can work through in active learning teams. Students then combine energies to reach common group objectives. Whether it's finding out about new concepts, solving problems, or questioning factual information, a collaborative approach has shown that it helps develop academic skills, while promoting understanding and self-esteem (Kagan, 1986). The new wave of school reform moves organizational structures from top-down management to teacher empowerment.

Changing classroom organizational patterns and teaching strategies works best when there is systematic staff development and association with like-minded colleagues. It also takes time, practice, and systematic support for the vital energy inherent in new skills to become part of teachers' repertoire. Such basic changes in the organization of learning requires a school environment where it is safe to make mistakes and where it is safe to learn from those mistakes. Remember, to succeed you have to put up with a few failures.

The approaches described here are all fairly easy to try. When students push two or three desks together they can begin helping each other learn. This kind of learning is seen as social, fun, and under their control. With the teacher acting as a resource person, learners create a climate of acceptance and a spirit of camaraderie.

Suggestions for Improving Small Group Collaboration

It often takes several attempts with cooperative learning techniques to get groups working effectively. If children are not used to responsible group interaction, it may take some getting used to. Like teachers, students must be gradually eased into the process through a consistent routine. The more teachers and students work in groups, the easier it becomes. Some students may encounter initial problems because they are accustomed to being rewarded for easy to come by answers that require little thinking. It may take some time and teacher assistance for them to become comfortable working cooperatively with more ambiguity.

Some useful strategies for helping students adjust include:

- Adjust the group size to suit the activity. Groups of 2, 3, or 4 work well for many activities like mathematics problem solving. (For teachers new to the technique, the smaller groups usually work best.)
- Groups of 5 or 6 may work better for activities that require larger group participation (creative dramatics, larger social studies projects, certain writing projects, etc.)
- Experiment with different group patterns and size.
- Accept a higher working noise level in the classroom.
- Do not interrupt a group that is working well. If a group seems to be floundering, ask a student to describe what the group is discussing or what part of the problem is causing difficulty. Try not to speak loudly to a group across the room. Go to them if you want to say something.
- Try interacting with the groups from time to time. *Listen* to their discussions.
- Give students rules for group work. Some suggestions:
  - Individuals must check with other members of the group before they may raise their hands to ask the teacher for help. Help can then be given to the group collectively.
  - Try to reach a group consensus on a problem.
  - All students should participate.
  - Be considerate of others.
  - Students are to help any group member who asks.

Some Activities for Working Cooperatively

1. **Stress Cooperative Work.** Some of the more successful cooperative multicultural models view collaborative intimacy as a natural condition between teachers and students. The collaborative process works best when teachers provide students with the larger meaning (or purpose) for learning cooperative group skills. Students of mixed ability, gender, race, and ethnic groups can learn to function as a team that sinks or swims together. The basic idea is to have the group take responsibility for the learning of individual members. And within this collaborative framework, individuals are held accountable.

Learning how to search out, share, and receive information to continue progress on a group task are important skills in working collaboratively. Students also need to learn how to summarize and clarify that information so as to move the group towards completion of their task or goal.

2. **Assign Roles.** This teamwork approach with specific roles can be useful when analyzing videos, newspaper articles, or literary works. After viewing a video clip or reading together a literary work, students can learn to construct a coherent argument or support a particular point of view through debate and compromise. Two or more groups of four and five can be assigned to argue conflicting points of view and to gather evidence to support their particular argument.

This activity works particularly well when analyzing a poem, which is often more open to interpretation than other literary works, and, because of its length, can more easily be discussed within a classroom hour. The following poem by Langston Hughes, for example, can provoke a lively classroom discussion. The class can be divided into groups of three consisting of: (1) a **checker**/animator, who makes sure everyone understands the directions (see below) and keeps the discussion lively, but also focused on the questions; (2) a **reader** who reads the poem and the directions to the group; and (3) a **recorder** who explains/defends the small group's interpretation of the poem to the rest of the class.

3. **Group Poetry Reading.** Present the following poem to the class. Students may begin by reading it orally in a group. On the second reading assign roles. Let students decide what roles there are.

Mother to Son

Well son, I'll tell you:
Life for me ain't been no crystal stair.
It's had tacks in it.

And splinters,
And boards torn up,
And places with no carpet on the floor —
Bare.
But All the time
I'se been a-climbin' on
And reachin' landin's,
And turnin' corners,
And sometimes goin' in the dark
Where there ain't been no light.
So, boy, don't you turn back.
Don't you set down on the steps
'Cause you finds it's kinder hard.
Don't you fall now —
For I'se still goin', honey,
I'se still goin' honey,
I'se still climbin',
And life for me ain't been no crystal stair.
                                — Langston Hughes

After reading the poem, students work together to complete the task assigned in the following directions.

Directions: Write three different answers to the questions below and try to reach a consensus on the best possible solution. Work cooperatively: everyone must agree and be able to explain the group's responses to the following questions:

1. What are the emotions/attitudes expressed by the mother in the poem?
2. What are your reactions (feelings and thoughts) to the poem?
3. What do you think are three key words in the poem?
4. What is the poem saying?

4. Sample Management Plan. Divide the class into groups of three. Explain that they will be involved in solving a hypothetical problem of school children living in New Jersey. These children have a real problem. Everyday they complain about slow cafeteria service. Your task is to help them solve their problem. The problem is divided into sections: fact finding, problem finding, brainstorming, coming up with a solution, coming to consensus. Join them in solving this real life problem.

Group Task: To solve the problem of slow grill service.

1. *Fact Finding*
What do we know? Lunch time is a problem.
What would we like to know? Whether other people see it as a problem (teachers, principal, cafeteria workers). Why is it a problem?
What resources might help us? Talking with children and adults involved in the noon hour service. Checking with other schools who have a similar lunch service.

2. *Problem Finding*
What do we see as the problems? Can we rank them?
Older children pushing in.
Too many children buying things.
Not enough cafeteria helpers.
No teachers on duty at the grill.
Students get tired of waiting.
Bad manners.
Slow grill service.
What is the most important problem?
Slow grill service.
Restate the problem so that we can work on ideas for it.
How to improve grill service so that it's fair to all children, teachers, and helpers.

3. *Brainstorm as many ways as you can think of to solve the problem.*
Remember accept all ideas, don't judge.
Schedule times children can use.
Get more volunteers for the grill.
Open the grill only on certain days.
Use fast food service goods in the grill.
Open two grills.
Teach students better manners.
Write to school council and ask for more helpers.

4. *Solution*
How will we judge or analyze ideas? What criteria will we use?
How much will it cost?
Is it fair to everyone?
Is it difficult to organize?
An analysis grid or scaffolding to help: Give ratings to the ideas expressed in the criteria:

3—good
2—fair
1—poor

Put a check in each box:

	A	B	C

Total

Set up a schedule of times.
Get more voluntary helpers.
Open 2 grills.
Teach better manners.
Have school council pay.

5. *Acceptance—Consensus*

How will we put our plan into action?

Plan: To get more voluntary helpers.

Step 1: Interview principal, grill helpers, students—do a survey, graph results.

Step 2: Verbal and typed report to principal and grill supervisor, gain support for plan.

Step 3: Design posters to hang in community places.

Step 4: Write and duplicate letters to send home with each student.

Step 5: Write a report on grill investigation and outcomes for school newspaper and local newspaper.

What problems might we have? How can we deal with them?

(Dalton, 1991)

Cooperative Learning in a Multicultural Environment

An important finding of recent research is that cooperative learning improves social relations between racially and culturally different students. In a pluralistic society, we have in the United States various mixed racial, gender, ethnic, and ability group structures that can help students understand each other. After working in cooperative groups, all group members became more accepting of classmates who were different (Davidson & Worsham, 1992). Sports teams have long had a similar unifying effect on teammates.

Interracial or diverse cultural learning teams can be useful for organizing classrooms in support of multicultural harmony. Studies from social psychology suggest that dividing the class into interracial learning teams reduces prejudice by undercutting the stereotyped categories while encouraging group members to pull together (Costa, 1991). Other researchers (Davidson & Worsham, 1992), have found that cooperative groups are particularly beneficial for Hispanic, African-American, and other minority students.

Since the basic plan for cooperative learning revolves around the idea of active small group learning environments, it is a natural vehicle for promoting multicultural understandings. Positive interdependence, shared responsibilities, social skills development, and heterogeneity separate cooperative groups from traditional work in groups. Students at various "ability" levels cluster together, discuss topics, and learn to take charge of their own learning. They can also look for common ground, rather than emphasizing differences.

The American educational system must accommodate the demographic shift in the direction of increased diversity. Recognizing the evolving multicultural faces of school children means implementing a range of strategies for insuring a high-quality education that does not segregate students by class or "ability." Cooperative learning can be a powerful instructional tool for enabling students to meet standards that are high, universal, and equitable. To make educational opportunity a reality for all requires holding students, staff, school systems, and American society accountable.

Educators have been searching for techniques to teach today's students to think clearly, creatively, and cooperatively. By actively engaging students in the collaborative process, teachers have been able to integrate social skills and critical thinking with academic content. With the support of teachers and a solid research base, it is becoming the most widely used instructional innovation in American education (Clarke et al., 1990). Cooperative learning brings students to the edge of many possibilities— sharing visions and understandings that can enhance individual learning.

Building a Sense of Community

As students and teachers learn to conduct their communications with a collegiality (bordering on civility) collaborative teams can help build a broader sense of community and even stimulate collaboration between teachers. Connecting mutual achievement and collegial relationships may be extended to staff meetings, committees, and relationships with parents. Traditional teachers and parents must come to understand that it is sometimes all right for students to share answers.

As students and teachers become participating members of a collegial team of peers both develop a joint sense of purpose and even more efficiently tap the possibilities of cooperative learning. Critics of cooperative learning will have to be satisfied with attacking the tendency to oversell, under train, and the occasional tendency to focus more on social settings than what is taught. Method certainly isn't all, but in general the empirical and practical evidence supports the use of cooperative learning techniques in the classroom. And once the main elements are understood, teachers can adapt cooperative learning to the needs of their students and their unique classroom situation.

In cooperative learning communities instruction can become personalized and mutual achievement and caring for one another become more important. Students and teachers can come to view one another as collaborators who help one another cognitively, emotionally, physically, and socially. Active team learning is more than an innovation in itself, it is a catalyst for other changes in curriculum, instruction, and schooling. Slavin goes so far as to suggest that becoming a contributing member of a collegial team promotes self-discovery, higher level reasoning, and the "having of wonderful ideas" (Slavin, R.E., 1990).

In cooperative learning communities, the teachers might be thought of as community leaders and the students might be viewed as citizens. Students and teachers can be rooted in a network of familial and community relationships that make up a civil society. Like an extended family, everyone cares about individual and mutual achievement. Individual rights are balanced by reciprocal obligation and mutual interdependence.

Cooperative learning can be used with confidence across subjects and grade levels to explore meaning and help students care for one another. As students come together in teams, they can look at academic, social, and personal issues and jointly ask: "Where can we go with this?" and "How might it make our world better?" By building on the group energy and idealism of youngsters the thinking, learning, and doing process can be pushed forward.

By taping into student's natural curiosity and creating a learning community students and teachers can use cooperative methods to achieve academic goals. By working in successful cooperative groups both students and teachers can get better together. Cooperative learning can be more than a technique, by shifting thinking and organizational structures collaboration can be expanded to include the school and even the school district. Thus the democratic and consensus-making processes that stem from cooperative learning can influence education at every level.

REFERENCES

Abraham, S.Y. & Campbell, C. (1984). *Peer teachers as mirrors and monitors.* Detroit, MI: Wayne State University Press.

Burton, C.B. (1987). "Problems in children's peer relationships: A broadening perspective" in Katz, CG (Ed.). *Current topics in early childhood education,* Volume 7, Norwood, NJ: Ablex.

Carnegie Foundation for the Advancement of Teaching. (1986). Task Forum on education and the economy, Task force on teaching as a profession. *A nation prepared: Teachers for the 21st century.* New York: Carnegie Foundation.

Clarke, J., Wideman, R. & Eadie, S. (1990). *Together we learn.* Toronto: Prentice Hall.

Cohen, E. (1984). The desegregated school. In: N. Miller and M. Brewer (Eds.) *Groups in contact: The psychology of desegregation.* New York: Academic Press, 77–96.

Connelly, M.F. & Clandinin, D.J. (1988). *Teachers as curriculum planners: Narratives of experience.* New York: Teachers College Press.

Costa, A.L. (Ed.) (1991). *Developing minds: A resource book for teaching thinking.* Alexandria, VA: Association of Supervision and Curriculum Development.

Dalton, J. (1991). *Adventures in thinking: Creative thinking and cooperative talk in small groups.* South Melbourne Vic, Australia: Thomas Nelson Australia.

Davidson, N. & Worsham, T. (1992). *Enhancing thinking through cooperative learning.* New York: Teachers College Press.

Jager Adams, M. (1990). *Beginning to read: Thinking and learning about print.* Cambridge, MA: MIT Press.

Johnson, D.W., Maruyama, G., Johnson, R., Nelson, D. & Skon, L. (1981). Effects of cooperative, competitive, and individualistic goal structures on achievement: A meta analysis. *Psychological Bulletin* 89, 47–62.

Johnson, D.W. & Johnson, R. (1989). *Cooperation and competition: Theory and research.* Edina, MN: Interaction Book Co.

Johnson, D.W. & Johnson, R. (1994). *Joining together: Group theory and group skills.* (5th ed.). Englewood Cliffs, N.J.: Prentice-Hall.

Kagan, (1986). Cooperative learning and sociocultural diversity: Implications for practice. In *Beyond language: Social and cultural factors in schooling language minority students.* Los Angeles, CA: Evaluation, Dissemination and Assessment Center.

Levine, M. & Trachtman, R. (Eds.). (1988). *American business and the public school: Case studies of corporate involvement in public education.* New York: Teachers College Press.

Moore Johnson, S. (1990). *Teachers at work: Achieving success in our schools.* New York: Basic Books.

Nottings, N. (1984). *Caring: A feminine approach to ethics and moral education.* Berkeley: University of California Press.

Sharon, S. (1980). Cooperative learning in small groups: Recent methods and effects on achievement, attitudes and ethnic relations. *Review of Educational Research, 50,* 241–271.

Slavin, R. (1983). *Cooperative learning.* New York: Longman.

Slavin, R. (1986). *Using student team learning* (3rd ed.). Baltimore, MD: Center for Research on Elementary and Middle Schools, Johns Hopkins University.

Slavin, R. (1987). *Cooperative learning: Student teams.* Washington, DC: National Education Association.

Slavin, R. (1989). *School and classroom organization.* Hillsdale, NJ: Erlbaum.

Slavin, R. (1990). *Cooperative learning: Theory, research, and practice.* Englewood Cliffs, NJ: Prentice Hall.

Slavin, R., Sharan, S., Kagan, S., Hertz-Lazarowitz, R., Webb, C. & Schmuck, R. (Eds.) (1985). *Learning to cooperate, cooperating to learn.* New York: Plenum.

Chapter 2

CRITICAL THINKING
ACROSS THE CURRICULUM

"In our present age of invective and unreason, it is a daunting task to try and convey to the public the idea that critical inquiry and responsible revision remain the lifeblood of every serious intellectual enterprise." Critical thinking and reasoning skills are part of drawing "on new perspectives and data to reconsider and rethink received wisdom."

—John Dower

Developing methods that extend critical thinking across the curriculum is a reform strategy that is widely supported—and working. Like cooperative learning, critical thinking has shown both staying power and a dispersion of expertise. Both the strategies have quietly become part of the curriculum and national standards. Critical thinking involves the ability to raise powerful questions about what is being read, viewed, or listened to. Teaching thinking also involves developing the ability to assess information and make creative and critical judgments. Collaboration can amplify the application of reasoning skills—helping students talk about, draw, or use other methods to express what is going on inside their heads.

Although some of the concepts of critical thinking go back to Socrates, today's efforts to place critical thinking in the curriculum started in university philosophy departments in the 1980s. It was felt that philosophy had something to contribute to the school reform movement. Next, cognitive psychologists and educators began to build on critical thinking to advance their findings about how the human intellect operates. Rather than relying on demonstration or packing the concepts into a single subject, critical thinking can be infused into other subjects. This helped teachers quickly pick up on the concept as a way to improve the teaching of traditional subjects. Critical thinking is continuing to grow in popularity. A new awareness is taking hold: critical thinking is an academic competency as crucial to a child's future as literacy and numeracy.

Times of great change offer real opportunities, but you have to act because they don't last. The first wave of American educational reform (beginning in the mid 1980s) resulted in some incremental changes.

However, the basic patterns, structures, and methods were left in place. The new wave of reform is after something more fundamental, a kind of strategic change that requires restructuring the way schools are organized, the way subjects are taught, and the way elements like collaboration and thinking skills are embedded in the curriculum.

Teachers must work with students to set the conditions for critical thinking and collaborative problem-solving because these processes not magically occur in a vacuum. When used in unison, both concepts challenge students to collaboratively construct meaning by interpreting, analyzing, and manipulating information in response to a problem or question that requires more than a true application of previously learned knowledge. It is important to remember that words are not the only good expression of thought—pictures, semantic webs, painting, dance, and music are just some of the additional ways to express what we are thinking.

Today's educational change efforts involve dislodging thinking about teaching and learning from the places where they get stuck. This includes opening new spheres and imagining a better state of things. To formulate plans for the transformation of education also requires the best minds and accumulated wisdom of the nation. Laying the foundation for future educational practice requires a whole range of expertise. Educational researchers and social scientists can help by providing new insights into how people learn to think and organize knowledge.

Reasoning and Thoughtfulness: Making Meaningful Connections

When small cooperative groups show good group or individual reasoning skills and thoughtfulness, it usually indicates reflection, thinking problems through, flexibility enough to consider original solutions, a curiosity to pose new questions, and a mode of expression that moves beyond discussion.

The research evidence suggests that giving students multiple perspectives and entry points into subject matter increases thinking and learning (Sears & Marshall, 1990). The implication here is that ideas about how students learn a subject needs to be pluralized. Almost any important concept can be approached from multiple directions—emphasizing understanding and making meaningful connections across subjects. This means making available learning possibilities and resources (human and technological) that might appeal to pupils with very different learning styles and cultural backgrounds.

Tomorrow's schools will need to introduce new frameworks for learning that build on the multiple ways of learning. This means addressing the several ways of representing thinking and knowledge by organizing lessons around the ways students think and learn. A major goal will be to enhance thoughtfulness by creating a critical thinking and cooperative environment and making the school a home for inquiry. If many of today's dreams and possibilities are going to be put into widespread practice, we must all be more courageous in helping admired models move beyond the margins and into the schools, the media, and the home.

A child's critical thinking ability evolves through a dynamic of personal abilities, social values, and institutions. Taking this into account in the effort to revitalize the educational process means looking at recent advances in the understanding of child development. All children, for example, bring their own incomplete models of how the world works to school with them. From birth, children are busy making sense of their environment. By grappling with the curious and the confusing, they learn ways of understanding, develop schemes for thinking, and find meaning. Children sing songs, tell stories, and read the tiniest gesture accurately in a wide variety of contexts. By the time they come to school, they have already developed a rich body of knowledge about the world around them (Gardner, 1991).

The best beginning can be extended in school when the teacher cultivates a broad disposition to critical thinking throughout the year. Natural rhythms are one thing, but it will take learning-centered instruction to continue the process of working through misunderstandings and developing mature thinkers. It helps when teachers use the language of thinking. By using and explaining terms like "hypothesis," "reasoning," "theory," and "evidence," they can lay the groundwork for inquiry and enhancing intellectual development. Since thinking skills are directly involved in successful learning throughout the educational experience, the idea that thinking should assume a central place in the curriculum doesn't come as a surprise to most teachers. Piaget and his followers have insisted for over fifty years that memorization and factual knowledge were not true learning. Most educators now view learning more as *constructing knowledge* than memorizing information (Resnick & Klopfer, 1989).

Today's cognitive educators share with Piagetians a constructivist view of learning that teaches us to begin with real materials, respect knowledge, invite interactive learning, and the various dimensions of thoughtfulness. Constructivist teachers connect academic goals with practical problem solving and students' life experiences. Some of the elements of thinking encouraged are inquiry, self-regulated learning, collaboration, experimentation, metacognition, and the relationship between various subjects and the child's life. The best of the new approaches also suggest teaching content and the skills of thinking simultaneously (Damon, 1989). Rather than special classes, critical thinking works best when it is woven into all subject matter. The embedding of thinking skills and cooperation in the curriculum involves students intensely in reasoning, elaboration, hypothesis forming, and problem-solving activities.

The ability to raise powerful questions about what's being *read, viewed* or *heard* is a dimension of thinking that can contribute to the process of constructing meaning. Developing the motivation to think, solid decision-making, working together, elaboration, and insightful creations (that suggest possibilities for action) form the core structure of effective thinking and learning (Shoenfeld, 1982).

> *Better learning will not come from finding better ways for the teacher to instruct but from* giving the learner better opportunities to construct.
>
> — Papert

Developing mature thinkers who are able to acquire, work together, and use knowledge means educating minds rather than training memories. New curriculum designs recognize this and include strategies that develop thoughtful attitudes and perceptions. Critical thinking involves the ability to raise powerful questions about what's being read, viewed or listened to. Effective problem solving, solid decision making, insightful observations, and inventing are included in this definition.

Sometimes the acquisition of enhanced thinking skills can be well structured and planned; at other times, it is a chance encounter formed by a crazy collision of elements. It is little wonder that such innovative approaches pose a challenge—a few teachers even worry that neither they nor society can handle too many critical thinkers. They're wrong, without the magic of thinking, collaboration, and critical inquiry school work lacks much of its useful meaning.

The implementation of new possibilities depend on the teacher in the classroom. The elements of thinking are teachable, and teachers can learn to do it well. But professional development activities may have to go hand-in-hand with *organizing* instruction to accommodate new ways of representing knowledge and inviting reflective thinking. It is important to provide diverse staff development activities to expand knowledge, horizons, and organizational possibilities. If given half a chance, many teachers will collaboratively take what is now known about critical thinking and use it to support innovative practice.

Qualities of Good Thinking

Critical and creative thinking are natural human processes that can be amplified by awareness and practice. Both critical and creative thinking make use of specific core thinking skills. Classroom instruction and guided practice in the development of these skills will include the following:

1. *Focusing Skills* —attending to selected chunks of information. Some focusing skills include defining, identifying key concepts, recognizing the problem, and setting goals.
2. *Information Gathering Skills* —becoming aware of the substance or content needed. Observing, obtaining information, forming questions, clarifying through inquiry are some skills of information gathering.
3. *Remembering Skills* —are activities that involve information storage and retrieval. Encoding and recalling are thinking skills which have been found to improve retention. These skills involve strategies such as rehearsal, mnemonics, visualization, and retrieval.
4. *Organizing Skills* —arranging information so that it can be understood or presented more effectively. Some of these organizing skills consist of comparing, classifying (categorizing), ordering, and representing information.
5. *Analyzing Skills* —are used in classifying and examining information of components and relationships. Analysis is at the heart of critical thinking. Recognizing and articulating attributes and component parts, focusing on details and structure, identifying relationships and patterns, grasping the main idea, and finding errors are elements of analysis.
6. *Generating Skills* —involve using prior knowledge to add information beyond what is known or given. Connecting new ideas, inferring, identifying similarities and differences, predicting, and elaborating adds new meaning to information. Generating involves

such higher order thinking as making comparisons, constructing metaphors, producing analogies, providing explanations and forming mental models.

7. *Integrating Skills* — involve putting things together, solving, understanding, forming principles, and creating composition. These thinking strategies involve summarizing, combining information, deleting unnecessary material, graphically organizing, outlining, and restructuring to incorporate new information.

8. *Evaluating Skills* — assessing the reasonableness and quality of ideas. Skills of evaluation include establishing criteria and proving or verifying data (Marzano et al., 1988).

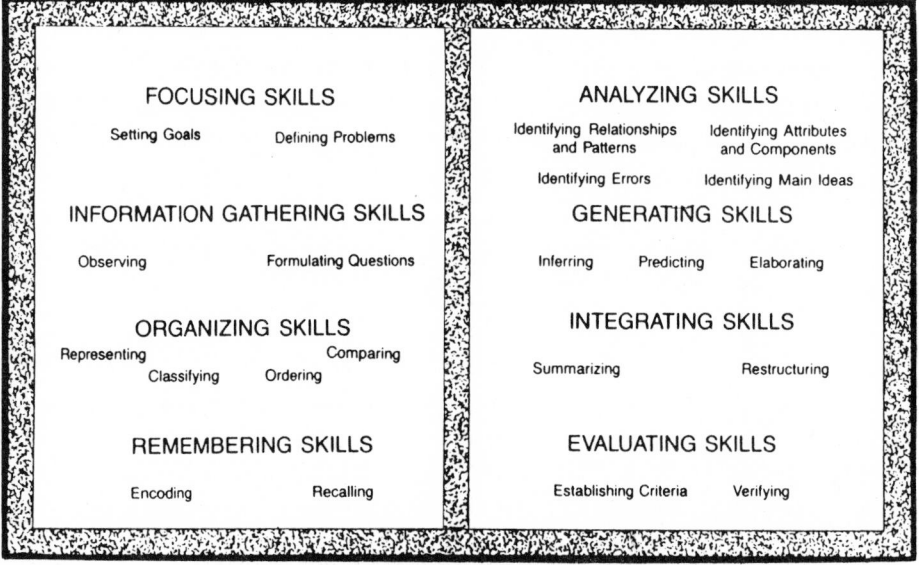

FOCUSING SKILLS

Setting Goals   Defining Problems

INFORMATION GATHERING SKILLS

Observing   Formulating Questions

ORGANIZING SKILLS

Representing   Comparing
Classifying   Ordering

REMEMBERING SKILLS

Encoding   Recalling

ANALYZING SKILLS

Identifying Relationships   Identifying Attributes
and Patterns   and Components

Identifying Errors   Identifying Main Ideas

GENERATING SKILLS

Inferring   Predicting   Elaborating

INTEGRATING SKILLS

Summarizing   Restructuring

EVALUATING SKILLS

Establishing Criteria   Verifying

To put thinking skills into classroom practice teachers need to consciously question how they can best be taught. Introspective questions such as: "How can I get students to express their thinking, become aware of new information, ask questions, retrieve and organize information, analyze and generate new ideas, summarize and evaluate?" At one time or another each of the elements will require some reflection, elaboration, and action. Remember that it is just as important for students to "think on paper"—or express themselves with physical models—as it is to think in their heads.

Proficient learners seem to automatically integrate elements of efficient thinking into their repertoire of techniques for making meaning. For those who don't find it quite so automatic, research has shown that most of these skills can be enhanced by effective instruction. There is also strong evidence that many students—especially the youngest and lower achievers—need explicit and sustained instruction to become skilled in thinking and monitoring their own thinking processes (White & Gunstone, 1992).

In addition to instruction in specific thinking skills, students also need guidance in how to use these skills. Thinking processes such as forming mental drawings, describing relationships which can be applied to many examples, comprehension, problem solving, oral discourse, and scientific inquiry are relatively complex sequences of thinking.

Mental autonomy, creative expression, and critical thinking must connect the child's home and school environment. For the process to reach its full potential, we need to teach in ways that can encourage good intellectual habits and arouse passion. Concept development, collaboration, and comprehension are thinking processes that can be directed toward knowledge acquisition—with one feeding on the other.

Creating and Using New Knowledge

The real voyage of discovery consists not in seeking new landscapes, but in having new eyes.

—Marcel Proust

Although knowledge acquisition processes are needed to form the base, that knowledge is useful to the degree it can be applied or used to create new knowledge (Marzano et al., 1988, p. 33). Thus students need opportunities to use their knowledge, compose, make decisions, solve problems, and conduct research to discover or create new knowledge. As teachers facilitate critical thinking activities they can help everyone to open their world and tap into the whole spectrum of intelligences—encouraging multiple "readings" of the world, media, and written text.

The infusion of thinking skill concepts into the curriculum can go hand in hand with the basic principles students must learn to be competent with a subject. Other thought patterns build on these foundations, stressing the production and application of knowledge. The process leaves spaces where students and teachers imagine better things and figure out where they need to repair gaps. Group discussion can add to this by providing social support that allows a number of thinking processes to merge in the student's personal repertoire of strategies.

It is important to make all students aware of the characteristics of critical thinking and provide experiences for its application. Extending and refining knowledge together can be very satisfying. Cooperative problem solving can help students identify central questions, pose strategies for solutions, evaluate alternative possibilities, and develop plans for implementing the best solution. Discussion and small group decision-making can be intricately entwined in this process of opening the world to wider and wider perspectives. Such shared thoughtfulness and search for meaning can connect to the struggles of our times, maintaining a vital link to those daily realities. Classrooms organized for active group work create a community that respects individual learners. Thinking does not thrive in a threatening, intimidating environment where either adult or peer pressure impedes independence.

Good teachers support diverse thinking styles and collaboration. The goal is often to help students focus on the thinking process, and step outside the boundaries of experience to construct meaning. This means that the teacher and students open themselves up to suggestions, styles of thinking, connections, and ambiguities previously unexamined. The potential for imaginative action grows out of this process. As Aristotle suggested, "*there are two steps to doing anything: (1) Make up your mind, and (2) Do it!*" How thoughtful and willful we become will determine the pathways we all travel tomorrow.

Newman has identified six key indicators of thoughtfulness in the classroom:

1. Students are given sufficient time to think before being required to answer questions.
2. Interaction focuses on sustained examination of a few topics rather than superficial coverage of many.
3. The teacher presses students to clarify or justify their opinions rather than accepting and reinforcing them indiscriminately.
4. Interactions are characterized by substantive coherence and continuity.
5. The teacher models the characteristics of a thoughtful person (showing interest in students' ideas and their suggestions for solving problems, modeling problem-solving processes rather than just

giving answers, acknowledging the difficulties involved in gaining a clear understanding of problematic topics).

6. Students generate original and unconventional ideas in the course of the interaction (Newman, 1990, 1992).

Some Suggestions for Fostering Critical Thinking in Learning Communities:

- Provide opportunities for students to explore different viewpoints and domains of information that arouse frustration or outrage.
- Conduct debates and discussions on controversial issues. Students work in groups to present an argument on a topic and present their view to another group. Sides can then be switched, the opposite view defended, and different routes to a better social order explored.
- Role play historical events or current news happenings from conflicting viewpoints. Examine some of the more questionable television news images, whose power is palpable but whose connection to reality is tenuous.
- Watch TV broadcasts that present different viewpoints. (For example, those that interview individuals with differing perspectives on a problem.)
- Have students write letters to the editor of newspapers, TV or popular journals expressing their stance on an issue of importance.
- When students express what they have been thinking it is important to open up the whole range of possibility—from poetry to computer modeling.

These suggestions open up the possibility for developing thinking by practicing argumentative thinking skills. The basic goal is to stimulate and encourage a wide range of collaboration, divergent thinking, and discussion. By arguing important moral dilemmas in history, politics, literature, art, music, or sports, students can learn content, reasoning possibilities, and extend ethical concepts. To have power over the story that dominates one's life means having the power to retell it, deconstruct it, joke about it, and change it as times change. Without this power, it is more difficult to think and act on new thoughts and open the doors to deep thinking.

Beyond specific teaching strategies the climate of the classroom and the behavior of the teacher is very important. Teachers need to model critical thinking behaviors—setting the tone, atmosphere, and environment for learning. Being able to collaborate with other teachers can serve as another formative contribution to how the teacher might better see and construct individual classroom reality. In collaborative problem solving, for example, teachers can help each other in the clarification of goals, and share the products of their joint imaginations. Thus perceptions can be changed, ideas can flow, and practice can be meaningfully strengthened, deepened, extended, *and changed.*

Learning different approaches to figuring things out (with peers) and connecting knowledge in meaningful ways are viewed as important elements in furthering new curriculum goals. Developing mature thinkers, who can work with others has always been a major goal of elite educational institutions. Today's task is to teach these skills within the schools. Whether we choose to value thinking—or even follow the path towards a quality educational system—is as much a societal issue as it is a pedagogical one (Baron, 1988). If we as a nation make the wrong choice and diminish educational possibilities, we lose something of incalculable value.

Thinking is more than acquiring knowledge; it's a quest for meaning and possibilities for collective action. In this context, learning can be viewed as an adventurous joint effort that connects invention, insightful reflection, and sound decision making. The process depends on a combination of mental habits, interpersonal ability, subject matter expertise, general strategic knowledge, and tenacity.

The fundamental search for meaning is made especially powerful when team efforts are connected to individual self-perception, attitudes, and accountability. Along with this, metacognitive awareness (thinking about thinking) can be amplified as small groups try to define, and construct their own understandings. Such a self-reflective thinking process can play a large role in the development of reasoning and interpersonal skills. Towards this end, students can work together to actively integrate new information with existing knowledge, select what is important, deal with the unexpected, and learn to make inferences beyond the information given.

"Relationships to others, like thinking, are as incoherent and difficult to measure as truth . . .
But when previously unassociated ideas strike together the result is a little stunning"
—Herman Melville

Improving Schools Is Only Part of Improving Educational Outcomes

Technology and communication have created a world economy where working smarter is just as important as working harder. Today's jobs require workers who are mentally fit and prepared to absorb new ideas, adapt to change, cope with ambiguity, and solve unconventional problems. Citizenship goes a few steps farther and requires the building of civic consciousness. Getting ready to be productive workers and citizens requires rigorous academic training, moral development, and the ability to think critically.

It is difficult to deal with education in isolation because the deficiencies in the schools often reflect the problems in the wider society. However, we don't just get the schools we deserve; the schools influence a whole range of issues that reach across society—from attitudes about learning to maintaining productive mental habits. This is especially true when the generative power of higher education is added to the mix.

Quality instruction involves spending more time on thoughtful discussions, reasoned discourse, criticism, reflection, collaboration, and asking insightful questions. Traditionally, things like logistics have gotten in the way of both process and content (Goodlad, 1983). In some schools, students are seldom asked for their opinions—nor are they encouraged to question each other, the teacher, or the textbook. This has to change. Higher level questions must be valued and students must be helped to go beyond unsupported personal opinions, to work together, to supply good argument with some kind of evidence to support their viewpoint. Argument, based on good information, can help form productive habits of the mind (White & Gunstone, 1992).

Schools play a major role in the development of critical and creative thinking (Wiggins, 1984). As schools continue to grope for valid solutions, it is important to recognize that improving the schools is only part of improving educational outcomes. Parents are the first teachers and today many of them need training—especially when one young parent is asked to do the work of two under extreme conditions.

As a child grows, the community can also play a major role. Schools can be assisted in organizing cognitive apprenticeships that allow older students to participate in work environments (Resnick & Klopfer, 1989). This means involvement in real tasks, like running a small business, figuring out how to run equipment in a biotechnology lab, explaining physical phenomena that is difficult to understand, or writing a message of explanation for an interested audience. Success in life outside of school is often quite dependent on cognitive tools (like computers or calculators) and the ability to work with others in ferreting out bits of information when it's needed. Interactions between specialized skills, general knowledge, interpersonal skills, and thinking ability are crucial to confronting uncertainty and solving such real problems.

> *The thought behind I strove to join*
> *Unto the thought before*
> *But sequence raveled out of reach*
> *Like balls upon the floor.*
>
> — Emily Dickinson

Dealing with exploration, experimentation, exceptions, mistakes, and ambiguity are part of the "work" description in both the school and the workplace of tomorrow. So is dealing with failure in a way that makes it a stepping stone to future accomplishment. A parental or social safety net is one thing, encouraging a dysfunctional dependency is quite another. The best teamwork, thinking, and problem solving is no guarantee — it just improves the odds. Students need nourishing support to get over the rough spots. A willingness to *take risks* and *persevere* turn out to be two of the most important attributes for eventual success. The most critical and creative thinkers make mistakes. The goal should be to learn from them. In the words of the pseudo rock band Spinal Tap "When you take a chance it's such a fine line between stupid and clever."

Opening to the Unfamiliar: Assessing Thinking and Collaboration

The role of teachers is changing along with thinking styles. The old view of teaching as the transmission of content is being expanded to include ways of helping students construct knowledge. Classrooms that invite thoughtfulness understand that knowledge is to be shared or developed rather than held by the authority. Teachers, administrators, and parents need to model interpersonal skills and think about thinking themselves.

Students can best come to critically think about — and understand — complex concepts by actively exploring them in cooperative groups. Recognizing the development of critical thinking is a good first step toward its application and assessment. Some possible guideposts for assessing development of thinking and collaboration include:

- A decrease in "How do I do it?" questions. (Students ask group members before asking the teacher.)

- Using trial and error discovery learning without frustration.
- Questioning peers and teachers (asking powerful why questions).
- Using metaphor, simile, allegory, in speaking, writing, and thinking.
- Developing interpersonal discussion skills for shared inquiry.
- Increased ability to work collaboratively in cooperative groups.
- Willingness to begin a task.
- Initiating inquiry.
- Comfort with ambiguity and open ended assignments.
- Synthesizing and combining diverse ideas.

It is hard to measure attitudes, thinking and interpersonal skills on a paper and pencil test. Another way is to observe the humor, antidotes, parental reactions, and teacher-student interaction.

The ability of both students and teachers to pull together as a team influences how well students reflect on their thinking, pose powerful questions, and connect diverse ideas. Failure to cultivate these aspects of thinking may be a major source of difficulty when it comes to learning content (Beyer, Berry, 1988).

The following are elements to look for in creative thinking:

Fluency	—Producing and considering many alternatives.
Originality	—Producing ideas which go beyond the obvious and are unique and valued.
Highlighting the essence	—Finding and expressing the main idea.
Elaboration	—Filling out an idea or set of ideas by adding details.
Keeping Open	—Delaying closure, seeing many ideas, considering a range of information, making mental leaps.
Awareness of Emotions	—Developing and expressing emotional awareness, perseverance, involvement, and commitment.
Combining and Synthesizing	—Seeing relationships and joining parts and elements to form a whole.
Visualizing—Richly and Colorfully	—Perceiving and creating images which are vivid, strong and alive.

Visualizing—The Inside	—Seeing and presenting ideas and objects from an internal vantage point.
Enjoying and Using Fantasy	—Making use of imagination in a playful way.
Using Movement	—Learning, thinking, and communicating kinesthetically.
Using Sound	—Interpreting and communicating ideas, concepts, and feelings through sound and music.
Breaking through and Extending Boundaries	—Overcoming limitations and conventions and creating new solutions.
Using Humor	—Combining incongruous situations with comical wit, surprise and amusement.
Imagining the Future	—Envisioning alternatives, predicting consequences, and planning ahead.

Students learn elements of creative thinking from interpersonal communication behaviors. Students can help develop these and other language skills in a variety of ways: listening, speaking, arguing, problem solving, clarifying, and creating (Dissanayake, 1992). Pairs of students can argue an issue with other pairs and then switch sides. The chaos and dissonance of group work can help foster critical thinking and imaginative language development. This way students learn to work creatively with conflicts, viewing them as possibilities for the improvement of literacy. Hopefully some of this will carry over to conflict resolution and peer resolution of other disputes.

Multiple Possibilities for *Process* and *Content*

The brain has a multiplicity of functions and voices that speak independently and quite differently for different individuals (Bandura, 1986). Howard Gardner and others have attempted to more broadly define different kinds of thought processes and abilities (Gardner, 1991). They suggest viewing mathematical and verbal ability as but two of seven crucial abilities or "intelligences." The other five: spatial ways of

PROMOTING CREATIVE THINKING:
A SELF-EVALUATION

_____ 1. I provide stimuli for as many of the senses as possible.
_____ 2. I guide students to recognize that creativity can be improved by working in a disciplined manner.
_____ 3. I verify that students understand the instructional objectives for the creative activities we do.
_____ 4. I teach a variety of strategies for overcoming blocks to creativity.
_____ 5. I make a conscious effort to provide opportunities for students to be creative, to be original, and to try to think of new ways to solve a problem.
_____ 6. I provide a nonthreatening atmosphere in which students are encouraged to raise questions.
_____ 7. I encourage students to develop criteria to judge the work of both their peers and themselves.
_____ 8. I encourage students to apply affirmative judgment and to make positive self-statements about their creativity.
_____ 9. I help students to defer judgment and to keep an open mind when new ideas are being presented.
_____10. I attempt to integrate divergent production into as many areas of science as possible.
_____11. I help students to recognize and value the components of convergent and divergent thinking in creative production.
_____12. I model creative thinking and apply it to the science curriculum whenever possible.
_____13. I provide opportunities for students to share their creative products with appropriate audiences.

knowing (art or navigation are two examples), bodily kinesthetic intelligence (movement and dance), musical ability, intrapersonal intelligence (self-reflection), and interpersonal intelligence (working in groups). There is nothing sacred about these categories. However, the point is that there is a wide range of abilities; no one is great at everything; and it is best not to restrict educational avenues to a single path of representing, knowing, or learning (Sternberg & Frensch, 1992).

To make learning more accessible to children means respecting multiple ways of making meaning. When a teacher settles on a single representation of either subject matter or pedagogical reality, many possibilities for learning may be shelved. This, in turn, shuts the door on other approaches that are capable of shaping students' learning in meaningful ways.

Introductory Activities for Helping Upper Grade Students, Teachers, or Parents Understand Multiple Intelligences

Try putting large numbers on four walls: 1,2,3,4. Explain that four is excellent, 3 good, 2 fair, and 1 poor. Have everyone stand up and move to a number that best describes their ability to swim, compute, write, dance, sing, paint, work in a group or understand yourself. Wait a minute or two after each item for a brief discussion. Have the group make some suggestions for qualities that might spread the group into each of the four categories. The point is that nobody is good — or bad — at everything. People have strengths in a wide range of areas and these strengths should be taken into account when approaching a subject.

Logical-Mathematical, Linguistic, Spatial, Musical, Interpersonal, Intrapersonal, Bodily-Kinesthetic

Put the "7 Intelligences" on the board in a random order and let the group guess which one is being demonstrated after the activity. Explain each intelligence after the experience.

Lingustic Intelligence: "Close your eyes and think of a poem that you knew or wrote. A passage in a book or a speech would also work. Take a moment and listen to the sounds. Share your imagery."

Logical-Mathematical Intelligence: "How long ago was a million seconds? Work it out any way that you want — calculator, ask others, use paper." Wait until at least one person gets close (about 11+ days). The right answer isn't the point; *share the process.*

Musical Intelligence: Either the presenter or a prepared member of the audience can hum a few bits of any well known song or jingle . . . have the group guess what it is. See if someone else in the audience can come up with a few bits of a melody for the group to figure out. Asking a few musically inclined students come into class prepared to hum a short segment can help here.

Spatial Intelligence: Close your eyes and try to visualize this room . . . the carpet, ceiling patterns, light fixtures, etc." WAIT (a minute or so) "Open your eyes and check the answer. How many of you had a good idea?"

Bodily-Kinesthetic Intelligence: "Stand up and walk in place (normally) using a few feet of space near you. Now pretend that you are walking on fresh tar . . . hot pavement to cool grass . . . Jupiter, with much heavier gravity." Throughout this you are using the body to express ideas.

Interpersonal Intelligence: "Stand up and find somebody with shoes like yours—introduce yourself." Wait a few minutes and ask how people went about the task.

Intrapersonal Intelligence: "Close your eyes and go back in life to a time when you felt most alive (defined any way that you wish). Experience the feeling of that time." Have a few of the participants share their stories.

After a discussion of the theoretical and practical implications of multiple intelligence you could ask if this approach might cause a rethinking of ideas about intelligence. How about a little critical analysis . . . Is there a lot of evidence to support the theory? If you believe Gardner did a good job of identifying the influential intelligences of the twentieth century, *are these the same ones most needed for the 21st century?*

A Sample Unit-Based Interdisciplinary Theory

A wide range of projects can build on these seven ways of doing an assignment. For example, basing an interdisciplinary unit about dogs on Gardner's theory of multiple intelligences might include the following:

- *Spatial:* maps of where dogs they identify walk if loose, kennel club charts of breeds, pictures of dogs, and student art.
- *Musical:* listening to tapes or videotapes of dog sounds and imitating them.
- *Kinesthetic:* ask other students about their dog's habits (where the dog sleeps and plays) hike to a dog's residence, play with the dog, you may wish to sketch or build a replica of a dog's sleeping area (or dog house).
- *Intrapersonal:* finding a place of solitude for dog watching. In many city parks, 5 p.m. is a great dog watching time.
- *Interpersonal:* working with a community project to protect local dogs. How might dogs get total strangers to talk?
- *Linguistic:* written stories, poems, book reports, oral presentations and video or tape recordings.
- *Logical-mathematical:* collecting statistics about dogs, breeds, and exploring how scientists have tried to figure out how dogs communicate. [Schools have traditionally emphasized linguistic and logical-mathematical intelligences.]

Dogs have been working closely with humans for at least 15,000 years. Even the earliest cave paintings show dogs helping in the hunt and guarding the encampment. Their sense of hearing, smell, speed, loyalty, and the possibilities for training in a large number of tasks assisted mankind with building civilization. In the twentieth century, we find dogs doing everything from herding and pulling carts to serving in the military and helping hearing impaired people. For children today, dogs can provide an opening to another world. They teach children many things usually not taught in school, including nonverbal communication. Interdisciplinary inquiry on dogs can examine everything from how different cultures treat dogs to training guide dogs for the blind—a wide range of possibilities for open-ended, learner-centered theme development.

Students whose thinking or learning styles happen to be different from the style of the teacher (or the textbook) frequently experience more difficulty than others (Shulman, M., 1991). When teachers identify their own thinking style and provide multiple possibilities for their students there is a greater likelihood of success (Bamberger, 1991). Reflective teachers who are aware of multiple paths to understanding can make suggestions that broaden a student's intellectual and cultural base without destroying student initiative.

Cultivating Thoughtfulness and Integrating Knowledge into Personal Experience

What's missed most isn't something that's gone, but possibilities that will never happen.
— Margaret Atwood

A curriculum that ignores the powerful ideas of its charges will miss many opportunities for illuminating the human condition. To teach content without regard for self-connected thinking prevents subject matter knowledge from being transformed in the student's mind. If the curriculum is to be viewed as enhancing *being*—rather than merely imparting knowledge and skills—then reasoned decision making is part of the process (Berman et al., 1991). A curriculum that takes students thinking seriously is more likely to be successful in cultivating thoughtfulness and subject matter competence. Respecting unique thought patterns can also be viewed as a commitment to caring communication and openness.

Breaking out of established patterns can be done collectively by those most directly affected. All of us need the occasional push or encouragement to get out of a rut. It is important for teachers to develop their own reflection and inquiry skills so that they can become students of their own teaching. When a teacher decides to participate with students in learning to think on a daily basis, they nourish human possibilities. Can teachers make a difference? Absolutely. The idea is to connect teachers with innovative methods and materials so that they can build learning environments that are sensitive to students' growing abilities to think for themselves. By promoting thoughtful learning across the full spectrum of personalities and ways of knowing, teachers can make a tremendous difference and perform a unique service for the future.

When the ideal and the actual are linked, the result can produce a dynamic, productive, and resilient form of learning. What we know about teaching and thinking is increasingly being put into practice in model classrooms and schools (Boomer, 1992). These exemplary programs recognize that powerful inquiry can help students make personal discoveries that change thinking and that critical thinking skills can turn an unexamined belief into a reasoned one. Thus the control people exercise over their lives can be enhanced by the teacher's support of inquiry and caring.

A constructivist approach in teaching builds on the idea that children learn by integrating observations and experiences into their personal framework (memories, associations, feelings, sounds, rules, etc.). If this learning framework is rich, students will have the ability to explain, predict, provide analogies, make connections, and provide new perspectives as they express what they have been thinking. As students learn how to actively apply knowledge, solve problems, and promote conceptual understanding they need to be able to use these processes to change their own theories and beliefs in ways that are personally meaningful. In this way they can develop conceptual understanding and the means for integrating knowledge into their personal experience.

Some Suggested Activities for Teachers:

1. **The jigsaw approach** to cooperative groups suggests setting up five or six groups to study the same topic and having an individual in each group take responsibility for investigating the same subtopic. Students investigating the same subtopic work together to study that topic before returning to their original groups. Once back in with their original team, they teach the subtopic to everyone in the group. It is most motivating and active when students know about their teaching responsibilities beforehand.

2. **Reasoning together with paired problem solving**
Students who are exposed to a variety of viewpoints through various media and authentic materials need to be able to view the varying

perspectives critically. One way to accomplish this goal is with paired problem solving. The ability to recognize the implicit argument in the explanation of their partner helps both individuals to compare the similarities as well as the differences among the various points of view. Active learning, the nurturing of critical thinking skills, rather than passive listening, will enable students to develop self-reliance in their problem solving across the curriculum. Encouraging active learning rather than passive listening shifts the focus from a teacher-centered approach to one that is student-centered and cooperative. Within this framework, the teacher serves as a facilitator of thinking, rather than an authority figure who transmits knowledge.

In paired problem solving pairs of students might be assigned a specific task. One student works on the problem while the other asks questions what they are doing and they help each other develop a plan for the symbolic support of their thinking (Lochhead, 1985).

3. Shift the learning emphasis

In the student-centered class, the emphasis shifts from product to process, from a goal-oriented approach to learning to one in which the learning process is itself the central focus.

Learning involves not merely the acquisition of information, but also the development of critical skills for evaluating facts and the interpretation of facts. Sharing various interpretations of a text adds an extra dimension in the learning process as students not only learn how others perceive a certain issue, but also appreciate the various reasoning processes and life experiences that support different interpretations.

4. Teach thinking skills

Critical skills that can be developed include questioning the presentation of information: the order in which facts are presented, the emphasis of certain facts over others, and the implicit slant of any "story," whether it be in literature, history books, or the news. Student groups also can learn to look for discrepancies between the facts and the conclusions drawn from them or inconsistencies among the various versions of a particular news story. When reading literature, they can discuss the varying perspectives among the characters and, for older students, the different points-of-view between the narrator and the characters. All these exercises should enable students to distinguish between fact and opinion and to question the possibility of any totally objective presentation of information.

5. Analyze stereotypes

As students learn about the perspectives of other cultures — including the varying interpretations of historical events, such as wars and political transitions and critically view their own culture's interpretation of such events, they can explore where stereotypes come from. In this framework, each student's cultural background is viewed as a valuable tool for learning, a bridge to another world view, rather than a barrier to understanding another individual.

Understanding the essence of the argument means understanding some of the universal truths that speak to everyone *and* recognizing how a diversity of new voices can add vigor to learning. As students learn about the perspectives of other cultures—including social and historical background—they can explore where stereotypes come from. This shouldn't stand in the way of supplying students with the common and universal roots of present conditions. Rather, it means including active learning techniques where students can collaboratively shape alliances that view each student's cultural background as a valuable tool for learning.

6. Use moral dilemma and debate activities

Argument (debate) may make some people uncomfortable, but it does result in an understanding of the issues. Bringing important controversial issues out into the open is central to the health and vitality of American education. Encouraging students to argue together can help them reason together (just make sure that each side has an equal chance to be heard). The goal is a more integrative understanding of human community and an appreciation of overlapping cultural experiences.

7. Using semantic maps, webs, and Venn diagrams

These are all visual representations that can be used in a wide variety of subjects. The process involves noting visually, sketching comparisons, contrasts, word associations, and the connections between subtopics. One way to do a semantic map puts the main idea in a circle in the middle with spokes radiating out for key concepts. Subtopics can branch off the spokes. Other possibilities include connected word association circles and Venn diagrams of overlapping circles where similarities are in the overlap and differences are in the part of the circle not overlapping. Maps can be used for predicting what is going to be in a unit based on subtitles or pictures. They can also be used for vocabulary development. But most often maps are used for expressing a summary of comprehension —with children connecting, sketching, and remembering concepts.

Clearing Our Own Pathways

Broad misconceptions, naive theories, oversimplified explanations, and stereotyped views are deeply ingrained. To bring such misconceptions to the surface requires an in-depth awareness of thinking and learning. We know that subject matter concepts make more sense to students when they are connected by a variety of paths to real situations. No concept is too difficult when the ideas at the heart of a subject have meaning for students' lives.

In a search for meaning, teachers and peers can help individuals to understand the nature of a subject—while leaving room to reshape concepts as new information becomes available. The personal search for understanding thinking (metacognitive awareness) is shaped by the students' attitudes, the subject matter, knowledge of themselves, and their ability to work with others. Subjects can be approached in different ways: descriptive accounts; logical analytical quantitative methods; and aesthetic expressions in art, dance, or music.

In learning how to think, children need something concrete to think about. There needs to be a connection between activities and subjects—allowing the thinking skills engendered in one area to serve as a bridge between subjects and the environment. For example, while watching a newscast about whales trapped in the ice, one fifth-grade class we worked with decided to find out more about the characteristics of whales and their migratory patterns. This led to an exploration of their status as endangered species. In the process of conducting research, the children did mathematical calculations and explored geographical, environmental, and social issues—generating their own ideas and potential solutions to the problem. Information from books was augmented by newspapers, video clips, and experts from the field. Editing a videotape and writing about the issues raised in these activities helped students think of new ideas and develop a habit for academic discourse. Lessons can follow a similar pattern of:

- topic formation
- exploration of prior knowledge
- sharing interesting new questions
- researching a specific knowledge base
- comparing, reporting and reflective thinking about a project
- expressing the results to an audience

Inviting Thoughtfulness

We are far from having all the answers needed to design a curriculum that invites thoughtfulness. But we do know enough to begin the intellectual adventure. And we know enough to institute educational practices that promote true understanding. A skilled teacher, open to new ideas, can open a number of doors to adventures in imaginativeness and creative perception. Reflection, discussion, and cultivating the disposition for critical thinking can inform and enrich our teaching (Sternberg & Wagner, 1986).

Integrating, extending, refining knowledge, and using that knowledge meaningfully requires teachers to integrate and use what is known about how this fits into the instruction process. Educators also need all the help they can get as they struggle to create vital learning communities that foster critical, creative, civic, and moral thought. Although improvements in teaching alone will not solve some of our dire social and educational problems, it is a factor that has an absolutely vital role to play in successful change. Teachers who have a substantial knowledge of pedagogy and subject matter can use that classroom expertise in a manner that gradually legitimizes new approaches.

No one can play it safe and easy when it comes to breaking down the barriers between social problems, and educational opportunity. Teachers need the courage and the support to take risks. If given the chance, good teachers, with good approaches (in the right environment) can push the process of more effective thinking and learning forward. They can make a real difference. Making mistakes has to be viewed as part of the process of change. Teachers can only bring about real change by having the freedom and support to succeed by occasionally failing.

Good teachers can't all be miracle workers and get it right every time — and they shouldn't have to. But a good teacher can provide an astonishing revelation. Good teachers put snags in the river of children passing by and, over the years, they redirect hundreds of lives.

— Tracy Kidder

Thinking skills are learned through interaction with the environment, mass media, peers, and subject matter. Some students pick it up naturally, while others learn reasoning skills with difficulty or not at all. It is clear that the following thinking skills can be taught directly: *generating multiple ideas about a topic, summarizing, figuring out meaning from context,* understanding *analogy,* and *detecting reasoning fallacies* (Segal, Chipman, & Glaser, 1985).

Thinking and its expression can take many forms—going beyond reading, writing, mathematics, and science. Painting, music, and dance (movement) can resonant with meaning and are just one set of neglected imaginative abilities that can be brought to the fore. The idea is to have students work with various media and subject areas so that they can go beyond the literal and linear to probe areas that are ambiguous in meaning and rich in illusion. Creative expression is not limited to print. Isadora Duncan made this point clear when she said "If I could write it, I wouldn't need to dance it."

Critical and Creative Thinking

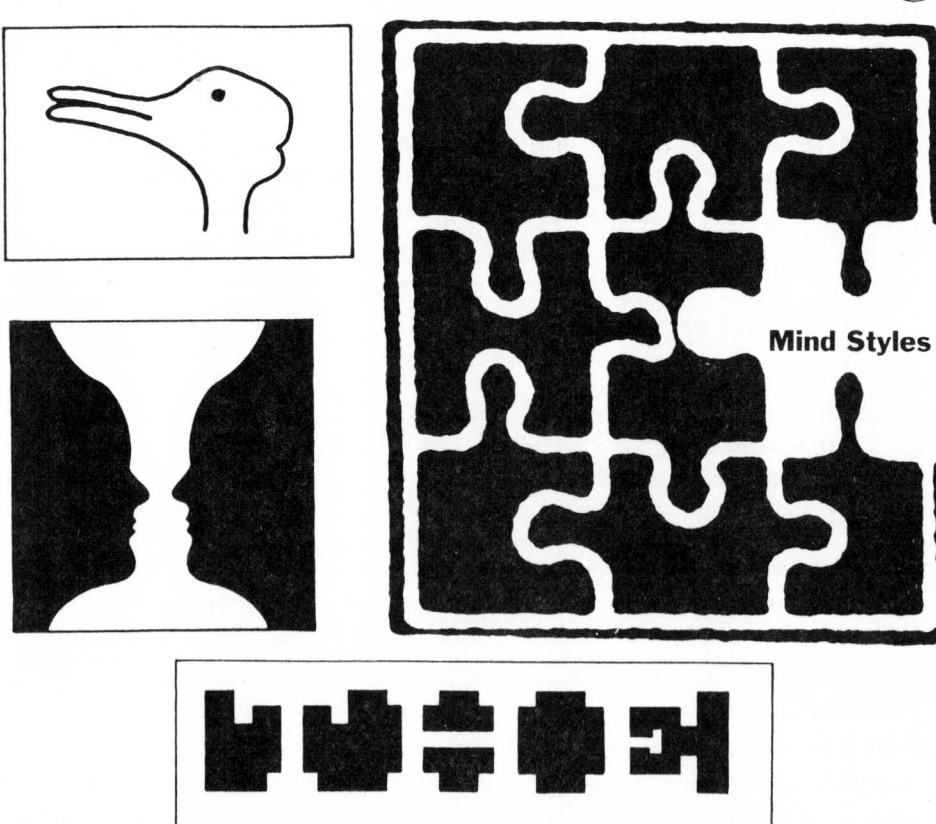

Mind Styles

Creating a Learning Culture That Values Thoughtfulness

Information and thinking are not antithetical. Information isn't a substitute for thinking. And higher level thinking requires some information to be effective. But this doesn't have to leave us content paralyzed. Time must be taken to be sure that student thinking can transform knowledge in a way that makes it transferable to the outside world (Siegler, 1985). There will *never* be enough time to teach *all* the information that we feel is useful. When there is time for inquiry and reflection, covering less can actually help students learn more.

In cultivating the reasoned mind, Hannah Arendt said that evil was not demonic but *the absence of thinking*—a kind of emptiness or blankness that leads to bad deeds. She also suggests that "thinking unfreezes what language has frozen into consciousness" (Arendt, 1958). To bring conflicts to the surface, where they can be transformed by thought, turns them into opportunities for new understanding. A partnership between thought, subject matter, and action can make a unique contribution to human progress on a number of levels.

Since it is so difficult to figure out what information will be crucial to students in the future, it makes sense to pay more attention to the *intellectual tools* that will be required in any future. It makes sense to focus on how models of critical thought can be used differently, at different times, and in different situations. The idea is to put more focus on concepts with high generalizability—like civic responsibility, problem solving, reflection, perceptive thinking, self-direction, and the motivation needed for life-long learning.

As the old lecture-for-recall methods of instruction are abandoned, new collaborative work structures are being offered to make our educational environments more open to thoughtful engagement, untangling the mysteries of learning. The primary goal is for learning to lead to deeper understanding.

Dealing with the changing realities of the late twentieth century is a shared responsibility. The need for educated public engagement is growing with participation in deciding crucial issues that require a broadly informed citizenry. This means that we have to educate *everyone* to think critically, creatively, and deeply. As science and technology transforms our physical and social world a more educated public is required to deal with a constantly evolving set of political, aesthetic, and moral issues. An education that ignores these new realities is incomplete.

Making Thinking Visible

Students come from a world where traditional supports have been weakened and the school must build a learning community that is concerned with the motivation, interests, academic goals, and cultural values. For students to learn how to think new thoughts requires creative teachers who recognize children's need to learn in meaning-centered explorations. Feeling and meaning can be turned inside out as children learn how to construct their own knowledge and absorb new experiences in ways that make sense *to them.* The basic idea here is to go beyond giving students the *truth* of others, making it possible for them to discover their own. These new approaches require teachers who are free to invent diverse approaches to helping students succeed.

We know that students learn in a variety of ways and can be encouraged to reach desired goals by very different paths. They can demonstrate what they have learned in a number of ways: videos, performances, photo-collage, stories for the newspaper, or other projects that can be shared with other students and members of the community. This process gets at the essence of what curriculum is: ways of engaging students in thought on matters that are believed to be important—and sharing what they find.

To be educated means knowing the depths that wait for us under the surface of things, whatever those things may be. As a society, we ignore the realm of the imagination and its impact on the future at our own peril. *Change,* as Louis Pasteur pointed out, *does favor the prepared mind.* The future may be unpredictable. But when the educational experience is better suited to the nature of the growing mind, students can do a better job of mapping the terrain.

> *Better thinkers, problem solvers, and readers are in control of their own future—and once there, they make better strategic decisions, based on what they expected to find.*
>
> —M. Pressley

Building Bridges to an Ambiguous Future

Tomorrow's realities will place an even higher tax on the familiar. What students need to survive in such a rapidly changing world is the mental flexibility to deal with an uncertain future. No subject or approach should be treated like a religious icon. Deep understanding involves more questioning than it does reverence. It also involves engaging students in critically analyzing, synthesizing, making judgments, creating products, and standing up for their rights without resorting to violence.

Students now have to go beyond knowing to understanding how to actually do something. Learning how to think sometimes means cognitive self-observation and taking part in language rich classroom interaction. Shared inquiry is a method of preparation, discussion, and problem solving that can help in developing knowledge. In the words of one sixth grader: "friends don't let friends write bad poetry . . . they figure better ways to do things together."

While collaboration can provoke thought, it can also conflict with basic (deeply entrenched) ways of making sense of the world. Traditional methods of teaching, like lecturing, listening, and working alone, were never effective for everyone. The old paradigm included strategies like "read it again" or "remember what I showed you." Even those who *could* sit still for it don't learn much about thinking, articulating questions, or solving problems along different paths. Lip service may occasionally be given to "teaching thinking skills," but there simply can't be much practice with higher levels of thinking when someone else does most of the important elements of it for you.

Contentment and self-satisfaction are the enemies of change. Real change most frequently comes during times when major players in a situation are simultaneously ill at ease—and focused on an issue. After years of dwelling in a state of sleepy social and educational self-contentment nearly everyone is now becoming concerned about what has happened to the once great American educational system. As part of reestablishing our national commitment to the future we can look forward to an interactive meaning centered curriculum that can develop the thinking skills appropriate for the beginning of a new century.

The goal of schooling should not simply mean reaching for higher levels of basic achievement. Rather there should be a concern with creating a learning culture that moves beyond rote learning to promote wider understandings that connect students to fulfilling and socially responsible lives outside of school. To cope and prevail students need thinking skills, and the mental flexibility for meeting and evaluating new circumstances. Building such inner resources can bring about a harvest of thoughtfulness, community, and possibilities for action.

As schools try to greet the future, curriculum models must shift to help students critically perceive, analyze, interpret, and discover a whole new range of meanings. The challenge for teachers is getting creative and critical thinking out of the heads of their students and into wide range of possibilities for concretely representing ideas. This is not easy amidst the dumbed-down glitter of electronic reality and the devastating social conditions that many students face. It is a new world, crying out for new definitions and people who can redefine and creatively express themselves in a rapidly changing new environment. Teachers and students *can* learn to ask insightful questions together, self-monitor, reflect on their own thinking, concretely express thought, and be able to plan ahead.

The new wave of American school reform is in the process of incorporating recent developments in educational theory, research, and practice. Diverse approaches for reinventing the schools are being respected. As part of reestablishing our national commitment to the future, we can look forward to an interactive, meaning-centered curriculum that can develop the thinking skills appropriate for the beginning of the new century.

> *The year's doors open like those of language,*
> *toward the unknown.*
> *Last night you told me:*
> *Tomorrow, we shall have to think up signs,*
> *sketch a landscape, fabricate a plan on the double edge of day and paper.*
> *Tomorrow, we shall have to invent, once more*
> *the reality of this world.*
>
> —Elizabeth Bishop

REFERENCES

Arendt, H. (1958). *The human condition.* Chicago: University of Chicago Press.

Bamberger, J. (1991). *The mind behind the musical ear.* Cambridge, MA: Harvard University Press.

Bandura, A. (1986). *Social foundations of thought and action: A cognitive theory.* Englewood Cliffs, NJ: Prentice Hall.

Baron, J. (1988). *Thinking and deciding.* New York: Cambridge University Press.

Berman, L., Hultgam, F., Lee, D., Rivkin, M. & Roderick, J. *Toward a curriculum for being.* Albany, NY: State University of New York Press.

Boomer, G. (1992). *Negotiating the curriculum.* Busingstake, U.K.: Falmer Press.

Bruener, J. & Haste, H. (1987). *Making sense.* New York: Routeledge.

Damon, W. (1989). *Child development today and tomorrow.* San Francisco: Jossey-Bass.

Dickens, C. *Hard times,* p. 93.

Gardner, H. (1991). *The unschooled mind.* New York: Basic Books.

Gardner, H. (1993). *Creating minds.* New York: Basic Books.

Goodlad, J. (1983). *A place called school: Prospects for the future.* New York: McGraw-Hill.

Henderson, J. (1992). *Reflective teaching: Becoming an inquiring educator.* New York: Macmillan.

Krosnick, J., & Alwin, D. (1989). Aging and susceptibility to attitude change. *Journal of Personality and Social Psychology,* 57, 416–425.

Lochhead, J. (1985). In Segal, J.W., Chipman, S.F. & Glaser, R. (Eds.). (1985). *Thinking and learning skills: Vol. 1: Relating instruction to research.* Hillsdale, NJ: Erlbaum.

Marzano, et al. (1988). *Dimensions of thinking: A framework for curriculum and instruction.* Alexandria, VA: Association for Supervision and Curriculum Development.

Papert, S. (1990). Introduction in Harel, Idit (ed.). *Constructionist learning.* Cambridge, MA: The Media Laboratory, MIT.

Piaget, J. (1962). *The language and thought of the child.* (Marjorie Warden, trans.) New York: The Humanities Press (Original work published 1923).

Pressley, Michael, et al. (1987). What is good strategy use and why is it hard to teach? Paper presented at American Educational Research Association, Washington, DC 121, 182.

Resnick, L.B. & Klopfer, L. (1989). *Toward the thinking curriculum: Current cognitive research.* Alexandria, VA: ASCD Publishing.

Salomon, G. (Ed.) (1993). *Distributed cognitions.* New York: Cambridge University Press.

Sears, J. & Marshall, J.D. (1990). *Teaching and thinking about curriculum.* New York: Teacher's College Press.

Schulman, M. (1991). *The passionate mind: Bringing up an intelligent and creative child.* New York: Free Press.

Siegler, R.S. (1985). *Children's thinking.* Englewood Cliffs, NJ: Prentice Hall.

Shoenfeld, A. (1982). Measures of problem-solving performance and of problem-solving interactions. *Journal for Research in Mathematics Education.* 13:31–49.

Short, E.C. (Ed.). (1991). *Forms of curriculum inquiry.* New York: State University of New York Press.

Sternberg, R. (1985). *Beyond I.Q.: A triarchic theory of human intelligence.* Cambridge, MA: Cambridge University Press.

Sternberg, R. & Frensch, P. (1992). *Complex problem solving: Principles and mechanisms.* Hillsdale, NJ: Erlbaum.

Sternberg, R. & Wagner, R. (1986). *Practical intelligence: Nature and origins of competence in the everyday world.* New York: Cambridge University Press.

Weinstein, C. & Mayer, E. (1986). The teaching of learning strategies. In M.C. Wittrock (Ed.) *Handbook of research on teaching.* New York: Macmillan.

White, R. & Gunstone, R. (1992). *Probing understanding.* Bristol, PA: Falmer Press.

Wiggins, G. (1987). Creating a thought provoking curriculum. *American Educator.* Winter, 1987.

Chapter 3

COLLABORATION IN THE LANGUAGE ARTS:

CONNECTING READING, WRITING, THINKING AND LEARNING

Teachers—like parents—form our minds, enlarge our visions, and elevate our aspirations. Language, literacy, critical thinking and learning are the very foundations on which cooperation is built in a democratic republic. By emphasizing these concepts good teachers prepare men and women, of all races and circumstances, to exercise the responsibility of citizenship.

—James Freedman

An educated and literate citizenry has always been essential to American democracy. As we move beyond pessimism (or cynicism) to a sense of possibility the nation faces some difficult choices. If the educational, social, and economic topsoil continues to blow away, America's bond with its children will be broken. Wise investments in education support the values we all claim to honor, while enhancing everyone's understanding of communications skills and the world in which we live. An absolute mastery of one's native language is essential to further education, the workplace, and citizenship. Everyone needs solid reading, writing, thinking, and teamwork skills to face the challenges of the future. For the schools to do their part in language development and literacy they must be sure that children frequently engage the language arts and its associates: reading, writing, speaking, listening, critical reflection, and collaboration.

In many language arts classrooms today, peer collaboration is seen as critical for helping students develop as literate people. Reading and writing are meaningful, constructive, human, and language-based processes which can be enhanced by social activity among peers. In reading, for example, students bring their world views and experiences to texts to evoke new meanings (Rosenblatt, 1993). Constructing meanings often involves sharing interpretations of texts with peers within literature discussion groups or literature circles. Writing is seen as a recursive process in which learners make successive approximations toward coherent, vivid writing through sharing their work with others in authors' circles and conferences (Graves, 1994). Students can share their reading and writing experiences to construct meanings, refine ideas, set goals, and assess their growth—all of these skills are necessary for literate growth.

Holistic teaching in the language arts classroom is grounded by a set of beliefs about teaching and learning. One central idea is that children grow as learners when they are treated like members of the same literacy club (Smith, 1986) rather than text bound pupils searching for "correct answers." While part of a community, students are also seen as individuals, developing in unique ways as they transact with the world. A holistic view of learning implies that there are no rigid, linear stages of literacy development. Students experience growth recursively, based on the developmental capacities of learners within particular environments.

Errors in reading and writing are not viewed as pathologies; rather they are seen as windows into how children think (Botel & Lytle, 1990). When a student has difficulty learning how to read or write, it is often a sign that the environment needs to be changed to allow students to take the risks necessary for development. One way of reducing risks is to encourage students to work with each other. Since peers share a similar age and ability status relative to the teacher, they may be inclined to take risks when interpreting a story or sharing advice about writing (Lazar, 1993).

New ideas about the significance of talk and the place of student authority also underlie the emergence of collaborative learning in the language arts classroom. Democracy in the language arts classroom means that students share the power and responsibility of teaching others how to read and write. In more traditional classrooms, peer talk is viewed as "insignificant noise," relegated to few and infrequent periods of the school day (Goodlad, 1983). Increasingly, many educators recognize the positive relationship between talk and intellectual growth (Vygotsky, 1962, 1978; Wertsch, 1991). Pairing students with each other allows them to engage in exploratory talk which is a critical component to learning. Structuring these opportunities also means that teachers come to see students as legitimate "teachers." When children work with peers to talk about a book, revise a piece of writing, or assess artifacts in a portfolio they become accustomed to social interaction and reaching for learning goals together.

Mixed Ability Groups

Increasingly, teachers and schools are setting up flexible or hetero-geneous groupings in reading/language arts classrooms. Traditionally, low-middle-high ability groups have been used to help teachers serve the needs of diverse learners in a classroom. Unfortunately, such structuring has often resulted in situations of permanent tracking; students who do not read and write on schedule with their peers were often placed in the bottom reading group and tended to end up in the lowest-ability groups or classes throughout their school years. Students in lower ability reading groups usually received instruction that emphasized decoding over meaning-making (Allington, 1983). Undoubtedly, issues of self-esteem, equity, and opportunity surface when children are seen by themselves and others as "less-able" than their peers.

Heterogeneous grouping allows groups of children of diverse abilities to read and write together, based on criteria like a group's mutual interest in a book or the desire of some students to learn a specific writing convention. Teachers who help children structure these groups must be mindful of the status differences between students and the ways in which students communicate in groups (Cohen, 1986). Experiences for helping to make these groups successful can include teaching learners to be responsive to group members or teaching students how to listen to and give specific feedback to group members. Helping students to monitor their own collaborative activity is an essential part of mixed-ability grouping in the reading/language arts classroom.

Recent innovations in classroom texts and materials have also influenced peer collaboration in the classroom. Educators are currently struggling to bring practice in literacy instruction into harmony with current knowledge by shifting from basal reading systems to literature-based approaches. Research and theory favor the use of whole, meaningful works rather than works excerpted from their original source. Nevertheless, many reading programs in elementary schools still depend on older basal reading systems that focus on discrete skills and the use of contrived stories that have a controlled vocabulary.

As a response to the literature-based trend, some textbook publishers have even developed literature anthologies. Many of these texts include original stories written by famous authors of children's books. Some of the newer anthologies do not include comprehension questions or vocabulary exercises. Instead, many emphasize meaning-making through collaborative learning. The newest Houghton-Mifflin series (*The Literature Experience Series,* 1994) offers specific suggestions for having students work in collaborative groups to respond to stories through talking or writing.

New assessment practices allow teachers to gather information about the ways peers transact with one another in the classroom. The current emphasis is on assessing reading and writing processes (as opposed to products), self-assessment, and observation (Rhodes & Shanklin, 1993). Many whole language teachers are assessing how students work with others, including peers, as they move through various reading, writing, talking, and listening experiences. Recognizing that literacy development happens between people (Taylor, 1993) and in many instances, between peers, teachers are writing descriptive anecdotal notes about the ways students help each other within collaborative groups. Students are also beginning to assess themselves as participants within reading and writing groups. These new ways of seeing students and documenting their growth can have a profound influence on the teachers' instructional decision-making.

Another component to holistic teaching is the emphasis on integrating all language experiences. Through "silent talk," readers make connections with authors as they read and writers connect with audiences as they compose. Readers share what they read with others in organized book clubs or through casual conversations. Writers in the world outside of school often collaborate to help the act of writing, insight, and feeling come together more powerfully. Communicating with others is a natural part of reading and writing. To help students recognize the social nature of writing, for instance, teachers can encourage them to randomly examine a library shelf, magazine, or scholarly journal to spot how many works are jointly authored. Published authors can also be invited to the classroom to discuss their collaborations with many people which have helped them along composing route—wives, husbands, children, friends, co-workers, associates, editors.

Many changes in language arts teaching have evolved over the last few decades and these innovations have shaped reading instruction in many classrooms. Instead of seeing round-robin reading and silent desk work, visitors to many of today's classrooms are likely to hear lively classrooms, filled with the voices of students talking about books and reading to each other. Recent research has provided a window into how teachers experiment with and nurture collaborative learning experiences within real classrooms. Emerging portraits from these classrooms continue to reflect new successes, spawning renewed enthusiasm for collaborative learning in the language arts classroom.

Could National Standards Be a Catalyst for Change?

Competence in all subject areas is dependent on competency in the language arts. As in other core disciplines, standards for classroom instruction and student learning should be based on the best research and most current knowledge about subject matter, learning, and human development (Ravitch, 1995). A major goal is to help teachers establish English language arts curricula that values language development, literature, composition, reading, and visual communication. How do subject matter standards fit in?

Setting the standards for English Language Arts proved more difficult than the other subject areas covered in this book. The mathematics standards were agreed to by 1990. The standards in Science and the Arts were ready in 1994. None were carved in stone, but they represent a comprehensible standards document that can be used to support instruction, insure quality assessment, and provide guidance for the future. In the language arts the standards are still not set in a manner that supports teaching. In 1993, the federal government funded the Standards Project for English Language Arts (SPELA) in cooperation with the National Council of Teachers of English (NCTE) and the International Reading Association (IRA). One of the professional organizations, NCTE, suggested that equity and *opportunity* standards to go along with *delivery* standards. Eighteen months into a three-year project the federal government criticized the professional associations for producing vague opinions and platitudes, focusing too much on process and not suggesting a coherent conceptional framework. Some neutral observers felt the disagreement had more to do with social and political issues—like giving all children an equal chance to meet the standards. Whatever the reason, the federal government withdrew funding (in 1994) and the IRA and NCTE decided to proceed on their own—hoping to have a set of useful standards ready by 1996.

Without a forum within the major professional associations, it will be difficult to arrive at a set of solid language arts standards that will really have an impact on the classroom. If Congress doesn't overturn the whole *Goals 2000* effort, national standards for every core K–12 subject area should be in place by 1996. In the meantime, we will have to rely on the literature, the research, and the goal statements of the professional associations. There is general support for a holistic, collaborative, integrated approach to teaching the language arts—helping students learn the language skills they need to deal with today's literacy-intensive environment. This includes an understanding of the features of electronic media and being able to comprehend the structural and symbolic conventions across the whole range of communication possibilities.

English Language Arts standards for *reading* will include the ability to read strategically, constructing meaning by self-monitoring comprehension— questioning, reviewing, revising, and rereading. Since students must make sense of literature, film, television, and content area exposition it is important that they be able to critically analyze and integrate concepts across information sources. A suggestion: help students become part of an active community of readers who understand, appreciate, and discuss what they read.

As far as *writing* standards are concerned, there are also common themes in the literature and the research that cannot be avoided. Writing can be viewed as a tool for learning across the curriculum and for fictional stories. Students need to understand the conventions of writing and be able to search out a variety of writing sources—composing with words, illustrations, video, and computer-generated graphics. Attention needs to be given to small group or pair collaboration using the writing process approach—prewriting, drafting, revising, and editing. As students become constructive and critical members of a community of writers they can help each other *and* add to the collective spirit.

Writing fiction is about allowing the reader to enter another dimension. As a species, we need stories to deal with the collective spirit.

—Isabel Allende

Integrated Language Arts

The language arts can be viewed as an integrated tapestry of reading, writing, listening, and speaking. It is generally agreed that students must be frequently engaged in all of these and more as they learn about mathematics, science, social studies, technology, and the arts. Thinking is sometimes viewed as the fifth language art and it can be used as a foundation for teaching the other four when taking an integrated language arts approach.

Here we use the term "integrated language arts" to describe a literature-based approach to language learning that connects students to real communication situations across a whole range of subjects. Such a program is designed to help teachers (or perspective teachers) make the transition to helping children explore other content areas through encounters with real text. While such an approach could be considered as much a philosophy as a methodology, we focus on ideas, issues, and practical methods for meaningful teaching and learning. In contrast to many basal reading programs, which provide step-by-step guidelines, an integrated language arts program calls on teachers to become more independent decision-makers.

The idea is to use literature-based language arts to make learning more active, dynamic, purposeful, and fun. We believe that language is best learned holistically (in context) rather than in bits and pieces. Putting a strong emphasis on reading real literature is the most likely path leading to a love of books. A rich literature base is essential even for those youngsters who need subskills to get started. Learning from practice exercises is less effective than reading real text or writing for a real audience. A fundamental premise is that students should frequently read, write, and speak throughout all areas of an integrated curriculum. In learning math, science, technology, or the arts children must discuss, read, and write about what they experience. Thus, integrating the language arts throughout the curriculum makes instruction in all subjects more effective.

Literacy Circles and Meaning-making

An integrated language arts approach that connects with cooperative groups can have a profound effect on children's work in other content areas. Those most competent at reading also tend to be competent when it comes to speaking, writing, and doing science and mathematics (Barr, Kamil, Rosenthal, & Pearson, 1993). If children *read* good writing about content, it has a positive effect on their own writing across the curriculum (Burns et al., 1988). Students need good books that challenge personal perspectives, stimulate thinking, and clarify intellectual relationships. Good books, like good art, let us enter into unexplored territory and jointly explore the range of human possibility. By taking part in "literacy circles," students can discuss what they are reading, investigating, and composing. The whole range of language skills can be helped by

Life experiences

Topic choice

Uninterrupted reading, writing

Language strategies instruction

Discussion, input from peers

Publishing, sharing

Revision, self-editing

Outside editing, refinement of product

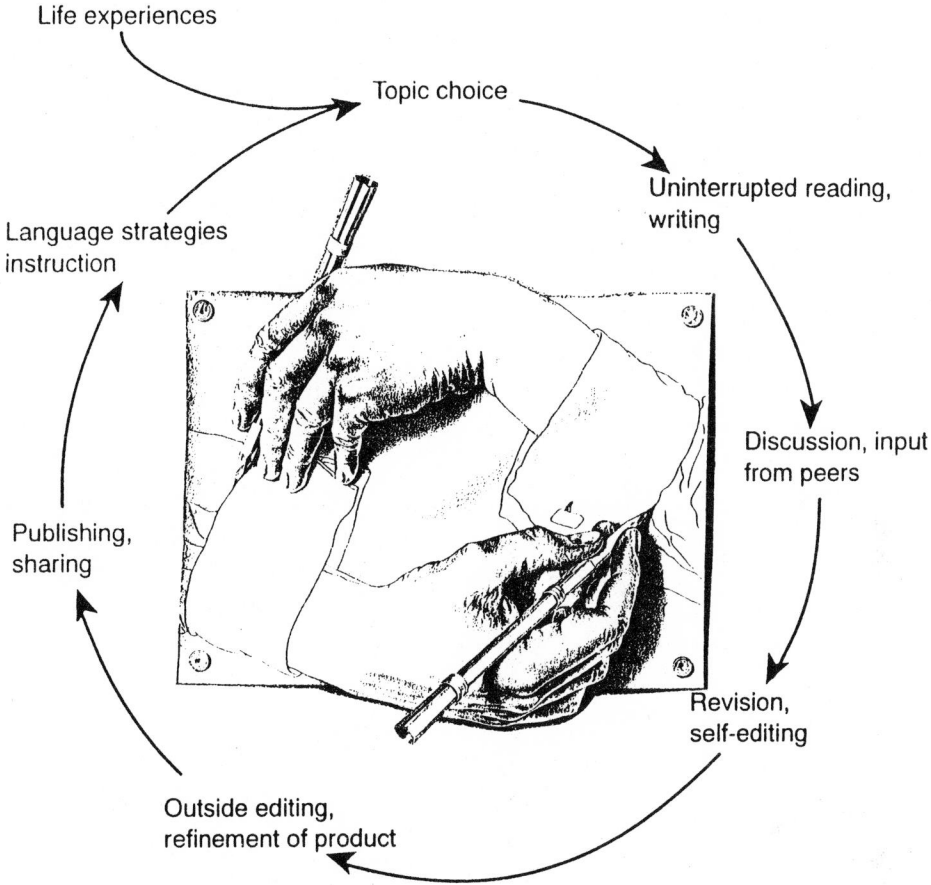

Computer composite image containing an element from M. C.Escher's "Drawing Hands" (1948) Michael Sachs Collection.

communicating with peers who provide immediate feedback during reading, analysis, writing, and revising.

Reading is much more than extracting facts; it involves the making of meaning (from the printed word) and connecting with a rich literacy tradition. Helping readers develop means teaching them to bring prior knowledge to stories, anticipate story outcomes, make connections between stories and their own lives, and read critically. This section includes a description of several collaborative learning experiences that are specifically designed to promote meaning-making before, during, and after reading.

Collaborative Experiences Before Reading

For students to make meaningful connections with print, they must be given opportunities to bring their own world views and experiences to texts. Structuring *before-reading experiences* is a way teachers activate students' prior knowledge. The purpose of before reading experiences is to get students to talk or write about what they already know about a particular subject or theme contained in the text. Once students have explored what they know, they are better able to relate to the text and make predictions about story events.

Most before-reading experiences lend themselves to collaborative learning. As a practical example, let's use the novel *Julie of the Wolves* by Jean Craighead George (Harper & Row, 1972) to show the variety of prereading activities that can be structured collaboratively. This is a novel about a 13-year-old Eskimo girl who communicates with wolves to survive a long journey across the tundra of Alaska. The main character, Miyax, shows great courage during the journey, and she also learns to identify with the Eskimo way of life. A novel for mature readers (5th grade+), this story is packed with rich themes—old vs. new, nature vs. technology, white vs. native American communities, man vs. nature.

Prior to reading *Julie of the Wolves,* students need to talk about what they know about the setting (Alaska) and culture (Eskimo) if they are to make important connections with the book. They can also talk about important themes in their own lives which relate to those presented in the book. Working together, students can make predictions about the characters or events in the book after reading the story title. The following is a brief list of specific collaborative activities which students can engage in to activate prior knowledge.

1. Partners can tell each other stories about surviving a difficult journey, or accomplishing a difficult job.
2. Partners can generate vivid descriptions of life in the Arctic.
3. Partners can brainstorm the meanings of key words like "survival."
4. Partners can tell each other about their own scary experiences being alone.
5. Small groups can discuss how they would survive alone in the Arctic.
6. Small groups can illustrate a giant map of the Arctic.
7. Small groups can generate questions about the book.
8. Small groups can dramatize an experience about the Arctic.

9. Small groups can preview the text illustrations and make predictions.
10. Small groups can discuss what they would bring on a trip to the Arctic.

These before-reading experiences can help students make important connections with this book prior to reading it. Careful monitoring and observation of groups will help teachers determine how particular students participate in before-reading experiences.

Collaborative Experiences During Reading

The primary purpose of during-reading experiences is to help readers make meaning as they progress through the text. Readers can read esthetically, by directing their attention to the lived-through images and feelings that they evoke while reading, or they can read primarily to take away information, as in efferent reading (Rosenblatt, 1978; 1993). Often, particular types of texts will influence a reader's purpose for reading. Literary texts such as poetry, short stories, or mysteries are more likely to inspire aesthetic reading. Conversely, students may read informational texts such as newspapers, recipes, or prescriptions efferently. Other factors though, like teacher expectations, classroom environment, or student intentions will shape how readers direct their attention during reading, irrespective of the text genre. Any text can be read aesthetically or efferently, and students can read with their attention directed with some combination of ways.

Teachers need to keep aesthetic and efferent reading in mind when they structure collaborative experiences as students read together, or between moments of independent reading. Traditionally, teachers have emphasized efferent reading by having students read to answer comprehension questions. More recently, teachers have been interested in structuring aesthetic reading experiences by having students share their lived-through thoughts, images, and feelings about a text. Establishing reader response groups or group literature discussions is an ideal way to get students to simply enjoy good literature (Short, 1990). Students make personal connections with texts and share these with peers. They can compare different interpretations of texts and justify their views by finding supporting evidence in the text. To get reader response groups running smoothly, teachers must spend time modeling the process.

Generally, reader response conversations begin with personal responses and move toward higher levels of analysis. They often begin by having students write a personal response after they finish reading a passage or chapter. The written response can be informal—words, phrases, sentence fragments, or complete sentences which capture what students are thinking and feeling at the moment. Writing allows time for personal reflection and it also prepares all of the students for a speaking turn. Students are then invited to share what they have written. Inevitably, students will have diverse responses to texts and this inspires another level of conversation around comparing and contrasting viewpoints. This often leads to students' defending their interpretations by looking back at the text to find specific descriptions or actions which "prove" their point. Students can also analyze how they arrived at certain conclusions, based on their own prior experiences. They may even critique the writing and think of new story variations.

One possible format for helping students write and talk about their interpretations is shown below. Using inductive reasoning grid, students can write about specific evidence from the text so that they can then make more informed interpretations.

Inductive Reasoning Grid

Name of character _____

Reading Clues: *Interpretation:*

1. Statements by the character:

   _____   _____

   _____   _____

2. Character's actions:

   _____   _____

   _____   _____

3. Character's thinking patterns:

   _____   _____

   _____   _____

4. What others say about this character:

   _____   _____

5. Situations the character becomes involved in:

   _____   _____

   _____   _____

6.   Other important information about the character:

_____   _____

_____   _____

Summary of the character: *My generalizations about the character:*

Collaborative groups are often used to help students refine their interpretations by gathering and considering evidence as they read. In a directed reading-thinking activity (DRTA), students try to predict future story events on the basis of a few clues that they have been given. Students can read either independently or aloud, stopping to predict what might happen in the story and refining their predictions as they gather new evidence through continued reading. Divergent responses are encouraged—although opinions must be justified by finding supporting evidence from the text. After the story, students can demonstrate their understanding by talking to each other about how their predictions changed as they progressed through the text. The goal of DRTA is to get students actively searching for evidence to support their predictions so that they can eventually internalize this way of processing texts while reading independently.

Literature Circles (Daniels, 1994) is another way of structuring the classroom for independent reading and collaborative work. Students assume particular roles such as *discussion director, literary luminary, connector,* and *illustrator* while engaging in literature discussions. Prior to these conversations, all group members choose a text and read it (or a portion of it) silently. They then fill out sheets which outline specific duties of each role:

Discussion Director: develops discussion questions for the group.
Literary Illuminator: guides group to revisit some sections of a text.
Connector: relates text to other readings and experiences.
Illustrator: creates and shares a visual display of a text.

These are some of the suggested roles for literature circles. There are others which can be added, such as *summarizer, vocabulary enricher, or investigator.* Note how each role describes how each group member can transact with story content. They do not suggest a particular status as would be the case for roles such as *group checker* or *monitor;* these roles tend to pit students against each other because one student assumes the role of evaluator of other group members. Roles like these should be avoided.

Teachers should model all roles and allow initial practice sessions so that children can experiment with roles and ask clarifying questions about them. Ultimately, the aim of Literature Circles is to give students a foundation for conducting conversations about books with the goal of withdrawing the role sheets when students have internalized a variety of ways to talk about literature with each other.

Some teachers even like to assign different group roles so that students can experience and develop the strategies for dealing with isolated, overly talkative, or nontask-oriented group members. This allows them to practice strategies of good listening, clarifying, or disagreeing in a nonthreatening manner. Smooth and successful peer interactions depend on clearly defined roles for individual group members.

During-reading experiences are also aimed at helping students become more fluent readers. Younger students especially love to read aloud so that they can practice reading more smoothly and with intonation. This is why partnered reading, buddy reading, or shared reading are popular forms of collaborative reading in the early grades. Working in partners, students take turns reading a portion of the story, sometimes making predictions, or sometimes to simply enjoy a story together.

Collaborative Experiences After Reading

After-reading experiences help students deepen and extend their understanding of texts. Students can relive parts of the text through retelling, writing, drawing, dramatizations, and discussions. All of these experiences can be done collaboratively, with small groups or pairs of students. Some activities are more appropriate for groups of two, like dialogue journals, while other activities, like skits, are better designed for larger groups of four to six. The following is a list of ten after reading experiences which involve peer collaboration.

1. Retellings, with each group member contributing part of the story.
2. Retellings, with each group member taking a different viewpoint.
3. Skits, groups perform a scene from the story with movement and props.
4. Reader's Theater, group members divide text and read portions aloud.
5. Pantomime, silent performance using movement and facial expressions.
6. Readers response discussion, groups share personal responses.
7. Video project, group members enact scene on video tape.

8. Diorama, groups create a particular setting from the book.
9. Dialogue Journals, students can write as themselves or as characters.
10. Concept maps, groups create and complete giant concept maps showing literary elements, characterizations, mood, theme, event time-line.

These collaborative after-reading experiences help students consolidate their understanding of texts, while prompting positive associations with reading. Teachers do not need to rely on comprehension questions or book reports to assess student's comprehension of reading material. These traditional closing activities are primarily for individual seat work and are often uninspiring. Providing a choice of various collaborative projects for after reading can get students talking and moving together. Not only are these stimulating ways for students to put closure on a book, but they can also provide teachers with important information about how students transact with others about print.

Using Big Books to Help Teach Reading

Children can learn skills within the context of good literature with large print and big colorful illustrations. Big Books can help connect the positive effects of group reading experiences by letting children observe someone (the teacher) engaged in a desirable activity that they can emulate. Teachers may make the Big Book available for group readings and small books for the children to use independently. Students might be encouraged to take the small book version home to share with their family. Activities may be suggested that help children use their interest in the science/math topic covered to move directly into other books or themes. For example: *Pumpkin, Pumpkin* could lead to a unit on plants or how living things grow and change. Related Big Books include *The Carrot Seed, The Reason for a Flower,* and *The Little Red Hen.* A theme on the growth of living things could connect to other Big Books—*The Very Hungry Caterpillar, Animals Born Alive and Well, Little Salt Lick and the Sun King, The New Baby Calf,* and *Chickens Aren't the Only Ones.*

Many Big Books will fit into a teacher's current theme plans *and* suggest new topics to explore. Whole classrooms can share memorable stories and interesting facts and small groups can use Big Books to encourage listening and speaking. The teacher models reading and risk-free participation by teaching science/math skills within a literary context. Such a meaningful teaching of skills within context is a powerful learning experience. An abundance of good literature about science and mathematics is a key to independent reading.

Big Book example in science: Pumpkin, Pumpkin by Jeanne Titherington (Scholastic Inc. 1-800-325-6149) This book has detailed illustrations that blend science with a simple informative story line exploring a child's wonder at watching a seed grow. It is for younger readers who may need to hear the story several times to build confidence and link the book to common human experiences.

Big Book example in mathematics: Bunches and Bunches of Bunnies, by Louise Mathews, helps children understand multiplication with a story of rhymes that allow for counting, dramatization, and rapidly multiplying rabbits. Teachers often like to read the story through once and go back to look at the changing rhyme pattern and organizing what is happening on a large chart. (The book goes through the numbers one to twelve as the bunnies multiply.) Children may be encouraged to creatively strike out on their own with rhyming couplet patterns that predict the answers to other multiplication questions. *The Silly Song Book* would connect some of these concepts to music.

On occasion students might build their own Big Book in a small group, laminate, and show off in class. This way the science/math and reading program is to be extended to include writing and art. The same possibility exists when using Big Books like *How much is a Million?* or *Ten, Nine, Eight.*

Using Big Books for interdisciplinary inquiry in science and mathematics helps accommodate different learning styles by and encouraging children to use many and varied resources. In *Ten Little Ducks,* for example, children could take the lead from one of the little ducks and go outside to blow some "magnificent bubbles." This encourages children to piece together meaningful patterns from many sources—literature, science, mathematics, their friends, and the world outside of school. Let's turn to the upper grades.

Bookmarks: A Teaching Strategy

Active readers respond to text as they read by monitoring comprehension, predicting, asking questions, recalling related experiences, and self-monitoring comprehension. Good readers also connect life with text and make connections across texts. Strategies that encourage the reader to interact with both the text and peers can result in higher levels of understanding and increased reader involvement. *Bookmarks* is a simple technique for quickly capturing reactions to text as on small pieces of paper as they work to understand a text. Readers can use their brief *Bookmarks* reactions to note their struggles with the unfamiliar and their transactions with vocabulary and concepts. Students can continue to read if they know that they will have a chance to talk about their problems and interpretations after reading.

Procedure:

1. Give students opportunities to talk about their responses to the concepts described in the text before the strategy is introduced. It is often helpful for the teacher to join in the discussions as a reader who has personal responses to the material.
2. Cut construction paper or notebook paper into strips about two inches wide.
3. Teachers do a better job with teaching content areas if they actually read some books and explore issues themselves. To model the strategy the teacher can demonstrate by using *Bookmarks* while doing their own reading. The teacher can then share their own responses and demonstrate the process themselves.
4. Students can be given about a dozen *Bookmarks* and asked to choose a piece of literature to read. Ask them to note the page number when they are responding. By having an uninterrupted reading time it is possible to generate a fair number of responses; these can be stapled together. If you ask the children to always have two books they like (in their desk) it helps with classroom management.
5. Children can share examples of their responses with a small group and selected examples can even be shared with the whole class.
6. The teacher can read through the bookmarks and respond to questions, share their own reactions, and encourage rethinking or rereading. Some of the *Bookmarks* can be included in portfolios and brief teacher responses can be included on the *Bookmark* and handed back to the reader. (Don't grade.)

SQ3R

The SQ3R strategy can be used on a regular basis to help students get ready to read (prereading). The basic process has five steps: survey, question, read, recite, and review. Students *survey* the passage to be read by headings, italicized words, highlighted items, questions, introductory and concluding paragraphs. Next students come up with questions based on the headings and reads the passage to find the answer. In the final review step the student looks back over the text and any notes they jotted down while reading to determine the author's major points.

Language Experience Approach

The language approach (LEA) is often used in the lower grades to integrate children's knowledge and experience with interdisciplinary inquiry in reading, writing, social studies, the arts, science, and mathematics. This method is based on the notion that what children experience (say a visit to the science museum) they can write about or have someone write for them. What is written can then be read by everyone. With first graders, for example, teachers can print student generated ideas on a large chart, have the children do some painting, laminate, put some rings through the top, and *presto* the class has a LEA big book.

Reciprocal Teaching

Reciprocal teaching works well from the middle grades on up and requires the use of four strategies in summarizing content area material. First the student reads the passage and summarizes it in one sentence. The next step is to ask one or two higher level questions about the material read. In the third step, the student explains or paraphrases the most difficult parts of the passage. The final step involves predicting what will occur in the next part of the text to be read. Reciprocal teaching focuses on student dialogue and collaboration in bringing meaning to what's being read in the content area.

A variation of reciprocal teaching is the generating reciprocal inferences procedure (GRIP). Here students are taught to look for clue words for inference types like location, time, category, action, object, attitudes, instrument, agent, solutions, cause and effect. Although some of the work must be done alone, students can be divided into pairs so that they have someone to respond to the inferences made from cue words or reading selections. In the beginning it is often best for the teacher to model the process to show how to find cue words and justify inferences. Two students can also coauthor their own inference paragraphs (including cue words) and exchange their work with other partnerships. The authors can later check to see the inferences are correct.

Reading-on-the-Go

This technique is related to the kind of content area reading that people do (outside the classroom) when quickly reading everyday things like directions for taking medicine, reading the thermometer, understanding highway mileage signs, mixing paint, figuring out a sports column, or calculating the savings in a sale. This kind of reading requires quick judgments. As they work through some real problems in their community or from the newspapers and magazines students can confirm assumptions or note mistakes. This allows children to develop content reading strategies that apply in the world outside of school.

Sketch a Concept

The visual arts can connect to reading passages about science, mathematics, literature, or stories written by classmates. (Einstein, for example, used a similar technique to sketch out the theory of relativity when he was a young man working in Bern, Switzerland.) The idea is to use colors, lines, symbols, and shapes to convey meaning. This can be done with a partner or in a small group that focuses on reframing their understanding of the text by sketching a visual representation of the concept. Teachers can set up a whole class sharing session that integrates the language arts as students think through concepts, listen, speak, "write," and "read" in a visual mode.

Using the Media to Enhance Language Learning

Teachers can encourage student involvement in the real world and literature by supplementing the text with related topics in magazines, newspapers and on television (Adams & Hamm, 1989). *The New York Times,* for example, has a special science section on Tuesdays. Every newspaper has at least some material that relates to math and science. Even the lower grades can do a little of this by making use of the pictures and weekly reader type newspapers that bring things down to their level. The average local paper is written at the fourth or fifth grade "reading level" and with a little background upper grade students can comprehend the evening news. This kind of reading, viewing, and discussion can help students above the third grade level keep up with current events topics that bypass out-of-date or boring information in some textbooks.

Newspaper Scavenger Hunt

> *"I read the news today, Oh Boy."*
> — John Lennon

This activity is a good way to get to know what is in the newspaper and how to find the information you want. Upper grade students can compare doing the activity using a local newspaper with using a national paper like *The New York Times*. "Newspaper Scavenger Hunt" can be applied to a variety of reading levels—with younger students should using newspapers with a lot of pictures. Pick a day of the week or a newspaper that has a high content of things that you would like your students to know more about. (Many papers have special days for science, the arts, literature, or whatever.) Before class, make a list in two columns of words and phrases extracted from a sample newspaper. You could list cartoons, pictures, graphs, words, concepts, and short phrases in the newspaper. Make enough copies and give one to each pair of students along with the paper. Be sure to have enough newspapers (they must all be the same paper) and give one complete paper to each partnership.

The hunt: Students work with their partner to find the page where the item is located . . . they put the page number on the answer sheet and circle the item in the newspaper. A time limit is set for the search to take place . . . you don't want more than one or two groups to finish. When time is up, the students can compare their "success" rates and check some controversial possibilities. The teacher may focus the discussion on several areas of interest in mathematics and science. This exercise can be modified for a range of ability levels and is a good way for students to get to know the parts of a newspaper and to get ready to actually read some stories in the news.

Reading the newspaper: After reading a section or article in the print media students can work in pairs to write a critical analysis using the following questions as guides:

1. Describe the author's basic point in one short paragraph. Note the date, title, publication, page number, and author's name (if given).
2. What have you learned that is unique?
3. What new questions might you raise after reading the article?
4. How do graphs, statistics, illustrations, or pictures back up the main points? Explain one major concept in the passage and point out its connection to math or science.

5. How does the passage you read change your attitude towards the subject and how would you like to solve some of the problems discussed?

Writing a fictional story using headings and subheadings: In this activity students work in pairs or small groups to write a story based on the vocabulary, headings and subheadings that they find in the newspaper. Encouraging humor and wild connections works well here. When finished the coauthored stories may be read to the group or to the whole class. An example of one line in a news headline/subheading "story" by middle school students: "WORLD ENDS: WOMEN AND MINORITIES HARD-EST HIT."

As they come into contact with what is going on in the world around them, students should be encouraged to unlock the mysteries lying behind the daily headlines. Its much more than language arts. Gaining a familiarity with current events through collaborative experiences with the news media breeds curiosity, enthusiasm, and critical thinking. By improving "world knowledge," understanding in all of the basic subjects is amplified.

Readers Theater Can Connect to the Language Arts

Readers theater is the oral presentation of prose or poetry by two or more readers. Complete scripts can be provided or students can write them after reading a story or a poem. The actual story or chapter may be ten or twenty pages long—the finished readers theater script may only be one, two, or three pages of print. If pictures are used, there may be ten or twelve large illustrations. We recommend trying some prepared scripts first (so that children get the basic idea) and then have the students work as a small group to transform a story or poem into a script.

The typical readers theater lesson involves script writing, rehearsal, performance, and follow-up commentary for revision. Before the class presentation, children need a chance to practice and refine their interpretation. Everybody eventually gets their own copy so that they can read their role from a hand-held script. (A few mistakes in reading are good for a laugh.)

When reading, students stand up (from a chair) or turn to face the audience; when their turn is over, they sit down or turn their back to the audience. If there are four roles and five children, then two read the same thing at the same time; if there are four students and six roles, then two members of the group read two roles. Lines, gesture, intonation, and movement are worked out in advance. Individual interpretations are negotiated between group members. The performance in front of an audience can intensify the experience and connect the reader to the audience.

Readers theater can be a good informal cooperative learning activity where students not only respond to each other as character to character but in spontaneous responses that ties the group together with the situation of the text. The idea is to use a highly motivating technique to engage children in a whole range of language activities.

A good script for teaching animals, colors, and sight concepts to first graders is *Brown Bear, Brown Bear, What Do You See,* by Bill Martin. A somewhat similar book (emphasizing sounds) by the same author is *Polar Bear, Polar Bear, What Do You Hear?* Remember that lines and pictures may be changed and shortened by the students to make it work in *their* readers theater. Each child gets two large pictures and words that have been painted, sketched, or copied (enlarged) from the original book. The group gets a chance to practice in the small group on get ready to take their turn in front of the class. When a student turn comes they turn to the class and read the words on their picture.

1st child shows the Polar Bear:

Everyone: Polar Bear, Polar Bear, what do you hear?
1st child: I hear a lion roaring in my ear. (lion turns around)
Everyone: Lion, lion, what do you hear?
2nd child: I hear a hippopotamus snorting in my ear. (hippo turns)
Everyone: Hippopotamus, Hippopotamus, what do you hear?
3rd child: I hear a flamingo fluting in my ear. (flamingo turns)
Everyone: Flamingo, Flamingo, what do you hear?
4th child: I hear a zebra braying in my ear. (zebra turns)
Everyone: Zebra, Zebra, what do you hear?
5th child: I hear a boa constrictor hissing in my ear. (boa turns)

The first five pictures may be quickly laid out on the floor and students go on to the second student created picture (with words)

Everyone: Boa Constrictor, Boa Constrictor, what do you hear?
1st child: I hear an elephant trumpeting in my ear. (elephant turns)
Everyone: Elephant, Elephant, what do you hear?
2nd child: I hear a leopard snarling in my ear. (leopard turns)
Everyone: Leopard, Leopard, what do you hear?

3rd child: I hear a peacock yelping in my ear. (peacock turns)
Everyone: Peacock, Peacock, what do you hear?
4th child: I hear a walrus bellowing in my ear. (walrus turns)
Everyone: Walrus, Walrus, what do you hear?
5th child: I hear a zookeeper whistling in my ear. (zookeeper turns)
Everyone: Zookeeper, Zookeeper, what do you hear?
5th child: I hear children.

[Pictures put quickly onto the floor in order.]

The group of five pointing at each picture in turn: "I hear children: growling like a polar bear, roaring like a lion, snorting like a hippopotamus, fluting like a flamingo, braying like a zebra, hissing like a boa constrictor, trumpeting like an elephant, snarling like a leopard, yelping like a peacock, bellowing like a walrus . . . *that's what I hear.*"

Collaborative Learning and Writing

The Writing Process

Since the mid- to late-1980s, the process writing model has had a major impact on language arts instruction. Teachers who have adopted this model help their students see writing as a process by having them experience various dimensions of the writing process—inventing, drafting, revising, editing, and publishing. Each of these processes is recursive in nature in that students often revise as they draft or edit as they invent. In fact, problems can occur when teachers see writing process as a series of rigid steps to be followed in a prescribed sequence (Labbo, Hoffman, & Roser, 1995). The ultimate goal of process writing is to guide students toward developing meaningful written pieces over time.

To write meaningfully, students are encouraged to choose topics that are relevant to their own lives (Graves, 1994). Consistent with the whole language movement, functional and aesthetic aspects of writing are emphasized. Students write to inform, entertain, persuade, reflect, criticize, summarize, etc. Depending on the purpose for writing, students are encouraged to experiment with a variety of written genres—expository, fiction, or poetry. Regardless of the genre used, students are encouraged to draw from their own experiences to write.

For the teacher, process writing means writing along with students, modeling not only enthusiasm for writing, but the thinking and composing processes that are an integral part of what real authors do. Teachers share rich literature with children and discuss the literary styles of a variety of authors. They also demonstrate the use of conventions through "mini-lessons" which are tailored to small groups of children who share a particular writing need.

Woven throughout the process writing cycle are opportunities to share writing with others. Talking about topics, drafts, or finished pieces with peers allows students to gain a sense of audience as they think about developing their written pieces. Teachers can stage many collaborative experiences for students across any dimension of the writing process.

Prewriting

Inventing texts is a social process (Lefevre, 1987); our ideas for composing texts often come from our experiences with others. That is why group sharing is a particularly important part of the rehearsal process. If teachers can stage opportunities for students to first talk about their ideas for composing texts with caring others, students will have a stronger foundation from which to begin composing.

Groups of students can generate ideas for topics in a small group or with a partner. For instance, grade school children often talk to each other about the kinds of stories they would like to write based on their favorite books, superhero characters, movies, or personal experiences. Calkins (1994) suggests that students use a writer's notebook to jot down the things they notice in and out of school, their memories and ideas, their favorite words and responses to reading, or their conversations with other students. When these notes are shared, peers can then ask questions about these experiences and thoughts, eliciting more information. Such talking opportunities prior to writing can provide authors with a beginning frame from which to begin drafting.

Drafting is a first attempt at writing ideas down in a narrative form. Many teachers invite young authors to turn off their "internal editors" and just allow all of their ideas to flow onto the paper. Once an author is finished with a first draft, they can begin the sharing process which is so essential to refining written pieces.

Peer Revision and Editing

Revision involves making changes in the content of a draft. As previously stated, revision happens as students are thinking of new ideas to write before they draft, or as they are drafting a piece. Writers tend to revise naturally, without prompting, and at any time during the composing process. Teachers can see this happen as students erase and cross out

information as they draft a story. To get students to revisit a piece of writing after they have drafted requires a lot of teacher modeling and peer feedback. This kind of revision should only happen once students are more experienced in drafting (grades 2 and beyond). It is not recommended for younger students who are just learning how to form letters and write words. The focus of instruction at this level should be to develop interest and purpose for writing (Graves, 1994).

Peer revision requires comprehension, reasoning, and reflection. Peers can provide a sense of audience to a fellow writer who wishes to make a piece of writing clearer or more vivid. One kind of format for peer revision is the Authors' Circle (Harste, Short, & Burke, 1988). While working with three or four students, peers help each other clarify what they want to say. Students are encouraged to bring their pieces to Authors' Circle when they have come to a point in their writing where they need audience feedback. The process is as follows:

1. The author reads a piece aloud. (When writers are more experienced, they can: (a) state what they like about the piece, (b) identify
   problems, and (c) ask for specific kinds of feedback.)
2. The listeners tell the author what they heard in the piece and what
   they found most effective.
3. Listeners raise questions about parts that were unclear or confusing,
   or parts that need more information. The author can take notes to
   remember peer comments.
4. Authors can consider the suggestions made by the peer group.

Through modeling, teachers can demonstrate ways to participate in
Authors' Circles so that students can learn how to listen and give helpful
suggestions to their peers. Once students understand how to give positive
feedback on the meaning of pieces, they can then run their own revision
groups independently. Students should be able to give feedback on the
extent to which:

1. The piece is focused around one central idea.
2. Ideas are supported by details.
3. One part flows smoothly to the next part (organization).
4. The author's voice is present.
5. Words and phrases are lively and descriptive.

Feedback like this helps students become more aware of how others
receive their pieces. During circle time, students can make notes and
place asterisk marks in places where a part of their writing needs further
refinement. Author's Circles should be combined with teacher-student
conferences so that students can get both peer and adult feedback to
enhance their written pieces.

As students are working on refining the language in their pieces, they
also need to consider the clarity and meaning of their message through
the use of conventions. Donald Graves (1994) uses the metaphor of sign
posts, to illustrate the relationship between conventions and meaning:
As I sit at my computer keyboarding these words, every letter that
follows every other letter, the spaces in between groups of letters to
indicate words, the capital letter at the beginning of each sentence, the
period or stop to end an idea, the spaces between lines, all of these are
acts of conventions. Like sign posts, they help you, the reader, enter
familiar ground so that you can concentrate on the information without
distraction. (Graves, 1994, pg. 191)
Teachers need to help students understand the relevance of conventions

for conveying meaning. While authors can look at their own pieces to assess spelling, punctuation, or capitalization, sometimes a fresh perspective is needed to help students read their pieces with conventions in mind. Peers can give each other feedback on the conventions of written language through the process of peer editing. Working in pairs, students can swap drafts and give each other feedback on their use of certain conventions.

Another format for peer collaboration would be to set up an editor's desk as a work station in the classroom. Students who enjoy helping others use conventions can take turns sitting at the desk during writing workshop and assisting other students who need help with conventions. This part of the room can include several reference books and wall charts that explain certain conventions.

Peer collaboration can also be used for more explicit teaching of conventions. Graves (1994) suggests the use of a collaborative game which helps students become familiar with the use of conventions. Working in heterogeneous groups of three, children refer to their own work and a book they are reading to locate specific conventions. Using the following game format, children help each other understand why certain conventions are used:

1. The teacher writes a sentence on the board that shows a particular convention and underlines it.
2. The teacher asks students to look for the convention, first in their work folders, then in a book they are reading.
3. When one team member finds the convention, the other members look at it and discuss its purpose using the questions, "How does this convention help the meaning of the sentence? How does this help readers?"
4. When everyone in the group thinks they know how the convention helps the meaning of the sentence, all three group members put up their hands.
5. These group members are asked to explain what the convention is and how it helps readers to understand the sentence better.

Graves plays this game with students for ten to fifteen minutes every eight to ten school days. The advantage of this game is that students *help each other* learn about conventions using their *own work*. Students act as teachers and use relevant materials for instruction.

The success of peer collaboration in writing groups will depend on the way teachers model the use of conventions during mini lessons (see

Graves, 1994). Clear, meaningful modeling, using real work-in-progress, will help students understand the use of conventions so that they can draw from the teacher's examples to assist peers. Yet modeling different ways to write and revise is only one consideration for teachers. Teachers need to also understand the ways students feel about themselves and their writing, if they want to support students' efforts to help each other.

To a large extent, the view that developing writers come to have of themselves as students and writers is reflected from the response they get to their work. Elementary school children attend carefully to how teachers react to them, and they compare their progress with those around them. They can count stars and smiley faces on their written work or the absence of them. Comparison with peers affects the way students view themselves as readers and writers and many adolescent writers remember being humiliated in their very early attempts at reading or writing, and these responses caused later struggle in writing.

Before peers can work with each other to revise and edit their written pieces, teachers need to work on establishing trust between students. This involves permitting students some say in the way they are grouped and in the audiences to which their work is exposed. Many teachers permit students to select groups using preset criteria. Some teachers simply say, "form your own groups of three, making sure that there is a male and a female in each group." Neil Witikko, a Minnesota teacher, forms on-going groups by having students turn in confidential group preference lists. Each student writes down three peers with whom they would like to work and if necessary the name of one person with whom it would be difficult to work. Trying to accommodate their requests, he keeps groups small (3 or, if necessary, 4) to permit a diversity of opinion at the same time as making trust more possible. If a problem group surfaces, he works with the group to raise trust or changes membership to solve the problem.

Teachers can enhance environments for writing by organizing classroom spaces with quiet isolated corners where students can discuss their work. Supporting each other in observation, critical thinking skills, and the art of writing can help lead to literacy in the fullest sense. Designing writing curricula so that students are writing for peer audiences that they trust, utilizing the workshop model, and designing writing tasks so that peers can work collaboratively towards a common goal fosters intrinsic motivation in writing at all levels.

The Writing Process Approach

In the process approach to teaching writing teachers use a workshop format where students may bring in writing that they have produced elsewhere. Students can collaborate or work alone on short stories, poems, a television script, or oral histories with elders. The focus can be on newspaper generated issues, science fiction, personal experience, or anything else. In the workshop, children talk about their writing, get suggestions, develop new ideas, and are made to feel part of a community of supportive writers. As writers and responders students are encouraged by the teacher to say something positive, suggest titles, comment on the lead sentence, ask about the authors favorite part of the story and how it could be made clearer. Students engage in prewriting activities, write, rewrite, and help each other with editing. After proofreading, students can decide what to "publish." Illustrations may be added, the "book" bound, the cover decorated, a card made up for the classroom card catalog, and the book is placed in the class library to be checked out and read by others.

Social Processing and Written Expression

The development of a writing community is a very powerful way for students to collaborate in developing their writing voice (Heilbrun, 1989). Whether writing is self, peer, or teacher evaluated, it is important not to lose sight of the connection between what is valued and what is valuable. Jointly developed math/science writing folders (portfolios) have a major role to play in student assessment. By selection samples these folders can provide a running record of students' interests and what they can and can't do.

To work toward less control teachers need to help students take more responsibility for their own learning. The ability to evaluate does not come easily at first, and peer writing groups will need teacher developed strategies to help them process what they have learned. The ability to reflect on being a member of a peer writing team is a form of metacognition— learning to think about thinking (Calkins, 1994). The skills of productive group work may have to be made explicit. This requires processing in a circular or U-shaped group where all students can see each other. Questions for evaluative social processing might include:

- How did group leadership evolve?
- Was it easy to get started?

- How did you feel if one of your ideas was left out?
- What did you do if most members of your group thought that you should write something differently?
- How did you rewrite?
- Did your paper say what you wanted it to?
- What kind of a setting do you like for writing?
- How can you arrange yourself in the classroom to make the writing process better?
- What writing tools did you use?
- How do you feel when you write?
- Explain the reasoning behind what you did?

Remember, it's just as important for students to write down their reasoning as it is to explain their feelings, content understanding, preferences, and solutions to problems.

The recognition of developmental stages in social skills must be taken into account as teachers incorporate literature-based writing concerns into their classroom routines. For the younger students, the writing process can take the form of jointly produced language experience stories that make connections between various elements of the language arts as it is found in the real world. This real world connection is important in helping students to value reading, writing, listening, and communicating as a way to understand that world and as tools for solving problems. As children work together with concrete materials, they can translate them into stories, pictures, diagrams, graphs, charts, and other symbolic forms. Some of these can be placed on large charts with the teacher or an upper grade student doing the writing. As soon as they can write on their own the children can keep a private journal where they label drawings, experiences and writing samples.

As students learn to expand their perspectives they can begin to carry a story from one page (or day) to the next. Time may be set aside each day for a personal journal entry. Although it is important that the language be in a student's own words, the teacher can make comments without formal grading.

Collaborative Experiences with Poetry

Poetry is not just "bad prose." To read or write it involves awareness of certain elements that make it unique. Teachers must have some basic

A Personal Coat of Arms

Write the following **4** questions on the blackboard or make copies for each child and hand them out.

1. What do you regard as your greatest personal success to date?
2. What are you trying to become or what do you wish to be?
3. What one thing would you want to get done by the time you are 65?
4. What are three things you are good at? If you had one year to live and were guaranteed success in whatever you tried, what would you do? What is your family's greatest achievement?

Give the following instructions:

1. Make a drawing to answer each question. Make the pictures colorful and do them large enough to be seen from twenty feet away.
2. You can change the questions if you like or you can answer less than all six (but at least three or four) of them.
3. Cut out a coat of arms (a family crest) and paste it on a large square piece of colored paper. Glue your drawings to your family crest and write a motto.

When all the children have finished, display the coats of arms so that everyone can see them. Then ask each child to explain his or her drawings to the class.

knowledge of the vocabulary of poetry in order to help children enjoy and mature in their understanding and appreciation of it. Some characteristics include:

1. Poetry uses condensed language; every word is important.
2. Poetry uses figurative language (e.g., metaphor, simile, personification, irony).
3. The language of poetry is rhythmical (regular, irregular, metered).
4. Some words may be rhymed (internal, end of line, run-over) or nonrhyming.
5. Poetry uses the language of sounds (alliteration, assonance, repetition).
6. The units of organization are line arrangements in stanzas or idea arrangements in story, balance, contrast, build-up, surprise, and others.

7. Poetry uses the language of imagery (sense perceptions reproduced in the mind) (Denman, 1989).

Before introducing children to collaborative poetry experiences, teachers need to expose children to a wide variety of poems and poets. Many children prefer poems that are humorous with clear-cut rhyme and rhythm. The narrative is the most popular poetic form and favorite topics are familiar experiences and animals. Some of the following poets write primarily for younger or older children, others for both—they all use content and forms that reflect the modern world.

Arnold Adoff	Dorothy Aldis
Byrd Baylor	Harry Behn
Bodecker, N.M.	Gwendolyn Brooks
John Ciardi	Aileen Fisher
Eleanor Farjeon	Elizabeth Coatsworth
Beatrice de Regniers	Zhenya Gay
Eloise Greenfield	Nikki Giovanni
Mary Ann Hoberman	X.J. Kennedy
Patricia Hubbell	Langston Hughes
Karla Kuskin	David McCord
Marci Ridlin Livingston	Myra Cohn Lilian Moore
Ogden Nash	Richard Hughes
Lillian Morrison	Jack Prelutsky
Mary O'Neil	Kay Starbird
Shel Silverstein	Wm. J. Smith
Zilpha Snyder	James Trippett
Judith Viorst	

Anthologies of contemporary poems by a variety of poets:

Stephen Dunning	Lee Bennett Hopkins
Nancy Larrick	

When reading poetry to children, teachers may have students respond to the images and meanings evoked by sharing their personal interpretations with a partner, similar to the reader-response discussions suggested earlier in this chapter. Students gather in small groups once a week to share poetry books they have been reading. The groups are structured so that each student:

1. reads the author and title of each book
2. tells about the book

3. reads one or two pages aloud
4. receives responses from members of the group, specifically pointing out parts they liked and asking questions (Nell, 1989).

Poems for older children and adolescents often include figurative language or abstract themes which can be difficult for students to decipher. Sharing interpretations is an excellent way for them to make important connections with poetry.

Poems are also a wonderful medium for helping students develop fluency and confidence in reading. Teachers can model ways of reading poems aloud by experimenting with voice, pitch, and intonation. They can invite students to read their favorite poems to each other by trying out various ways of reading modeled by the teacher. Students sign up and read aloud at the start of each day. Other students "point," commenting on parts of the poem that catch their attention. A classroom anthology of poetry can be illustrated and laminated.

Through a rich exposure to poetry, children will often want to write their own poetry (Sudol & Sudol, 1995). There are many types of poetry students can write that can be enhanced through peer discussions. Students can share their ideas about composing fixed forms of poetry like limericks, haikus, couplets, or free verse poems that can be humorous, serious, nonsensical, sentimental, dramatic, or didactic. Teachers can also structure collaborative poetry writing sessions as described in the following examples:

1. Wish Poems:
   Each student writes a wish on a strip of paper. The wishes are read together as a whole for the group. Students then write individual wish poems which are shared.
2. Timed Poems:
   Divide the class up into small groups, or teams. Each team is given a short time (one or two minutes) to compose the first line of a poem. On a signal from the teacher, each team passes their paper to the next group and receives one from another. The group reads the line that the preceding team has written and adds a second line. The signal is given and the papers rotate again—each time the group reads and adds another line. Teams are encouraged to write what comes to mind, even if it's only their name. They must write something in the time allotted. After 8 or 10 lines, the papers are returned to their original team. Groups can add a line if they

choose, revise and edit the poem they started. The poems can then be read orally with team members, alternating reading the lines. Later, some of them can be turned into an optic poem (creating a picture with computer graphics using the words of the poem) or acted out using ribbons or penlights (while someone else reads the poem).

3. Optic Poetry:

Students can make a picture with their poem, repeating lines if need to fill in the picture. They can be colored in or painted on larger pieces of colored paper and put up around the room. The teacher may ask students to focus on a science/math concept; coauthoring is encouraged.

4. Using Art Reproductions for Poetry:

Teachers or older students may cut up some art magazines. We often use *Art in America* and *Art Forum* and only bring to school those pictures that we wouldn't mind our children seeing. The cost of excellent color copying has really come down and the reproductions can be laminated at school. Each student gets to choose a picture and working alone comes up with:

1. *one word that describes* what they think is happening in the picture
2. *Two adjectives* (while looking at the picture)
3. Three verbs ending in *ing*
4. *A four word phrase that says something* about the picture
5. *one word to sum up* "What is it?" Finish before saying it's a cinquain poem.

The second half of the activity involves having students in small groups, they share their pictures and interpretations. Each group sends a member up to choose a large picture and the group places it on a large piece of poster board. Each student gets a large piece of construction paper and uses a felt pen to write their own cinquain about the one group picture. (These should be large enough to be seen from across the room.) After cutting out and taping down around the picture the whole group construction is put up as public art (with elements of language arts).

Alternative format: One word, giving title
Two words, describing the title
Three words, expressing an action
Four words, expressing a feeling
One word, a synonym for the title

5. Poetry with Movement and Music:

   Poems can be put to music and movement. One student can read the poem and the rest of the group moves around using streamers, penlights in a darkened room.

   Penlight Poem

   The Sun comes up,
   The Sun goes down.
   The Stars come out and twinkle.

   The Moon is full,
   But . . . sometimes not.
   The Sun will rise tomorrow.

   Birds will fly,
   And Fish will swim,
   The Bees will buzz about.

   But soon they'll rest,
   'Cause the Sun sets,
   And the Stars again are shining.

                            —Stephen Leggett

6. Diamente:

   This is a poem that takes the shape of a diamond. It has seven contrasting lines. The first line is a noun; the second line has two adjectives describing the noun; the third line has three ed or ing verb forms relating to the noun. The fourth line begins to make a transition by having four nouns that refer to both the opening and closing noun (line seven). (The noun in line seven must have an opposite or contrasting meaning to the noun in the first line.) The fifth line has three *ed* or *ing* verb forms relating to the noun in line seven. The sixth line has two adjectives related to the last noun.

7. Lantern:

   This poetry form takes the shape of a Japanese lantern. It has five lines with eleven syllables in a one-two-three-four-one pattern.

   One syllable _____
   Two syllables _____ _____
   Three syllables _____ _____ _____
   Four syllables _____ _____ _____ _____
   One syllable _____

8. Metaphor Comparisons:

   Poems containing metaphors used in mathematics and science are read aloud. Students may bring in metaphors used in science/math, social studies, popular songs, film, literature, and an object that could serve as a personal metaphor.

9. Creating Poems from Words in the Environment:
   This activity is designed to increase students' observation of words connecting to their environment and create poetry from printed words they observe around them. This can be in the classroom, at school, on field trips, at the bus stop, or walking down the street.

In whole language classrooms, teachers are using poems for integrated reading, writing, and talking opportunities as in the following lesson:

A Sample Poetry Lesson

A lesson developed from *Dinosaurs,* a poetry anthology for children edited by Lee Bennett Hopkins.

1. Teacher reads poems aloud.
2. Students brainstorm reasons why the dinosaurs died, and words that relate to how the dinosaurs moved.
3. Models of dinosaurs and pictures are displayed and talked about.
4. Students write poems and share them.
   Children may also wish to include personal school or family history in their poem. Math and social studies could be incorporated by using population, or area size of a state.

Poetry Share Time

Students gather in small groups once a week to share poems in books they have been reading. The groups are structured so that each student

1. reads the author and title of each poem
2. tells about the poem
3. reads one or two passages aloud
4. receives responses from members of the group, specifically pointing out parts they liked and asking questions.

Cooperative Group Activities Using Creative Drama

Creative drama has many facets and applications in the language arts classroom. It emphasizes spontaneous, intuitive, and natural responses to literature in the classroom as opposed to prepared or staged theatrical productions that require much advance preparation (Stewig & Buege, 1994). Creative drama allows students to bring their own world views and experiences to texts by using movement, facial expressions, or language through interpretive or improvisational activity. *Interpretive* experiences allow students to evoke their own renditions of characters or events that bear a relationship to a given story. *Improvisational* experiences allow students to explore characterization or plot by adding new conditions or considerations to stories, thereby reinventing stories in creative ways.

Creative Drama:

- Adapts to many types of lessons and subjects (English, Social Studies, Health, Creative Writing, Science, etc.).
- Encourages the clarification of values.
- Evokes contributions and responses from students who rarely participate in "standard" discussions.
- Evaluates, in English classes, how well students know the material (characterization, setting, plot, conflicts).
- Provides a stimulating prewriting exercise.

Creative dramatics emphasizes four fundamental educational objectives:

1. provides for self realization in unified learning experiences
2. offers firsthand experiences in democratic behavior
3. provides functional learning which is related to life
4. contributes to comprehensive learning

Drama is a natural way to improve vocabulary, listening, observation, and speaking ability. Skills learned through creative dramatics can carry over into the writing process in part because it engages students in the rough equivalent of prewriting, writing, conferencing, and rewriting. Creative drama can also help motivate students to clarify concepts, pay more attention in reading, and explore the deeper meaning in the text. Within these activities students can be viewed as performers required to demonstrate their collective knowledge. The teacher's role is like that of a coach—helping students know and interpret the standards provoking thought. The following is a list of ways creative dramatics can be used.

1. *Stimulating Exploration of the Environment*
   A stimulating environment for language learning includes tools for observation like microscopes, maps, thermometers, and telescopes. These materials stimulate the reasoning, explanation, comparison, drama, and the language of observation. Teachers tend to think of

these materials and methods as parts of the science or social studies curriculum. They are also crucial to language learning.

2. *Personification* (This can also be used as a pre-writing activity)
   Each student draws the name of an inanimate object (pencil sharpener, doorknob, waste basket, alarm clock, etc.) Students pick a partner and develop an improvisation from objects in a story or in the environment.

3. *Increasing Research and Journalism Skills*
   Using techniques of role playing and creative drama, have student groups show *how to* interview (Give good and bad examples). Short excerpts from TV news or radio information programs provide good models for discussion and creative drama activities.

4. *Showing Emotions* (nonverbal communication)
   Assign an "emotion" to each student (anger, jealousy, shyness, nervousness, nerdiness, arrogance, etc.) Students must act out the emotion without actually naming or referring to it. The class notes significant details and discusses which emotion was being portrayed.

5. *Extend a Story*
   Let students speculate on "what's next" in the life of a character based upon what we know from the literature.
   Ask: "What happens to _____ next?"
   Ask: "What if _____ and _____ met a year later . . . ?"
   Ask: "What advice would _____ give to someone in a similar situation?" Have students act out what they think should go in the blank—or come up with a new ending to a story they already know.

6. *Character Transpositions*
   Students can imagine the story they have just read in a town or city that they have seen. Take a character from some historical period and present him or her with a dilemma of the 1980s. Design a skit around one of these situations.
   The King Arthur Tales:
   • Merlin working in a used car lot.
   • Lancelot at a rock concert.
   • Guenevere at a NOW meeting.
   • Arthur interviewing for a job on Wall Street.

7. *Using Creative Drama to Increase Vocabulary*
   Assign five words to a group and let them use them in a skit. Look for patterns and rhyming in words. Students can also do research on the origins of prefixes and suffixes found in subject areas.

8. Send Students Back Through Time
   • The Crucible
   • What happens to an eighties teenager (with Walkman® & black T-shirt) who somehow lands in Salem at the height of the witch hysteria?

9. *Creating Character Transpositions*
   Students can imagine the story they have just read in a town or city that they have seen. They can also dramatize an incident in the life of a famous person. For example, if you are studying space travel, students can improvise a scene between one or two astronauts and those in charge of the mission.

10. *Superstition, Interesting Fiction, or Reality*
    Students act out an example of superstition vs. reality.

Teaching Story Dramatization

1. Select a good story—and then tell it to the group
2. With the class, break the plot down into sequences, or scenes, that can be acted out.
3. Have groups select a scene they wish to dramatize.
4. Instruct the groups to break the scene or scenes into further sequence, and discuss the setting, motivation, characterizations, roles, props, etc. Encourage students to get involved in the developmental images of the characters—what they did, how they did it, why they did it. Have groups make notes on their discussions.
5. Meet with groups to review and discuss their perceptions. Let them go into conference and plan in more detail for their dramatization.
6. Have the whole class meet back together and watch the productions of each group. Instruct students to write down five things they liked and five things that could be improved in the next playing.
7. Let the players return to their groups at the end of all group performances and evaluate the dramas using the criteria in number 6.
8. Allow groups to bring back their group evaluations to the whole class. Discuss findings, suggestions, and positive group efforts.

Reminders and Pointers

1. Do not rush students. Side coach if necessary, examples: "take your time." "You're doing fine."

2. Try to keep an environment where each can find his own nature without imposition. Growth is natural to everyone.

3. A group of individuals who act, agree, and share together create strength and release knowledge surpassing the contribution of any single member.

4. If during sessions students become restless and static in their work, it is a danger sign. Refreshment and a new focus are needed.

5. Become familiar with the many resource and game books useful in this work.

6. Be flexible. Alter your plans on a moment's notice.

7. While a team is performing, the teacher must observe audience reactions as well as the play work. The interaction of the audience is part of the creative dramatics experience.

8. Avoid giving examples. Too often the students become bound to that example and don't try new things.

9. If the environment in the workshop is joyous and free of authoritarianism, everyone will "play," and become as open as young children.

By connecting creative drama to the discussion of literature and writing students can share imaginative ideas with their peers and create an atmosphere where unconscious thought can flow freely.

Conclusion

Peer collaboration is an essential component to learning in the language arts classroom. Staging successful collaborative learning experiences requires time and practice. Teachers need to try different ways of structuring collaborative learning so they can assess what works and what does not work with specific groups of students. Through active "kidwatching," teachers can carefully observe and take note of how children engage in peer talk. By reflecting on these observations, they can consider ways to revise and improve collaborative experiences for the future. Above all, language arts teachers need to be given encouragement to experiment with student collaboration and engage in a process of critical inquiry which is so necessary for improving this mode of learning. Support from administrators, parents, and colleagues would help teachers feel that their efforts to promote collaborative learning are valued.

Graphic Organizers

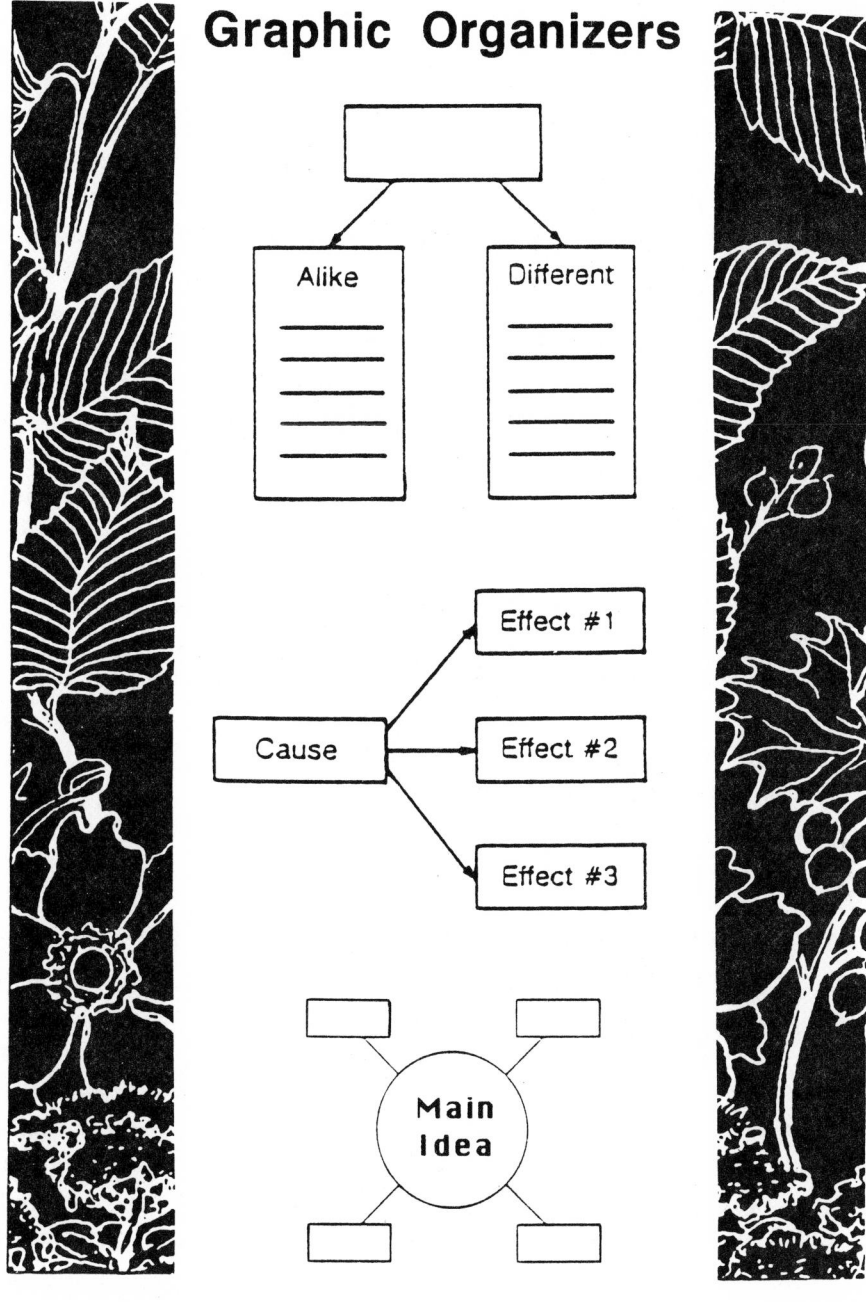

To grow as readers, writers, and thinkers, students must be given opportunities to engage in exploratory talk with peers. Incorporating cooperative learning structures into the classroom routine is consistent with holistic notions of social learning, student empowerment, and improving all of the language arts. Collaborative learning allows students to see each other as legitimate literacy partners and "teachers." Having multiple peer-teachers is critical for meeting the diverse needs of developing readers and writers in today's language arts classroom. Of course, it helps if students can express themselves well. This means that teachers may have to give a little more attention to speaking, a neglected element of the language arts curriculum.

Much of the language that students encounter today is communicated by the telephone, popular music, and television—not exactly good models of eloquence and reasoned debate. The consequences of waning articulateness is related to functional illiteracy and sloppy writing. Although the schools and the workplace are still very literacy-intensive, our culture is moving away from the written word and is becoming increasingly dependent on speech. (Do you write as many letters as you used to?) As the quality and civility of speech is shredded at the highest levels, it becomes ever more difficult to face up to the substantial and sustained educational, social, and economic efforts required to move beyond intellectual and moral chaos. By toning down the rhetorical extremes and encouraging more articulate behavior we might be able to have more reasoned conversation, less verbal combat, and more articulate public expression.

As far as public investment in education (the future) is concerned, it is time to stop watching as American education and culture continue their slow but sure slide downward. When it comes to the language arts, this means developing a comprehensive language arts program that will work for every child—even those who may need some systematic subskill instruction. The fact that the National Assessment of Educational Progress found a small decline in reading proficiency in 1990s does not help educators deal with the sociopolitical forces pressuring the language arts field (NAEP, 1995). Many schools have shown that with a high level of public support and on-going staff development they can do a better job of teaching language arts skills—helping students master what they need to know to become productive and self-reliant members of a democratic society.

Collaborative groups can extend the atmosphere and excitement of group work to imaginative language development. As the philosopher Ludwig Wittgenstein has suggested, the skills of the language arts can be developed through collaborative language games, informal conversations, brief exchanges, rationally persuasive oratory, and allowing good literature to influence the writing process.

> *Dust as we are, the immortal spirit grows,*
> *Like harmony in music;*
> *There is a dark inscrutable workmanship*
> *that reconciles discordant elements,*
> *Makes them cling together in one society*
> —Wordsworth

REFERENCES

Adams, D. & Hamm, M. (1989). *Media and literacy: Learning in an electronic age.* Springfield, IL: Charles C Thomas.

Adams, D. (1984). What children read influences how they write *The Leaflet,* NCTE.

Allington, R. (1983). The reading instruction provided readers of differing reading abilities. *Elementary School Journal* (May).

Barr, R., Kamil, M. L., Rosenthal, B. P., & Pearson, P. D. (Eds.) (1993). *Handbook of reading research* (Vol. 2, pp. 630–640). White Plains, NY: Longman.

Botel, M., & Lytle, S. (1990). *PCRP II.* Harrisburg, PA: The Pennsylvania Department of Education.

Burns, P., Roe, B., & Ross, E. (1988). *Teaching reading in today's elementary schools.* Boston, MA: Houghton Mifflin.

Calkins, L. M. (1994). *The art of teaching writing.* Portsmouth, NH: Heinemann.

Cohen, E. G. (1986). *Designing group-work: Strategies for the heterogeneous classroom.* New York: Teachers College Press.

Daniels, H. (1994). *Literature circles: Voice and choice in the student-centered classroom.* York, ME: Stenhouse.

Denman, G. (1989). *When you've made it your own: Teaching poetry to young people.* Portsmouth, NH: Heinemann.

Freedman, J. O. (1989). Commencement Address, Dartmouth College.

George, G. C. (1972). *Julie of the wolves.* New York: Harper and Row.

Goodlad, J. I. (1983). A study of schooling: Some findings and hypotheses. *Phi Delta Kappan,* 64, 465–470.

Goodman, K. (1986). *What's whole in whole language?* Portsmouth, NH: Heinemann.

Graves, D. H. (1994). *A fresh look at writing.* Portsmouth, NH: Heinemann.

Harste, J. C., Short, K. G., & Burke, C. (1988). *Creating classrooms for authors.* Portsmouth, NH: Heinemann.

Hollander, J. (1989). *Melodious guile: Fictive pattern in poetic language.* New Haven, CT: Yale University Press.

Labbo, L. D., Hoffman, J. V. & Roser, N. L. (1995). Ways to unintentionally make writing difficult. *Language Arts, 72*, 3. pp. 164–170.

Lazar, A. M. (1993). *The construction of two college study groups.* Unpublished doctoral dissertation. University of Pennsylvania.

LeFevre, K. B. (1987). *Invention as a social act.* Carbondale, IL: Southern Illinois University Press.

National Assessment of Educational Progress (1995). High school students ten years after. *A Nation at Risk.* Washington, DC:

Nell, V. (1989). *Lost in a book.* New Haven, CT: Yale University Press.

Ravitch, D. (1995). *National standards in American education.* Washington DC: *Brookings Institution 1995,* p. 163.

Rhodes, L. K. & Shanklin, N. (1993). *Windows into literacy.* Portsmouth, NH: Heinemann.

Rosenblatt, L. M. (1978). *The reader, the text, the poem: The transactional theory of the literary work.* Carbondale, IL: Southern Illinois University Press.

Rosenblatt, L. M. (1993). The literary transaction: Evocation and response. In K. Holland, R. A. Hungerford & S. B. Ernst (Eds.), *Journeying: Children responding to literature.* Portsmouth, NH: Heineman.

Short, K. G. & Pierce, K. M. (Eds.) (1990). *Talking about books: Creating literate communities.* Portsmouth, NH: Heinemann.

Smith, F. (1986). *Insult to intelligence: The bureaucratic invasion of our classrooms.* Portsmouth, NH: Heinemann.

Stewig, J. W. & Buege, C. (1994). *Dramatizing literature in whole language classrooms.* New York: Teachers College Press.

Sudol, D. & Sudol, P. (1995). Yet another story: Writers' workshop revisited. *Language Arts, 72*, 3. pp. 171–178.

Taylor, D. (1993). *From the child's point of view.* Portsmouth, NH: Heineman.

Vygotsky, L. (1986). *Thought and Language.* Cambridge, MA: MIT Press.

Vygotsky, L. S. (1978). *Mind in society: The development of higher psychological processes,* M. Cole, V. John-Steiner, S. Scribner, S. Souberman (Eds.), Cambridge, MA: Harvard University Press.

Weintraub, S. (Ed.). (1988). *Summary of Investigations Relating To Reading.* Newark, Delaware: International Reading Association.

Wertsch, J. V. (1991). *Voices of the mind: A sociocultural approach to mediated action.* Cambridge, MA: Harvard University Press.

Wordsworth, W. (1967). The prelude. In *English Romantic Writers.* D. Perkins (Ed.). New York: Harcourt Brace Jovanovich.

Chapter 4

SCIENCE, MATHEMATICS, AND COLLABORATION:

MAKING SENSE OF OUR WORLD
THROUGH A PROCESS OF GROUP INQUIRY

There was once a state legislator in Wisconsin who objected to the introduction of daylight savings time despite all the good arguments for it. He maintained sagely that there is always a trade-off involved in the adoption of any policy, and that if daylight savings time were instituted, curtains and other fabrics would fade more quickly (because an extra hour would be provided for sunlight).

— John Paulos

Many Americans who would never admit that they have trouble reading are not ashamed to admit that they are really ignorant of science and mathematics. Our growing science and mathematical "illiteracy" problem results in misinformed governmental policies, an acceptance of pseudoscience, confused personal decisions and trouble in the workplace. When students finish their schooling without a reasonable understanding of science and mathematics it puts them at a distinct disadvantage relative to their counterparts in the other industrial nations. How might we improve quality of teaching and learning about these subjects? Here we suggest an active inquiry-based approach for teaching science and mathematics that uses small cooperative groups to give students experiences with current issues and real phenomena.

This chapter introduces you to an integrated approach for teaching science and mathematics within the context of cooperative groups. It examines some of the advantages to integrating the two disciplines and identifies common process skills. Whether you want to connect science and mathematics or not, most of the principles presented here remain the same and almost any lesson at any level can make good use of cooperative groups. Traditionally science and mathematics have been presented as a body of knowledge to be remembered by rote, rather than a process of inquiry the intellectual and technological tools to make sense of the world. Teachers are now moving away from a "telling" model to structuring experiences encourage children to interact within the context of valued social relationships. We recognize the collaborative culture of learning and suggest hands-on/minds-on experiences that can help students become effective investigators.

Although it's best for children to construct knowledge for themselves, it should be recognized that they frequently have false understandings about scientific and mathematical concepts. Some of their misconceptions are natural, others were learned. The *National Institutes of Health* recently released a report that outlines a resurgence of belief in magic and psychic phenomena (N.I.H., 1995). Some Americans even reject the Western scientific tradition and share a hostility to modern science and its tools (like mathematics and technology). They list horrors like nuclear bombs and radioactive waste while avoiding any mention of positive examples—like the fact that life expectancy in the United States has doubled in the 20th century.

As citizens and political leaders are called upon to make decisions regarding everything from power plants to medical ethics, it becomes increasingly important to recognize "voodoo science" when it is encountered. Everybody should understand that we live in a universe shaped by natural laws that can be understood and used to benefit or harm humanity. What can be done to move from pseudoscience to helping youngsters understand science and its mathematical associates? On a practical classroom level, students can work together to study these subjects within the context of social and personal applications. Cooperative groups are a proven technique for getting students actively involved, motivated, and competent as they learn about modern science and mathematics.

Scientific Literacy

Shamos suggests that science should be taught "as a cultural imperative, and not primarily for content." He believes that only those seeking to become scientists need an in-depth science curriculum (Shamos, 1995). Of course, science is more than just content. It would be an educational mistake not to help students understand the scientific method and at least a little of the theory, laws and facts of natural world. Science is too important to be left to the experts. Without a minimal level of scientific literacy citizens are not only open to the foolishness of magical pseudo-science but will fail when they attempt to evaluate decisions that effect us all. Helping students become scientifically literate does not mean putting everyone on the graduate school science track in fourth grade. It means by the time students graduate students should:

- Be familiar with the natural world, recognizing its diversity and unity.
- Understand the key concepts and principles of science.
- Understand some of the important ways science, math and technology depend upon each other.
- Know that science, mathematics and technology are human enterprises (creations) and what this implies about their strengths and weaknesses.
- Have a capacity (ability) for scientific ways of thinking.
- Be able to apply scientific knowledge and ways of thinking to achieve personal and social purposes.

(This list is similar to the definition of "scientific literacy" in *Science for All Americans,* Project 2061 AAAS, 1989.)

A common theme in new science programs is helping children make connections between subject matter and real-life experiences. The "big ideas" of science, the scientific method, reasoning, and collaborative inquiry are emphasized. Big ideas are the themes of science, larger than facts and concepts, they integrate the theoretical structures of various scientific disciplines. For example, the theme of energy can link the properties of physics to life science and earth science. All of us can think of ways energy is connected to these scientific disciplines; a person has energy, plants have energy, so do the earth, the moon, and the stars. "If curricula and instructors are successful in developing themes for students in connecting scientific concepts and facts, then this intellectual habit will carry over and enrich other fields and disciplines.

What are some of the differences between teaching science today and in the past. To begin with, science teaching is no longer viewed as an inert body of detailed information with a specialized vocabulary and procedures that must be committed to memory. The emphasis is now on open-ended problem solving, scientific inquiry, experience, and active peer collaboration. Another difference in the 1990s is that boundaries between traditional subject matter categories are softened and thematic connections are more common. Concepts are chosen that make sense at a simple level but provide a solid foundation for learning more. As children move from the concrete to the abstract details are treated as enhancing understanding. For example, instead of saying the water evaporated. It would be much more engaging for students to watch the process. Questions such as: "How long do you think this water just spilled will stay on the table?" "What will make it disappear?" After studying maps and weather charts, students can build on concrete representations to collaboratively answer more abstract questions like: "How does the evaporation rate affect the climate?" Although children usually get off to a better start if they can begin by touching, feeling, or seeing something, in the world of modern science it is common to move back and forth between the concrete and the abstract.

New curriculum standards suggest devoting time to understanding *what the scientific enterprise is* and how science, mathematics and technology relate to each other and to the social system. This includes some important historical information about these subjects. All have roots going far back into history into every part of the world. Although modern science is only a few centuries old, elements (especially in mathematics and astronomy) can be traced to early Egyptian, Greek, Chinese, and Arabic cultures.

The Dimensions of Mathematical Power

The language of nature is written in mathematics.
— Galileo

With new national mathematics standards in place, many teachers have come to accept the new goals for mathematics teaching. Now to move from acceptance to more widespread *doing*. The 1993 National Survey of Science and Mathematical Education, by Horizon Research, Inc., showed that the vast majority (more than 80%) of teachers agreed with using hands-on active inquiry, moving from the concrete to the abstract, and encouraging students to use the intellectual/technological tools of mathematics to explore real world problems. However, the same survey found that the classroom reality usually didn't approach what teachers thought should be happening (Horizon Research, 1993).

On both the national and state level, mathematics reform is concerned with making students mathematically powerful (California Department of Education, 1992). This is defined as empowering students to think and communicate using mathematical ideas, drawing on the techniques and tools of mathematics.

Thinking refers to intellectual activity. This includes analyzing, classifying, planning, comparing, investigating, designing, inferring, and making hypotheses. It involves making mathematical models and testing and verifying them.

Communication is the coherent expression of one's mathematical processes and results.

Ideas refer to content: concepts such as addition, proportional relationships, geometry, counting, and limits.

Tools and Techniques extends literal tools such as calculators, compasses and their effective use to metaphorical tools such as computational algorithms and visual data representations.

Thinking, an important dimension of mathematical power, refers to intellectual activity. Students who are mathematically powerful are involved in thinking activities such as analyzing, classifying, planning, comparing, investigating, designing, inferring and making hypotheses. Mathematically powerful students make meaningful connections, construct mathematical models, raise questions, test and verify them (Silver, 1985). Communication is essential. Communication is the coherent expression of one's mathematical processes and results. When children or adults communicate they generally use ideas that make sense to them. Students should be encouraged to talk about and express their ideas orally or in writing during early conceptual development.

Ideas refer to content: concepts such as addition, proportional relationships, geometry, counting, and limits. Many mathematical concepts express relationships (equation, more, addition, fraction). Concepts such as square, triangle, quantity, seven, and million do not. An idea that is fully understood can be extended more easily to learn a new idea. A student who understands basic number concepts will have a much easier time mastering basic addition and subtraction facts. Mastering a new idea is measured to its connectedness to existing ideas. In geometry, the formulas for finding the areas of squares, rectangles, parallelograms, trapezoids, and triangles are interconnected with the single idea that area can be arrived at by multiplying the base and the height. That idea is built on an understanding of multiplication concepts and area units.

Mathematics tools and the techniques of mathematics go beyond the idea of literal tools such as calculators and compasses to understanding the procedures behind them, making connections (Burns, 1991). Procedural knowledge is knowledge of the symbolism that is used to represent mathematics and the rules and procedures that are used in doing mathematical work. Making connections implies that the rules and processes must have a meaningful rationale and make sense to students. Students need to understand the reasoning behind the rule or algorithm. Figurative tools such as computational algorithms and making visual representations of data need to be well grounded in conceptual knowledge so that students can explain not only what they are doing, but why. For example, many students know and can use the rule for dividing fractions (invert the divisor and multiply the numerators and denominators) but cannot explain what $1/2 \div 1/4$ means. They have no idea why they are doing what they're doing and are unable to make up a scenario where the computation would be appropriate. To be mathematically powerful is to *understand* the tools and the mathematical procedures behind them.

> *Knowing is not enough; we must apply.*
> *Willing is not enough; we must do.*
>
> --Goethe

The Impact of Mathematics, Science, and Technology

Science, mathematics, and technology have always assisted us in revealing hidden patterns for understanding the world. They are not just the building blocks of arcane academic domains. Now they comprise an important part of a much larger framework of technologically intensive society. Citizens are increasingly called upon to participate in decisions ranging from building electrical power plants to approving distribution of genetically engineered life forms. Today's fast-paced technological and communications culture also requires workers who can go beyond machine calculations to think and solve problems related to real world situations. More than ever, everyone must understand the basic outlines of science and mathematics to grasp patterns, solve problems, and deal with the ambiguity of a constantly changing world.

Science, math, and technology are having an increasing impact on education, the civic process, and American culture in general. But just when the importance of science and mathematics education is growing, most American students are pushed further and further from intelligent participation. Recent international comparisons rank American fifth graders eighth out of 17 countries in science achievement. By ninth grade, we are in 15th place (out of 17) and sliding. When compared to our industrial competitors, we look even worse. Even advanced placement high school physics students scored ninth and advanced chemistry students 11th on a 13-country comparison. Results on mathematics tests are similar. American eighth grade students scored well below other industrial countries in solving problems that require analysis and higher levels of thinking (National Assessment of Educational Progress, 1989).

Do current trends suggest improvement? Not yet. As the twentieth century comes to a close, the demographic make-up of the United States is rapidly changing. In many respects the U.S. is becoming a very fragmented community. In many of the largest U.S. cities, ethnic minorities now make up the majority of the school-age population. The National Research Council reports that white males, thought of only a generation ago as the mainstay of the economy, will comprise only 15 percent of newly hired positions between 1985 and 2000. The other 85 percent—women and people of color—are precisely those sections of the population that are widely underrepresented in the sciences, mathematics, and engineering. These students simply aren't studying much math and science. Research recently gathered by the U.S. Education Department found a majority of girls, disadvantaged students, and minorities are lost to these subjects by the time they leave elementary school. Lack of effective instruction and loss of student interest are major factors in this loss of talent (Clewell, 1987). Bringing science and mathematics into the lives of these students must be given the highest priority.

All is not gloom, doom, and ill-earned pessimism. There are some successful models out there. A good example is California Academy of Mathematics and Science, which is a joint venture of the California State University system, eight school districts in the Los Angeles area, and several high-technology companies. The program focuses on promising minority students and the results have been excellent. Science and mathematics are often integrated, students work in teams, and the focus is on problem-solving (Gross, 1994).

Integrated Inquiry in Science and Mathematics

To improve science and mathematics education for *all* students requires new approaches. We suggest connecting student inquiry in science and mathematics by emphasizing quantification, data collection, measurement, space-time relationships, collaboration, and hands-on problem-solving. Learning these science/math subjects involves the construction of meaning by learners as they interact with each other, the teacher, and the curriculum.

There is a mismatch today between the science and mathematics curriculum found in schools and that which most students want and need for the world outside of school. Current curricula consist largely of textbooks, teacher talk, and fill-in-the bubble testing — in spite of general agreement that science and math curriculum for the 1990s should emphasize thinking skills and model methods of cooperative inquiry. The best new programs move beyond the textbook to providing an active group examination of the nature of science, mathematics, and technology.

Why should we connect the science and mathematics curriculum? Many researchers have grappled with that question. Attempts to integrate mathematics and science instruction have appeared in the literature since the beginning of the twentieth century (Breslich, 1936, Moore, 1903, Kolb, 1968, Wandersee, 1992). McBride and Silverman (1991) have listed four reasons that help to answer the question *"Why integrate science and mathematics?"*

1. Science and mathematics are closely related systems of thought and are naturally correlated in the physical world.
2. Science and technology can provide students with concrete examples of abstract mathematical ideas that can improve learning of mathematics concepts.
3. Mathematics can enable students to achieve deeper understanding of science and technology concepts by providing ways to quantify and explain science relationships.
4. Science and technology activities illustrating mathematics concepts can provide relevancy and motivation for learning mathematics (pp. 286–287).

If integration of science and mathematics is to occur, changes will have to happen in teacher preparation programs at colleges and universities. This requires a new way of thinking. Issues such as course content, pedagogical issues, student beliefs, and identifying sources of guidance.

Standards developed by the National Council of Teachers of Mathematics and the National Science Teacher's Association suggests common science, and mathematics process skills:

1. Sorting and classifying
2. Communicating
3. Solving Problems
4. Measuring
5. Interpreting data
6. Formulating and interpreting models
7. Using spatial and time relationships

The science curriculum increasingly emphasizes process. Currently, science trade books and published commercial science kits and materials are used as a major source of hands-on science activities and interdisciplinary inquiry. In mathematics, the National Council of Teachers of Mathematics has developed curriculum standards which provide guidance for incorporating recommended mathematics concepts—what is to be taught and how to teach it effectively.

Goals of science and mathematics education now include helping students learn how to apply knowledge and solve problems as they gain conceptual understanding. Students need to be able to use science processes and mathematical tools to change their own theories and beliefs in ways that are personally meaningful and consistent with scientific explanations.

This way they can develop conceptual understanding and the means for integrating science/math knowledge into their personal conceptions.

To really learn science and mathematics, students must construct their own understandings, examine, represent, solve, transform, apply, prove, and communicate. This happens most effectively when they work together in groups to discuss, make presentations, and create their own theories (Hamm & Adams, 1992). Such an environment encourages students to engage in a great deal of invention as they impose their interpretation on what is presented and create theories that make sense to them.

Learning about science and mathematics involves learning to think critically and create relationships. How these relationships are structured in a student's mind depends on such factors as maturity, physical experience, and social interactions. The ability to inquire, think, collaborate and investigate fuels personal autonomy and self-direction in learning. The inability to do these things leads to inequality of opportunity, weakens our capacity for productive competition, and undermines American civic culture.

Tomorrow will bring different solutions to the best that we can envision today. Consequently, innovation and planning for the future must occur without too many preconceived notions and provide for flexible change. No curriculum should be chiseled in stone. Once programs are in place, new pictures emerge and programs will have to change with changing social and individual needs. Whatever new realities fall into place to change our views, there is no reason why scientific literacy cannot be achieved by all students in the United States. It is a matter of national commitment, determination, and a willingness to collaborate towards common goals.

Thinking and Problem-Solving

An important goal of science and mathematics instruction is to stimulate critical and creative thinking. The reason is simple: instruction in these subjects is most successful when lessons are geared to students' thinking processes and natural solution strategies. As the new standards make clear, science and mathematics instruction should be taught in the context of reasoning and problem solving.

Inquiry in science and mathematics involves many critical and creative thinking skills—including observation, inference, questioning, analysis, interpretation, prediction, and the use of metaphor. Inquiry is made more effective by highly developed reasoning ability. It also contributes to more effective thinking by getting students involved in science/math investigation and applying inquiry processes to these subjects.

Today's fast-changing world provides few occupational or academic opportunities for explicitly defined problem-solving. Now students must be ready to deal with ambiguity while employing a wide range of interdisciplinary skills, technological tools, and collaborative approaches. New standards place *problem solving* at the heart of the science and mathematics curriculum. They provide the context for learning other concepts and skills and follow the following four steps: understanding the problem, devising a plan, carrying out the plan, and looking back to review the solution.

The difficulties encountered in problem-solving may be found everywhere and provide a convenient link to other subjects. Humorous examples from outside the science/math content area are one good place to start. An example is this popular children's poem:

Recipe for a Hippopotamus Sandwich

A hippo sandwich is easy to make.
All you do is simply take
One slice of bread,
One slice of cake,
Some mayonnaise,
One onion ring,
One hippopotamus,
One piece of string,
A dash of pepper—
That ought to do it.
And now comes the problem. . . .
Biting into it!

—Shel Silverstein

Another example of a problem that young children might problem-solve: "How could Jack have resolved his conflict with the giant in *Jack and the Beanstalk?*" The interests of children are not content specific, and their acquisition of thinking and problem-solving skills cross traditional disciplines.

One way for teachers to approach a topic is by providing a realistic problem situation that would serve as a vehicle for inquiry by students as a group. After the problem has been identified, the students work as a scientific team that is seeking a solution.

A Cooperative Learning Model for
Teaching Science and Mathematics

Cognitive views of learning emphasize thinking processes *within* the learner and point towards changes that need to be made in the ways that educators have traditionally thought about teaching, learning, and organizing the school classroom (Garofalo, 1988). Central to creating such a learning environment is the desire to help individuals acquire or construct knowledge. That knowledge is to be shared or developed— rather than held by the authority that holds teachers to a high standard, for they must have both subject matter knowledge and pedagogical knowledge based on an understanding of cognitive and developmental processes.

The cooperative learning model for inquiry in science and mathematics emphasizes the intrinsic benefits of learning rather than external rewards for academic performance. Lessons are introduced with statements concerning reasons for engaging in the learning task. Students are encouraged to assume responsibility for learning and evaluating their own work and the work of others. Interaction may include a discussion of the validity of explanations, the search for more information, the testing of various explanations or consideration of the pros and cons of specific decisions.

The characteristics that distinguish new collaborative science and mathematics learning revolve around group goals and the accompanying benefits of active group work. Instead of being told they need information, students learn to recognize when additional data is needed. They jointly seek it out, apply it; they see its power and value. In this way, the actual *use* of science and mathematics information becomes the starting point rather than an add on. The teacher facilitates the process, instead of acting as a knowledge dispenser. Student success is measured by performance, work samples, projects, application or synthesis. Simple recall is not as important.

A Model of Mathematics and Science Instruction

Model Characteristic	Traditional	Mathematics and Science Textbook Model
Active Learning Model		
Theory	Behavioristic rewards/grades	Cognitive internal/self enhancement

Goals	product	process, learning, knowledge
Method	textbook, lecture memorization	joint group project inquiry, research skills
Skills	memorization resolving, presenting alternative solutions	communication, negotiation presenting a problem, reporting
Student's role	knowledge recipient	student as researcher reporting, synthesizing
Teacher's role	teacher as expert	teacher as learner
Authority	teacher	individual/shared
Evaluation	external	joint
Learning Setting	competition teacher validates thinking, recitation	collaboration self reliance group reliance higher level thinking

Cooperative science and mathematics learning models place an emphasis on exploring a problem, thinking, and the collaborative challenge of posing a solution. This involves peer helping, self-evaluation, and group support for risk taking. This also means accepting individual differences, and having positive expectations for everyone in the group. Students understand the purpose of their tasks as contributing to their own learning and self-development. If the teacher can help children push these elements together the result will be greater persistence and more self-directed learning. To reach these goals also requires viewing classrooms as learning places where teaching methods build on cognitive perspectives.

Emphasizing topic-centered, group-based instruction allows students to address common topics at a variety of levels of sophistication. The usual procedure is to have all students work on the same topic during a given unit, but the work is divided into a number of investigatory or practical activities on which the students work in groups. Activities are organized to include basic required work and optional enrichment work so that less able groups accomplished the requirements and were able to choose some of the options, but the more able groups moved on to more challenging assignments after completing the basic tasks. Because topics are not sequenced linearly, each new topic may be addressed provided opportunities for differentiated instruction. The brighter students tend to do much more writing, for example.

Combining Subject Matter and Effective Instruction
in a Technological Age

Cooperative learning is more working in groups of three or four. It is a small social unit (community) that makes a commitment to all group members. As a strategy for interdisciplinary inquiry in science/math it builds on the sharing of problem-solving strategies to help children learn that when everyone learns the whole group benefits.

In science and math, teaching both pedagogical and content area knowledge is important. Without the essential content base, teachers cannot focus on student thinking, or provide appropriate feedback. Without some knowledge of pedagogy, it is difficult to make mathematics and science more personally relevant and interesting for students. Teachers must know the content and the characteristics of effective instruction.

Traditionally, there has been a gap between what was taught in science and mathematics and what was really learned. Interpreting and understanding the real world—and how it relates to personal experience—is different than the interpretations and understandings advanced in school science and math courses. Typical school programs have produced students with increasingly negative attitudes about science and mathematics as they progress through the grades. This is especially true when math and science courses do not consider needs, interests, motivations, or experiences of the learners, or when the material being covered is not viewed as useful or valuable (Good & Brophy, 1994).

The teaching of science and mathematics today requires students to think skillfully and monitor their thinking processes as they work. Constructing a hypothesis, problem solving, and cooperative group work can replace traditional chalk, talk, and textbook methodology. It also helps to connect each learner's reality to the subjects by paying attention to individual and group understanding. When these elements are in place, science and mathematics *can* be used to solve interesting problems in unique ways.

In teaching children to think scientifically and mathematically, it is important to help them to apply their understanding and skills in solving problems, discovering relationships, analyzing patterns, generalizing relationships, and using numbers with confidence. Adding thinking skills and cooperative strategies can assist them in taking responsibility for their thoughts and provide an inner confidence.

Science, Mathematics, and the Shape of Thinking

In the sixteenth and seventeenth centuries, the scientist was viewed as a hunter, searching for new knowledge gained from direct experience. The scientist was viewed as someone who explored the hidden causes of things "the secrets of nature" remain "secrets" only until they are exposed through persistent research and experiments. In the sixteenth century, knowledge passed from being guarded by its owner (alchemists, physicians, or metalworkers) to the public domain. As the secrets of nature came to the public's view it excited the imaginations of many people. The result was an explosion of scientific, mathematical, and technical knowledge (Eamon, 1994).

Still, through the nineteenth century, much of religion and philosophy were set in the past or in heaven. We're so much more sophisticated and aware than that now (aren't we?) In the twentieth century progress in science and technology have moved them to the near future *on earth.* Beginning early in this century, science and its technological associates were viewed as capable of preventing hunger, disease, poverty, war, and even evil itself. Unfortunately, there is a benign indifference in the universe and things often don't progress in a positive manner that we expect. There is something to be said for those who can see the dark side of human possibility. Pessimism isn't fatalism.

In spite of the aggravations, science and technology have freed much of humanity from some of its more mundane tasks and changed in the process our relationship to physical and social reality. Recently, technological innovations, like calculators and computers have changed the way science and mathematics is taught and learned. New models of instruction that encourage using technology and collaboration have sprung up to deal with this new aesthetic. We are now at a stage where teachers and students must move from seeing technology as a source of knowledge (coach and drill) to viewing it as a medium or forum for communication and intelligent adventure. Using technological innovations intelligently requires more thinking, problem formulating, and interpersonal communication skills.

A substantive knowledge base now exists regarding the social and psychological characteristics of how children learn about mathematics, science, and technology. Yet studies indicate that even experienced teachers are not familiar with this knowledge. The challenge is to make research-

based knowledge accessible to both practicing teachers and students in teacher education programs (Lonning & DeFranco, 1994).

Factors that Influence Science, Mathematics, and Technology

It is becoming increasingly clear that being able to think scientifically and mathematically requires more than large amounts of exposure to content. Students need direct decision-making experiences so that their minds can be broadened by applying science and mathematics. By actively examining and solving problems, children can become flexible and resourceful, as they use their knowledge efficiently and come to understand the rules which underlie these domains of knowledge.

Shoenfeld (1985) examined traditional programs and found that students' foundations (cognitive resources) for problem solving far weaker than their performance on tests would indicate. His studies suggested that even mathematically talented high school and college students (who experienced success in upper division math courses) had little or no awareness of how to use math heuristics (rules of thumb). When faced with nonstandard problems which were not put in their textbook, students experienced failures and ended up doing distracting calculations and trivia instead of applying the basic concepts at their disposal. Even students who received good grades in memory-based programs frequently had serious misconceptions about mathematics and science. Implementing well-learned, mechanical procedures (in domains where little is understood) is one thing—deep learning of a subject is quite another.

The difficulties the American educational system is having in teaching science and mathematics connects to yet another problem. The home, the media, and the social environment all play a role in determining what students extract from their math and science lessons. The responsibility for developing citizens who are scientifically literate is a shared responsibility. And there are potentially dire consequences for schooling when you combine a society that doesn't understand science/math with a mass media that goes for dramatic pseudoscience.

Scientific Literacy

Knowledge of science, mathematics, and technology is valuable for everyone because it makes the world more understandable and more interesting. All students should have an awareness of what the scientific endeavor is and how it relates to their culture and their lives. This means understanding the union of science, mathematics, and technology, its roots, the human contributions, its limitations as well as its miracles. Recognizing the role of the scientific endeavor and how science, mathematics, and technology interact with society is one of the basic dimensions of scientific literacy. The National Council on Science and Technology Education identifies a scientifically literate person as one who:

- recognizes the diversity and unity of the natural world
- understands the important concepts and principles of science.

- is aware of the ways that science, mathematics, and technology depend on each other.
- knows that mathematics, science and technology are human endeavors and recognizes what this implies about the strengths and weaknesses of science, mathematics, and technology.
- has a capacity for scientific ways of thinking.
- makes use of scientific knowledge and ways of thinking in personal and social interactions (American Association for the Advancement of Science, 1989).

Scientific literacy also includes seeing scientific endeavors through the perspective of cultural and intellectual history and becoming familiar with ideas that cut across subject lines. This involves an awareness that most of the scientific views held today resulted from many small discoveries over time, and are a product of cultural and historical ways of thinking and viewing the world. Significant historical events, such as Galileo's perspective on the earth's place in the universe, Newton's discoveries of laws of motion, Darwin's observations of diversity, variety and evolving life forms, and Pasteur's identification of infectious disease stemming from microscopic organisms, are milestones in the development of Western thought and events.

People have always been concerned with transmitting attitudes, shared values, and ways of thinking to the next generation. With every part of contemporary life being bombarded by science, mathematics, and technology, it is wrong to avoid these issues. Part of scientific literacy consists of clarifying attitudes, possessing certain scientific values, and making informed judgments. Students need to cultivate scientific patterns of thinking, logical reasoning, curiosity, an openness to new ideas, and skepticism in evaluating claims and arguments. Positive attitudes are also important. Being able to understand the basic principles of science, being "numerate" in dealing with quantitative matters, thinking critically, measuring accurately, and using ordinary tools of science and mathematics (including calculators and computers) are all part of the scientific literacy equation.

To achieve this type of scientific literacy students need to be able to:

- develop and apply creative and rational thinking abilities
- develop values and attitudes that promote ethical and moral thinking.

QUIZ

Testing Scientific Literacy

How a national sample of 1,225 adults answered various questions on a test of scientific literacy. The correct answers are listed below.

1. Which of these is the nearest living relative of the dinosaur, Tyrannosaurus rex?

A chicken 10%
A crocodile 22%
A lizard 30%
An elephant 8%
Not sure 30%

2. About how much of the total area of the Earth is taken up by land surface?

5 percent 9%
30 percent 63%
70 percent 11%
95 percent 3%
Not sure 14%

3. The continents gradually change their positions. Is this true or false?

True 78%
False 12%
Not sure 10%

4. Human beings evolved from earlier species of animals, true or false?

True 45%
False 46%
Not sure 9%

5. The earliest humans lived at the same time as the dinosaurs, true or false?

True 35%
False 51%
Not sure 14%

6. Which of the following groups has the most living species?

Plants 34%
Birds 3%
Insects 42%
Mammals 8%
Not sure 13%

Answers: 1. A chicken; 2. 30 percent 3. True; 4. True; 5. False; 6. Insects

Sources: Louis Harris and Associates, The American Museum of Natural History

- develop a perspective that promotes the interdependent nature of the environment and global society.
- develop the ability for holistic thinking
- develop ability to use science concepts, facts and principles in the solution of problems.
- manipulate the materials of science and communicate science and mathematics information.

Numeracy

> *Numeracy is to mathematics as literacy is to language.*
> —Steen

We include numeracy under the general heading of "scientific literacy." Numeracy is defined as "those mathematical skills which enable an individual to cope with the practical demands of everyday life (Cockcroft, 1986)." Most of us put many mathematical skills to use every day. The ability to compare costs, understand graphs, calculate risks, estimate distances, and appreciate the effects of the deficient reflect the different dimensions in which mathematics and statistical ideas operate. No matter what one's job or standard of living, numeracy skills are directly linked to informed confident decision making. Those who lack confidence or skills lead their lives at the mercy of others. Advertisers, lotteries, or dishonest individuals "after a buck" prey on those who avoid examining exaggerated quantitative claims. Without practical numeracy, a person is left defenseless to those who would take advantage of their money and good intentions.

Society is also at a disadvantage with innumerate citizens. On issues such as acid rain, the federal budget, global warming, crime, population census, and AIDS, arguments and economics depend in essential ways on aspects of mathematical analyses. Being able to understand how large a billion is, comprehend the probability of winning the lottery, or estimating the likelihood of getting an infectious disease are essential skills. A public unable to reason is an electorate unable to discriminate between reasonable and reckless claims in public policy. Debates ranging from acceptable levels of radiation to waste management require a sophisticated level of numeracy.

The skills required for practical numeracy must be taught to most students during the elementary and middle school years. Yet traditional school mathematics programs have concentrated largely on fact-driven, didactic arithmetic. In some schools, neither science nor mathematics teaching has changed much in the last forty years. In these classrooms, science lessons are an hour or so a week of teacher-directed, textbook-driven instruction. Many students often don't encounter "real science" until middle or high school. Even mathematics, which gets more attention, often fails to help children see the relevance of math concepts in a wide variety of situations. *The good news:* at least some of the new math standards developed by the NCTM are in place in nearly half of the nation's schools. And there is general agreement that mathematics and science curricula for the late 1990s should emphasize thinking skills and model methods of cooperative inquiry (Aronowitz, 1989).

Emerging New Patterns

A new pattern for teaching science and mathematics is emerging which focuses on the nature of learning. It emphasizes concept relationships and views science and mathematics as a process or a journey that should focus on how to awaken curiosity, encourage creativity, and motivate students for lifelong learning. Students are now encouraged to relate and apply science/math to social problems, to mathematics, to technology, to creative innovation, and to their personal lives. Answering stilted, dry questions and memorizing facts just doesn't get it done anymore.

In the latest approaches, science and mathematics are seen as touching people, caring for the planet, becoming knowledgeable and socially responsible citizens. Today's best science/math teaching also emphasizes inquiry and builds on student understandings. A priority is given to improving students' self-image and self-concept viewed as indication of performance. Some of the newest methods include techniques such as creative visualization or mental imagery; keeping daily logs or journals; and expressing attitudes through creative endeavors such as writing, building, or art. Holistic creative thinking is encouraged as well as projects and presentations that combine experiential knowledge with theoretical understandings in science and mathematics. Emphasis is on exciting examples in everyday applications, and hands-on collaborative inquiry. The student is a participant and an explorer—reaching out to acquire the science/math skills they need now and in the future.

Contemporary mathematics recommendations have suggested a broader curriculum including estimation skills, problem solving, practical geometry, statistics, data analysis, calculator skills, probability, measurement and patterns. In science, the emphasis is on employing scientists' inquiry

"I Burned the Planet, Dear"

methods to discover and explain the mysteries of science. Students manipulate materials, make observations and draw inferences. Science and mathematics are viewed as complementing one another in everything from teaching about the metric system to using measuring devices. Whether it's problem-solving, communicating, reasoning or application, some integration of instruction improves both disciplines.

Today's students need opportunities to make connections, to work with peers on interesting problems. They also need to be able to apply the skills they are learning to real-life situations. Computational skills, the ability to express basic mathematical understandings, to estimate confidently, and check the reasonableness of estimates are part of what it means to be scientifically literate, numerate, and employable.

Increasingly, school learning is augmented by museum visits, community group meetings, outdoor education programs, peer teaching, and programs for parents. In the cooperative classroom, the science/math teacher is becoming more of a facilitator and a learner. Students are coming to share in some of the teaching chores. Science and mathematics are also coming to be seen as part of an interdisciplinary experience where emphasis is on relating to other subjects and the students world outside of school. This kind of teaching has implications for teachers. Some suggestions:

- allow time for creativity, incubation of ideas, and encourage students to imagine and question
- encourage the use of a variety of materials and sources
- use techniques such as brainstorming to generate ideas, open-ended discussions, collaborating with peers
- involve students in long-term collaborative projects
- integrate science/math processes and conceptual knowledge in ways that reflects the richness and complexity of the content.

Examining Learning

Problems in learning science and mathematics are major reasons why many students fail in school. Much of the failure is due to a tradition of teaching that doesn't match the way students learn. Forty years ago cognitive science combined the tools of psychology, philosophy, linguistics, neurobiology, and computer science. The communicative instinct to speak, learn, and understand is so tied in with human experience that we have trouble picturing what life would be like without it. Cognitive psychologists, such as Piaget and Bruner, explained long ago how students construct understandings based on their own experiences and that each individual's knowledge of science and math is personal (Bruner, 1987). Computing, listening, and memorizing abstract concepts or symbolic procedures leaves a bad taste for the subject.

Worksheets, homework, textbook pages, and repetition may help some students do well on standardized tests. But much of what is memorized is soon forgotten. And the possibility of transforming the skills to a different situation is practically nil. Lower order skills are generally ineffective for developing much needed higher order thinking and problem-solving abilities. The results are just as bad when students are trained to search for right answers or hints of "how to do the page." Neglecting thinking skills, conceptual understanding, and logical reasoning is neglecting scientific literacy. The true goals of science and mathematics education should be to help students learn how to apply knowledge, solve problems, and promote conceptual understanding. Students need to be able to use science processes to change their own theories and beliefs in ways that are personally meaningful and consistent with scientific explanations. This way they can develop conceptual understanding and the means for integrating science knowledge into their personal conceptions.

To really learn science and math, students must construct their own understandings, examine, represent, solve, transform, apply, prove, and communicate. This happens most effectively when they work together in groups to discuss, pose questions, analyze, create their own theories, and make presentations. The best environment for science/math learning encourages students to engage in a great deal of invention as they impose their interpretation on what is presented and create relationships between content and people. How these relationships are structured in a student's mind depends on such factors as maturity, physical experience, and social interactions. Science and mathematics *are* problem solving, communicating and reasoning, and making connections. Concepts in science and mathematics are to be valued for describing, explaining, making predictions, and gaining control over real-life situations. By providing realistic problems and examining applications outside of the classroom science/math content becomes more meaningful.

Correcting Misconceptions

Students often enter science classes with misconceptions about the content they will be studying. For example, most middle school students study plants that emphasize their role as food producers via the photosynthesis process. Students frequently know little about photosynthesis, but know a great deal about food, especially food for people. These beliefs may produce a great deal of confusion, if they lead students to assume that, plants, like people, must take in food from their environment in many forms. However, plants make their own food. Neither soil nor water nor fertilizers (despite their sometimes being called plant food) are taken in as food or consumed for energy. Nor do plants take in any other form of food. Their only source of food is that which they manufacture themselves through the process of photosynthesis. They transform light energy from the sun into chemical potential energy stored in food and available for use both by the plant and by animals. The matter they take in during this process (carbon dioxide, water, and soil minerals) is not food because it is not a source of energy. Students must go through a process of conceptual change if they are to attain understanding of photosynthesis and the food production function of plants. They must abandon their assumption about the metabolic similarities between plants and humans and restructure their thinking about the nature of food (focusing on the scientific definition of food as potential energy for metabolism).

The consequences of mathematical illiteracy ("innumeracy") contributes to an inability to deal rationally with large numbers and the probabilities associated with them. This increases the susceptibility to pseudoscience of all kinds—resulting in the confused social and personal decisions that go with such confusions. A sixth grader expressed her view on the national debt: "A billion, a trillion, or whatever, it doesn't matter, it's a big amount." Informed citizens really *do* need to know the difference. So do TV announcers and politicians, who sometimes confuse "million" with "billion."

Unless misconceptions are corrected, they are likely to persist and distort new learning and just about everything else. Unfortunately, teachers are usually not aware of common misconceptions that students are likely to harbor about scientific or mathematical content, so that the instruction they provide not only fails to confront these misconceptions directly but often is presented in such general terms that students can interpret the new input as consistent with their existing misconceptions.

Promoting Confidence & Motivation

Research findings continually point out that students need to *feel competent* if they are going to be motivated to do science and mathematics (NCTM, 1989). Much of the problem with competence is rooted in society's acceptance of poor attitudes about students' potential for success in mathematics and science. It is all too common to hear adults and parents point out the fact "I was never good in mathematics," or "I was never very interested in science"—and "I don't know much about either." Yet these same individuals would never admit to being unable to read. These are comparable skills! Poor attitudes about science and mathematics are passed along to children, with accompanying low expectations resulting in low motivation and low levels of achievement.

Motivation is a desire to learn, to explore, to find out, to share with others. To be motivated is to be active, moving, to have high levels of energy and a desire for personal fulfillment. Motivation is not such a big problem for most primary grade students, they arrive at school with it.

Most children have confidence that they are capable and feel good about their performance. Many report mathematics and science to be their favorite subjects. As students spend time in school, this attitude is diminished. By upper grades, many students have learned how to look good in relation to others, and feel successful when they have beat out their peers. They've developed the ability to monitor their performance and compete—at least on a superficial level. Teachers often encourage such competition. This is sometimes effective for top students who can perform better than their peers. But lower achievers most often feel defeated. Even many gifted students become bored by such social structures.

√ Collaboration, Not Competition

Good experienced teachers encourage students to complete a task adequately, regardless of how well other students do. Thus, students feel competent when they have learned something new regardless of what other students have done. In the cooperative classroom, competence is based on comparing their new knowledge to knowledge they possessed in the past. This promotes active involvement because all students can feel competent and motivated because they are improving. Team learning can help bypass individualistic and competitive structures by helping all students to feel competent and motivated to work without the external pressures of fear, retribution, or punishment.

Teachers may:

1. Use cooperative groups and encourage discussion of mathematics and science. Students are encouraged to work collaboratively on challenging problems and experiments. Students who work as a team do not spend as much of their time worrying about their own competence because success and failure depends on the group as a whole.
2. Let students know that you have confidence in their ability to learn mathematics and science. It is important that students develop a belief that with a reasonable effort they can learn. The belief that some people cannot learn math or biology is a myth popularized by American society that must be overcome (Dossey et al., 1988).
3. Praise students effort and performance when it is deserved. Praise for mediocre work gives students the feeling that the teacher

doubts that they are capable of anything better. It is often a fine line between encouraging and overpraising.

4. Stress the importance of self improvement over competition or "being the best." Students need to feel that success comes from personal involvement rather than outperforming others. It is better to say "Jane, you did much better today" than "Jane, you did better than Susan."

5. Let students know about the level of difficulty on assignments. A difficult exercise will require more effort, creative thinking and problem solving. Groups need to feel a level of satisfaction and accomplishment at solving difficult or challenging tasks. Poorly motivated students must be told success results as much from making a good effort as from getting the right answer. If they fail and made a valiant effort, checked out all possibilities that came to mind, it is not their own lack of competence that is to blame.

6. Grade on the basis of achievement of objectives rather than on a competitive curve. All students who achieve what they are supposed to, get passing grades. Groups are graded on how well they stuck to the task, worked together, used resources, experimented, tried out strategies, and presented their findings. If they did not arrive at the correct answer after a sincere effort, others should be encouraged to offer assistance or the group, after consultation with the teacher, may wish to try again rather than get frustrated or discouraged.

7. Stress the usefulness of science and mathematics. Students who believe that learning these subjects is important for success in school and the world outside of school will be more motivated than students who see no purpose or utility for science and mathematics. Discussing how careers connect to school subjects may help older students see the value of what they are studying.

8. Make connections between science, mathematics and current problems, environmental issues, recreation, school activities, sports, and other areas of high interest to students.

A Cooperative Learning Perspective

Through our extraordinary ability to question, learn, and above all collaborate with one another, we have built the remarkable edifice of modern science, which has allowed us to place members of our species on the moon. Yet we are at times both exasperatingly unable to behave rationally and abjectly powerless to solve some of our most pressing medical and social problems.

—Robin Dunbar

Contrary to popular mythology, *science* and its mathematical/technological tools does have its limitations. And these limits are an excellent location for collaborative inquiry by students.

Learning about science and mathematics is enhanced when students are given opportunities to explain their own ideas, interact with others, explore, question, and try out new approaches. There is substantial evidence that students working in groups can master material better than students working alone (Slavin, 1989). The more opportunities students have for social interaction, the more divergent viewpoints and perspectives can season their thinking. Through collaborative group explorations, students can be pushed to analyze what they think, discuss it, and clarify their own reasoning. Working in small groups also gives students a chance to interact with concepts and verbalize their conceptions within a relatively safe situation. It is often easier to ask questions of our peers. Structuring learning environments where working together is part of the classroom culture encourages more participation with less worry about "being wrong."

As teachers who have tried it know, cooperative group work is more than pushing some desks together. Students must have a reason to take one another's progress seriously and care about the team's success. When students are engaged in active group learning, everyone takes responsibility for the learning of individual members. This means that everyone has a chance to use equipment and manipulate materials to help solve the problem. All group members must learn and do. Cooperative learning means that suggestions from low achieving students are not to be pushed aside because they interfere with efficiency. Active cooperation is different. Group success is the sum of individual learning performances of all members.

A Cooperative Learning Model for Conceptual Change

The cooperative learning model for science, mathematics, and technology suggests that the intrinsic benefits of learning are more important than external rewards for academic performance. Lessons are introduced with the reasons for engaging in the learning task—the reasons might be learning to think critically or exploring the nature of an interesting topic. Students are encouraged to assume responsibility for learning and evaluating their own work and the work of others. Interaction may include a discussion of the validity of explanations, the search for more information, the testing of various explanations or consideration of the pros and cons of specific decisions.

The characteristics that distinguish new collaborative approaches to science and math revolve around group goals, individual responsibility, and the accompanying benefits of active group work. Instead of being told they need information, students learn to recognize when additional data is needed. They jointly seek it out, apply it, and see its power and value. In this way, the actual *use* of science and mathematics information becomes the starting point rather than just an add on. The teacher facilitates the process, instead of acting as a knowledge dispenser. Student success is measured on performance, work samples, projects, application, or synthesis. Simple recall is not the central feature.

Typically, collaborative science and mathematics lessons emphasize exploring a problem, reasoning, and facing the collaborative challenge of posing a solution. This involves peer helping, self-evaluation, and group support for risk taking. It also means accepting individual differences, and having positive expectations for everyone in the group. Students understand the purpose of the group task, contributes to their own learning and self-development. When the teacher helps children put these elements together, the result is greater persistence and more self-directed learning. The ability to inquire, collaborate, and investigate fuels personal autonomy and self-direction in learning.

New National Standards in Mathematics and Science

The National Council of Teachers of Mathematics (NCTM) has developed a list of standards which outline what is to be taught and how it should be taught. These standards are in place and influencing mathematics instruction in many schools. NCTM is widely credited with developing the first national standards. The NCTM's Curriculum and Evaluation Standards for Teaching Mathematics (1991) have been widely embraced by education leaders nationwide and have become the foundation for the current mathematics education reform movement. The goal of these standards is to shift student performance from a narrow focus on routine skills to the development of broad-based mathematical power.

In 1991, the Professional Standards for Teaching Mathematics outlined the support, training, and evaluation required for good teaching. Their goal was to move teacher performance from authoritarian models based on the "transmission of knowledge" and "drill and practice" to student-centered methods featuring "stimulation of learning" and "active exploration." Assessment Standards are scheduled to be completed at the end of 1994 (NCTM, Summer, 1994).

The national science education standards are still in a state of flux — due in part to the huge amount of science content available and some disagreement about which concepts are most important. The Standards Task Force and the National Research Council of the National Academy of Sciences is developing a comprehensive set of standards for curriculum, teaching, and assessment. In the meantime, textbook publishers, school district curriculum guidelines, commercial science kits, science trade books, and science museums are being built around inquiry-based science lessons. Although there is a great deal of variation in recommended science content, there is agreement on science process skills such as observing, collaborating, classifying, measuring, predicting, and linking related topics to other content areas. The National Science Education Standards are to be completed winter 1995. These concepts will be part of the science standards next year and into the next century. According to the 1994 outline of the science standards document, strands for the standards also include staples such as "physical and life science," "science as inquiry," "history and nature of science," and "unifying concepts and processes." Both science and mathematics educators have recognized the need to integrate technology content into their curricula (Kranzberg, 1991). The preliminary science standards document also includes "program standards," which will describe how content, teaching, and assessment are coordinated in school practice. Also included are what is called "system standards" which describe how policies and practices outside the immediate learning environment might support high-quality science programs.

Piaget tells us that learners must construct their own knowledge and assimilate new experiences in ways that make sense to them. Eleanor Duckworth's work also suggests that it is important to have prospective teachers examine their own process of learning by constructing and examining their knowledge about science/math phenomena. This active engagement helps new teachers think, wonder, and experience what they are about to teach (Duckworth, 1987).

How do new elementary teachers view the idea of integrating mathematics with science and technology? One hundred sixty-one graduate elementary education credential majors completed a ten-item questionnaire after putting integrated science/math lessons into practice in their school placement. They agreed that integrating math and science content was preferred over teaching the content separately. This may be influenced by the recent emphasis on whole language instruction at the elementary level (Lehman & McDonald, 1988). Nearly 70 percent *disagreed* with the statement that hands-on activities are more appropriate in science lessons than in mathematics instruction. This perception may reflect an increased awareness of available manipulative materials to teach mathematics concepts. Many of our student teachers were concerned about their background in mathematics and science. And there was general agreement about the need for more work in those subjects before student teaching. Along with increased science/math requirements before they enter their credential programs, it was recommended that teachers should receive instruction in the integration of mathematics and science and be given the opportunity to teach integrated lessons during supervised field experiences (Lehman, 1994).

Collaboration Activities for Math and Science

Learning is enhanced by presenting information in multiple formats including multisensory activities and experimental opportunities. Some of these include concrete manipulatives like geopieces, cuisinaire rods, blocks, fraction pieces, base ten blocks, pop sickle sticks, chips, etc. Other activities include TV programs, computer simulations, role playing problems, and instructional courseware. These cooperative group activities have proved highly motivational and effective at reaching multiple learning styles.

1. Math/Science Scavenger Hunt (Elementary)

Mathematics and science applications are all around us. Mathematical patterns in nature abound. Architecture, art, and everyday objects rely heavily on mathematical principles, patterns, and symmetrical geometric form. Students need to see and apply real world connections to concepts in science and mathematics. This activity is designed to get students involved and more aware of the mathematical/scientific relationships all around them, and use technology to help report their findings. Divide the class into four groups. Each group is directed to find and bring back as many objects as they can that meet the requirements on their list. Some objects may need to be sketched out on paper if they are too difficult to bring back to the classroom, but encourage them to try to bring back as many as possible.

Group One: Measurement Hunt

Find and bring back objects that are:

- as wide as your hand
- further away than you can throw
- half the size of a baseball
- smaller than your little finger
- thinner than a shoelace
- a foot long
- waist high
- as long as your arm
- wider than four people
- as wide as your nose

Group Two: Shape Hunt

Find and bring back as many objects as you can that have these shapes:

• triangle • circle • square • diamond • oval • rectangle • hexagon • other geometric shapes

Group Three: Number Pattern Hunt

Find objects that show number patterns. For example, a three leaf clover matches the number pattern three.

Group Four: Textures

Find as many objects as you can that have the following characteristics:

-smooth -rough -soft -grooved/ridges -hard -bumpy -furry -sharp -wet -grainy

When students return, have them arrange their objects in some type of order or classification. Using a graphing program on the computer or colored paper, scissors and markers, have them visually represent their results in some way (bar graph, for example).

2. Student Generated Problems

Have student groups construct their own problems on a topic of their choice. Encourage them to use survey data, newspaper stories, or current information (TV Guide is one source). Encourage calculator use.

3. Surveys and Graphing

A brief introduction of pie graphs, line graphs, people graphs, bar graphs, etc. These and other possibilities can be copied or cut from magazines and newspapers and used by the small cooperative groups as models. Many newspapers incorporate the graph into an illustration and a news story that shows scientific and mathematical implications in everyday life.

Procedure: Divide the class into small groups of two, three or four students. Have them brainstorm about what they would like to find out from the other class members (favorite hobbies, TV shows, kinds of pets, etc.). Once a topic is agreed upon and approved by the teacher, have them organize and take a survey of all of the class members. Remember five of six groups will be doing this at once so allow for on-task noise and movement. When the statistics are gathered and compiled, each group must make a large descriptive graph which can be posted in the classroom and understood from 20 feet away. We prefer tag board or construction paper mounted on tag board. Encourage color, originality, and creativity.

4. Bridge Building

This is an interdisciplinary activity which reinforces skills of communication, group process, social studies, language arts, mathematics, science and technology.

Materials:

Lots of newspaper and masking tape, one large, heavy rock, and one cardboard box. Have students bring in stacks of newspaper. You need approximately one foot of newspaper per person. Bridges are a tribute to technological efforts which employ community planning, engineering efficiency, mathematical precision, aesthetics, group effort, and construction expertise.

Procedures:

1. For the first part of this activity, divide students into three groups. Each group will be responsible for investigating one aspect of bridge building.

Group One: Research

This group is responsible for going to the library and looking up facts about bridges, collecting pictures of kinds of bridges, and bringing back information to be shared with the class.

Group Two: Aesthetics, Art, Literature

This group must discover songs, books about bridges, paintings, artwork, etc. which deals with bridges.

Group Three: Measurement, Engineering

This group must discover design techniques, blueprints, angles, and measurements, of actual bridge designs. If possible, visit a local bridge to look at the structural design, etc. Each group presents their findings to the class.

The second part of this activity involves actual bridge construction by the students.

2. Assemble the collected stacks of newspaper, tape, the rock and the box at the front of the room. Divide the class into groups of four or five students. Each group is instructed to take an even portion of newspaper to their group and one or two rolls of masking tape. Explain that the group will be responsible for building a stand alone bridge using only the newspapers and tape. The bridge is to be constructed so that it will support the large rock and so that the box can pass underneath.

3. Each group is given three to five minutes of planning time in which they are allowed to talk and plan together. During the planning time, they are not allowed to touch the newspapers and tape, but they are encouraged to pick up the rock and make estimates of how high the box is.

4. At the end of the planning time, students are given 10 to 12 minutes to build their bridge. During this time, there is no talking among the group members. They may not handle the rock or the box only the newspapers and tape. (A few more minutes may be necessary to ensure that all groups have a chance of finishing their constructions.)

Evaluation:

Stop all groups after the allotted time. Survey the bridges with the class and allow each group to try to pass the two tests for their bridge. (Does the bridge support the rock and does the box fit underneath?)

Discuss the design of each bridge and how they compare to the bridges researched earlier.

Follow up/Enrichment

As a follow up activity, have each group measure their bridge and design a blueprint (include angles, length and width of the bridge) so that another group could build the bridge by following this model.

5. Student-Generated Problems

Have student groups construct their own problems on a topic of their choice. Encourage them to use survey data, newspaper stories, or current information (TV guide is one source). Encourage calculator use.

6. Surveys and Graphing

Divide the class into small groups of four or five. Have them brainstorm about what they would like to find out from the other class members (favorite hobbies, TV shows, kinds of pets, etc.). Once a topic is agreed upon and approved by the teacher, have them organize and take a survey of all of the class members. Remember several groups will be doing this at once so allow for some noise and movement.

When the statistics are gathered and compiled, each group must make a clear descriptive graph which can be posted in the classroom. Encourage originality and creativity.

7. Collecting TV Data

Have students survey their families viewing habits. The survey questions could follow the same format as the Nielson survey data. This kind of survey includes what programs are watched, what time the TV is on, how many people are watching at a time, etc. Compose the survey instrument with the class based on information they would like to find out. (A note to parents outlining the intent of the activity and the assignment is helpful.) After the students have gathered the data for a week's time, have them summarize the information in their group. Compare such items as the average time spent watching TV for the group, most popular times for watching, most popular shows, etc. These are excellent ways to integrate charts and graphs into the technology curriculum. This kind of activity can also lead into social education and values clarification activities. Questions such as "How much TV viewing is good? What other things do you give up when you spend time watching television? How much talking goes on while the TV set is on?" can be explored.

Ask for volunteers to spend one week not watching television. This group should keep a record of what they did instead of watching television. Encourage volunteers to share their reactions to the experiment with the class.

8. Mathematics and Science in the World of Work

Have students gather information about mathematics and science in the workplace and careers that spark their interest. Draw up a simple survey form listing occupations that students are interested in, and spaces to gather data about ways mathematics and science is used on the job. Have student groups interview workers, parents, community professionals, and friends to find out how they use science and mathematics tools in their work. Have groups assemble and display the data in visual form (charts, graphs, etc.). Look for patterns and comparisons. Are there generalizations that can be made? Conclusions that can be drawn?

9. Using Community Resources

Museums are one way to link science and community resources. Students can play the role of curators. Working in pairs, have students investigate objects such as bones, fossils, shells, etc. Have students find out all they can about the object using the full range of resources available at the museum or naturalist center. To add an element of interest and adventure, have students in groups of four create a fictitious but plausible scenario to accompany an object of their choice. In one story students were told the bone was brought to them by the FBI who expressed concern that it might be human. (The Smithsonian actually gets many such cases each year.) Student groups must try to determine the origin. If not a human bone, then they are to find what animal the bone belonged to, what part of the skeleton, etc. At the end of the activity student groups return to the class and present their problem and the findings.

10. Using Video Segments to Teach

Tape short segments from science and technology programs which deal with issues and concepts in your curriculum. Excerpts from science programs like NOVA, Wild Kingdom, Science and Technology Week, 3-2-1 Contact, or even the Weather Channel and the evening news offer a wealth of material. Design short projects based on these segments. An endangered species mural, a chart of weather patterns for the country, a computer newsletter, an audiotaped radio news release, etc. Student teams are great at coming up with their own projects, especially once you've sparked their interest on a topic.

11. Using the Newspaper To Teach About Math, Science and Technology

Major newspapers, like *The New York Times* and *The Washington Post*, have weekly science and technology sections. Select a list of significant terms from the lead stories, pass out the papers or photocopies of the articles, and have students construct science fiction stories with the words and ideas from the feature science news page.

12. Graphing with Young Children

Instruct students to bring their favorite stuffed bear to school. As a class sort the bears in various ways, size, color, type, etc. Graph the results with the class. Have pairs of students sort the bears in another way and paste paper counters or stickers on paper to make their own personalized graphs.

13. Using Logo Programming

Seymour Papert developed the Logo language to teach geometric concepts. He believes students can learn mathematical relationships more efficiently if they can project themselves into the world of mathematics. Students who can program a computer to draw a square or circle must understand the nature of a square or circle well enough to "teach" the computer. Using a logo program, such as "LogoWriter," even young student teams can develop short procedures and program the computer. Here are a few sample procedures using "LogoWriter."

```
To Red Square
setc 3
repeat 4[fd 40 rt 90]
end
To yellow rectangle:
setc 4
repeat 2[fd 40 rt 90 fd 80 rt 90]
wait 60 cg
end
```

14. Group Problem Solving with Mathematical Patterns

This cooperative logic problem works best for groups of four or six students. Cut apart the set of clue cards (below). Make one set of cards for each group. Pass out a set of colored blocks to each table (pattern blocks, or cubes work well). Choose a group leader to pass out the cards, one for each person in the group. Each student may look at their own clue or clues but are instructed not to show their card to anyone else. Students work together to solve the problem. Students may talk while they are working but are not to reveal the information on their card except through actions and negotiations.

Clue Cards:

There are six blocks in a tower. The tower is six blocks high. There is a yellow block on top.
The red block is above the green block.
One of the yellow blocks is above the green block; the other is below it.
Each of the blue blocks shares a face with the green block.
There are two yellows, two blues, one green, and one red in the set of blocks.
No two blocks of the same color touch each other.

Sample Integrated Science & Math Group Lessons

The following lessons on weather are intended to involve cooperative groups and science and math content. A constructive learning method is used.

Clouds and Precipitation

Purpose: To provide a hands-on learning environment in which students can construct their own knowledge and better understand causes and changes in clouds and precipitation.

Objectives: Students will divide into groups and complete each experiment. Each group will then be responsible for demonstrating and explaining the activity and concept to the rest of the class.

Activities

1. Making a cloud
2. Creating a cloud in a bottle

3. Forming Mist
4. Determining how frost forms
5. Rain drops come in all shapes and sizes

Procedure:

These will be a cooperative group activities in which the students construct their own base of knowledge of how clouds and precipitation work. In this lesson, the teacher has already introduced the area of study: clouds and precipitation. The materials would be provided by the teacher, but the initiative and set-up would be the responsibility of the students.

1. Have the students count off by 5's. All 1's gather, 2's etc. until 5 varied groups are established. Assign one of the experiments to each group.
2. Groups are responsible to assign themselves the following roles:
   - Getters are responsible for all materials.
   - Reader must read the experiment to the group and understand it thoroughly.
   - Checker is responsible that the experiment is done thoroughly.
   - Encourager helps everyone do their roles, and is excited about the outcome.
   - Recorder communicates through writing the outcomes, trial and error and success or failure of their experiment.
3. Each group proceeds with their experiment and finds out as much as they can.
4. Each group then presents their experiment to the class. They become the expert group, the one who knows the most about this subject and can teach it to the other students.

Weather Lesson Content:

Clouds

Clouds are made up of millions of tiny droplets of water or ice crystals, formed when moist, warm air evaporates (turns into water vapor) and then is cooled. The air is cooled because it is moving away from the hot earth. The water vapor in the air condenses (turns back into a liquid) and sticks to the surface of all the dust particles in the air. This makes many tiny water droplets which all group together and form a cloud.

Clouds are named according to their shape, height, and weight. *Cirrus* clouds are high in the sky and have a feathery, wispy, wispy appearance (cirro means curl in Latin). They are usually made up of ice crystals because the air is so cold. *Nimbus* clouds are rain clouds, dark and gray. *Cumulus* clouds are rounded clouds with flat bottoms. They are often seen on dry sunny days but when they join together they can form huge, storm clouds called cumulonimbus. *Stratus* (strata-layered) clouds are the most likely to produce light rain and drizzle. Fog in the Bay Area is a form of stratus clouds.

Mist

Mist is really a surface cloud made up of many tiny droplets of water. It is formed when a deep layer is cooled by the underlying surface, like when warm air is cooled by the ocean. What is the difference between mist and fog? It depends on the density of the cloud. Fog is much thicker, and visibility is reduced. It is said to be "foggy" outside when visibility is less than 1 km.

Frost

Frost occurs when the temperature of the ground is below freezing. It forms when water vapor turns directly into ice as it comes into contact with a freezing surface. Why do you get frost in your freezer? When you open the door of a freezer, the water droplets in the warmer air outside touch the cold sides of the freezer and turn into frost.

Rain, Snow, Sleet, and Hail

Rain and other precipitation is caused by all the minute droplets of water in the cloud colliding and joining together forming larger droplets. This process is called coalescence. The droplets increase in size until they are too heavy to be kept up in the cloud by air currents and fall as raindrops. Each raindrop is made up of about a million droplets! The temperature of the air determines the type of precipitation (rain, snow, sleet, or hail). If the droplets fall through warm temperatures on the way to the ground, what we feel and see is rain. But if the air and ground is cold, the droplets will be snow. Sleet is formed when rain falls through a thick layer of very cold air and freezes before it hits the ground. Hail is formed in cumulonimbus clouds that have violent currents of air which toss the droplets around and they get coated with the layers of ice. You can cut a hailstone in half to count the number of times it has been tossed back into the cold currents of the cloud. It finally falls when it's just too heavy to be held up there any longer. Contrary to what most people think, raindrops are not tear-shaped blobs of water.

Science & Math Small Group Experiments:

Group 1. Making a Cloud

Materials:

large glass jar
ice
small metal baking tray
warm water

Procedure:

1. Pour approx. 1 inch of hot water into the jar. Measure by using a ruler. Use a thermometer to measure the temperature of the hot water.
2. Place some ice cubes in the baking tray and put the tray on top of the jar. Again use a thermometer to record and measure the temperature.
3. As the air inside the jar rises and is cooled by the ice, the water vapor it contains condenses into droplets and forms a cloud. Record what happens.

Evaluation:

1. Observe how fast the cloud is formed. How would this change depending upon the variables: how warm the water is, how much ice is placed in the tray?
2. Why do you think airplanes leave a white trail behind them? Does this happen when the air is very cold or very hot?
3. How did mathematics help you?

Group 2. Creating a cloud in a bottle

Air pressure changes cause changes in temperature. This experiment will show you that when the air pressure drops and the air becomes cooler, water vapor condenses and forms a cloud.

Materials:

cold water
matches
glass bottle with screw top

drinking straw
modeling clay
scissors

Procedure:

1. Make a hole in the bottle's screw top with scissors. Be careful!
2. Push the straw through the hole with just a small part sticking out the bottom and seal it in place on top of the cap with clay.
3. Pour a little cold water into the bottle and swish it around. Then pour it out.
4. Light a match. Blow it out, then hold the smoking match in the neck of the bottle so that the smoke is drawn inside.
5. Quickly twist the cap onto the bottle and blow into the straw as hard as you can. Stop blowing and pinch the straw so that no air can escape!
6. Let go of the straw. As the air rushes out, a cloud forms inside the bottle.

Evaluation:

1. What, in nature, could you compare this experiment to? Give examples.
2. Explain what happened in this experiment in your own words. Was math involved? How?

(The water vapor in the bottle condenses into tiny droplets, which cling to the particles of smoke and form a cloud.)

Group 3. *Determining How Frost Forms*

This experiment will show how frost forms due to these water vapor condensing on a cold surface and freezing, forming a thin layer of ice crystals.

Please read all directions before beginning and remember the roles of each group member; getter, reader, encourager, and recorder. Your group will be responsible for presenting this experiment to the rest of the class and sharing what you have found out about frost.

Materials:

spoon, cotton swab, Vaseline®, glass, crushed ice, salt

Procedure:

1. Dip the cotton swab in the Vaseline. Paint a design or your name on the outside of the glass.
2. Put the crushed ice in the glass. Cover the ice with salt and stir.
3. Wait a few minutes. A pattern of frost slowly forms on the outside of the glass. Measure the temperature.

Evaluation:

1. Have students offer an explanation of why things happened as they did. Encourage students to write their hypothesis in their science/math journal. (Vaseline is greasy and water cannot condense on it, therefore no frost forms.)

Group 4. Experiment Forming Mist

Have you ever wondered why you can see your breath in cold weather? This experiment shows how mist is formed when water vapor in the air cools and condenses, changing back into tiny drops of liquid water.

Please read all directions and perform the cooperative group roles; getter, reader, checker, encourager, and recorder. Your group will be responsible for presenting the experiment to the rest of the class and sharing what you have found out about mist.

Materials:

deep sauce pan or cake pan with dark silver stone lining
crushed ice, salt, spoon

Procedure:

1. Put the crushed ice in the pan. Cover the ice with plenty of salt and stir. Check the temperature.
2. Wait a few minutes. Then breathe gently over the salted ice. A mist appears!

Evaluation

1. Have the group presenting use this experiment to explain for the class the answer to the question "why can you see your breath in cold weather?"

(The air near the salted ice becomes very cold. The water vapor in your breath condenses in the cold air, forming mist.)

Science and Mathematics Group Investigations

1. French Fry Fun Science and Mathematics Investigation

Description:

Students use science and mathematical data they have collected about french fries to decide which local fast food restaurant has the best buy for a small order of fries. Statistics are used in the research to arrive at their judgment. Students then use this information to create an advertisement in their local newspaper describing their research and making recommendations about the best place to purchase french fries. This investigation involves the science and mathematics concepts and skills of: problem solving, communication, reasoning, making connections, number sense, computation and estimation, and statistics.

Materials:

calculators, graph paper, notebook, class recording sheet

Background Information:

Students will need to be familiar with the following statistics terms:
mean — the average of a set of data
median — the middle number or the average of the middle 2 numbers when the set of numbers are arranged in order.
mode — the number occurring most often in a set of data
range — the difference between the largest and smallest number in a set of data.
sample — a segment of a population selected for study to predict characteristics of the whole.
tally — a way of recording information

Objectives:

1. Student groups of four or five will be assigned a restaurant.
2. Groups will order a small bag of fries from the restaurant assigned.
3. Groups will systematically collect, organize, and describe their data on a class data sheet.

Class French Fry Data Sheet:

name of group:
name of restaurant:

restaurant price:
number of fries per small bag of fries:
total length:
mean length:
cm. per 11¢:

4. When all groups have entered their data then the class is faced with the following statistical challenges:
   - Find the average number of fries in the sample.
   - Determine the mode, range, median, and mean for lengths of fries.
   - Find how many centimeters of fries you get for an average order.
5. Student groups are to explain their strategies and reasoning.
6. Last groups are to create a local newspaper advertisement with the intent of making customers want to buy french fries at the restaurant they have just researched. Have students use the facts they have discovered to help sell the product.
7. Students will work as a team in a powerful, organized and purposeful manner.

Evaluation:

As a group, write a report about the investigation your class just finished. Include at least one graph. The report should describe how their group collected and compiled the data, explaining the information the group included in their graph or graphs. End the report by either recommending or rejecting one of the restaurants as the place to go for french fries. Be sure the students back their recommendation with facts from their research.

Connecting Science and Mathematics: Discovery, Exploration, and Teamwork

How can teachers avoid squeezing the pleasure out of science and mathematics instruction by connecting to the core of the subjects? Why do scientists and mathematicians want to devote their professional lives to this task? Of course, there are many responses to these questions, but most scientists and mathematicians would agree that it is the excitement of exploring the unknown, of discovering something new, of adding to the accumulation of knowledge, and creatively collaborating with colleagues.

The use of new curricula in science and mathematics classrooms can provide new and exciting opportunities for implementing the NCTM and AAAS standards. For example, the NCTM standards emphasize that students should be exposed to the connections between mathematics and other disciplines. The connections between mathematics and the sciences are clearly seen in historical materials. Indeed, in early civilizations, all scientists were mathematicians, and all mathematicians were scientists. Today we are ready once again to connect science and mathematics.

Given the level of stimulation and interest, you might conclude that discovery and exploration has always played an important role in integrated science and mathematics education. Unfortunately, the excitement was often missing. Fortunately, the research and new standards support breaking through the crust of tradition with active student-centered inquiry that has students work in teams—much as real scientists and mathematicians do. As Nobel Prize winner James Watson has said several times in television interviews, "Nothing new that is really interesting comes without collaboration."

Conclusion

Science and mathematics are more than content. As Nicholas Wade has suggested, they represent "a rational process in a largely irrational world"—generating "knowledge of intrinsic value and of equal and binding value to all races and cultures." Their "harvest has never been so rich as now." Although science and mathematics may sometimes be abstract and a little difficult, children who do not learn the central concepts may not be able to appreciate the role of science in society or be able to assess scientific experts when they put forward notions that affect all of us.

At the threshold of the Third Millennium we cannot be indifferent to general scientific/mathematical illiteracy in the American population. Science is, after all, how we sort out ideology and foolishness from truth. To move beyond magical cures, UFO's, and other pseudoscientific misconceptions requires educational solutions. When the graduates of our industrial competitors are getting better and better we cannot be resigned to mediocrity in science and mathematics education. Even if we are not sliding downward, being satisfied with staying at about the same

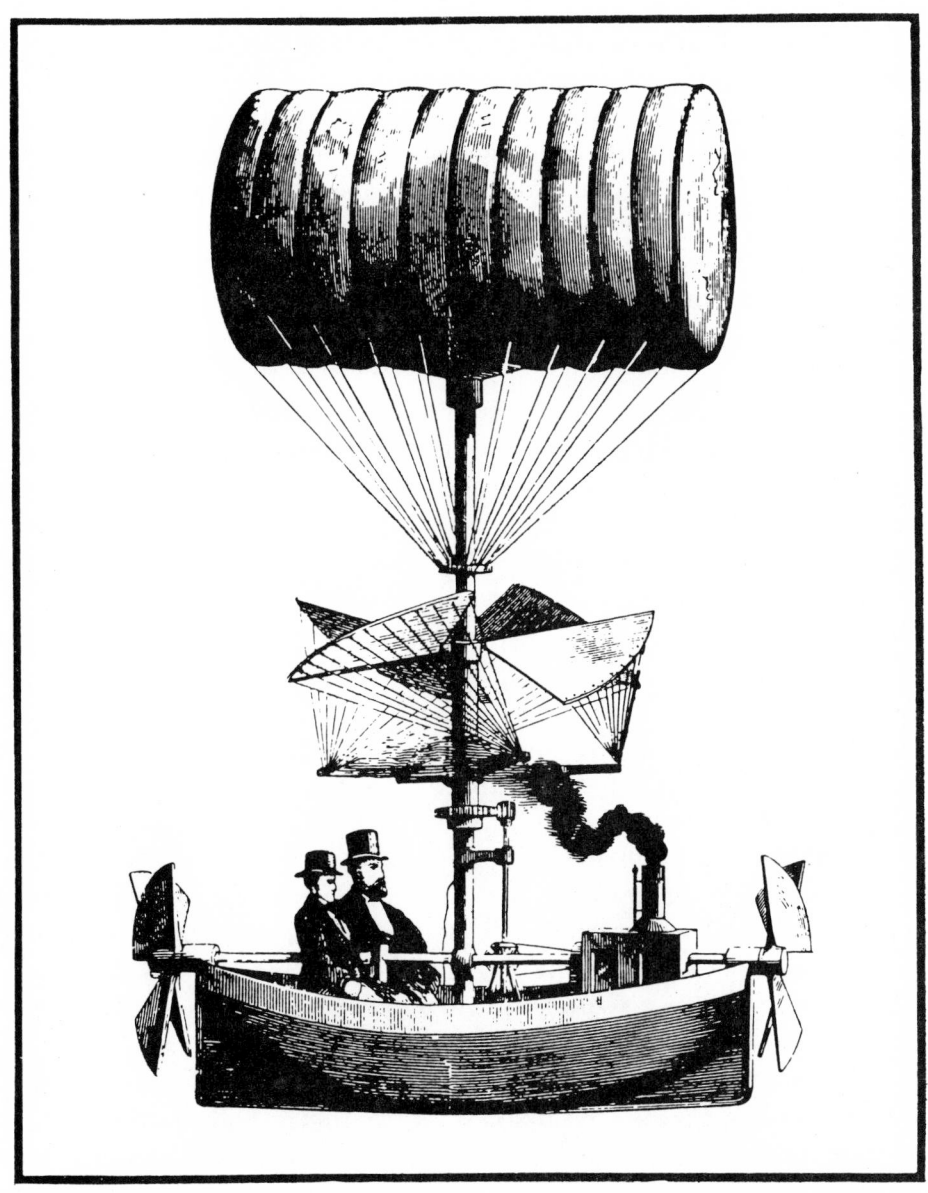

level is not very encouraging when others are improving. Everyone from the media to general public bears some responsibility for this state of affairs. However, we cannot overemphasize the importance of effective teachers in making improvements happen. In the early 1990s, it was educators who took the initiative and moved to implement the new standards in mathematics education. Some good news: the latest mathematics scores (unlike reading and writing) are inching upward (National Assessment of Educational Progress, 1995).

Bridging the gap between what informed educators want and public skepticism is sometimes a challenge. But when the public and parents see a new approach working to produce high quality work, they are usually supportive. By combining initiative and imagination with persistent effort, teachers can do their part in preparing students for a demanding future. As teachers change their practices and engage their students in increasingly complex content, they are acting as scholars in their own right.

Science, mathematics, and technology are at the center of changing and shaping the world. It is essential that all children become intellectually productive and excited about science and mathematics. As teachers, it is our collective obligation to draw on solid new approaches. This means building on active inquiry, higher-level questioning, cooperative learning, interdisciplinary reasoning, storytelling, and authentic assessment. If more teachers turn toward these possibilities, we may not make it to "first in the world," but we can at least continue to move in that direction and get children intellectually productive and excited about science and mathematics. If we were building the perfect teacher, we would also add some personal qualities like strength, courage, energy, political persistence, and a sense of humor.

Whether science and math are separated or integrated, cooperative learning is a proven approach. We argue for connecting many lessons in science and mathematics, in part because phenomena associated with the two subjects is often inseparable. Using big ideas to link subjects encourages students to visualize new possibilities and explore the deep themes that underlie content. "You cannot stir things apart," says a 13-year-old prodigy in Tom Stoppard's play *Arcadia.* By forming small cooperative groups, students can investigate related topics in science and mathematics as inquirers who "get better together." This is not to suggest that cooperative learning is not a full-time replacement for other methods, but it is a proven alternative to solitary individuals working in competition with each other. However, the mutual achievement and caring for one another that grows out of cooperative groups gives students support as they try to visualize new choices and possibilities. As diverse groups of students come together in a learning community something special happens.

REFERENCES

Americans Association for the Advancement of Science. (1990). *Science for all Americans.* Washington, D.C.: Author.

Aronowitz, D. C. (1990). *Science as power: Discourse and ideology in modern society.* Minneapolis, MN: University of Minnesota Press.

Breslich, E. (1936). Integration of secondary school mathematics and science. *School Science and Mathematics,* 36, 58–67.

Burns, M. (1991). *Math by all means.* New York: Math Solution Publications, Cuisinaire Company.

Bruener, J. & Haste, H. (1987). *Making sense: The child's construction of the world.* New York: Methuen.

California State Department of Education (1992). *California mathematics framework.* Sacramento, CA: California State Department of Education.

Clewell, B. C. (1987). What works and why: Research and theoretical bases of intervention programs in mathematics and science for minority and female students. In A.B. Champagne & E. L. Hornig (Eds.) *This year in school science 1987: Students and science learning* (pp. 95–135). Washington, D.C.: American Association for the Advancement of Science.

Duckworth, E. (1987). Teaching as research. In M. Okazawa-Rey, J. Anderson, & R. Traver. *Teachers, Teaching, & Teacher Education.* Cambridge, MA: Harvard Educational Review.

Eamon, W. (1994). Books of secrets in medieval and early modern culture. Princeton, N. J.: Princeton University Press.

Garofalo, J. (1988). Metacognition and school mathematics. *The Arithmetic Teacher,* 34(3), 22–23.

Good, T. & Brophy, J. (1994). Looking in classrooms. (6th Ed.). New York: Harper Collins.

Gross, J. (1994). In School, A school mixing math, science and minority students has impressive early results. *The New York Times,* Aug. 3, 1994, p. B-7.

Horizon Research, Inc. (1993). *A Profile of Science and Mathematics Education in the United States,* Chapel Hill, NC.

Kolb, J. (1968). Effects of relating mathematics to science instruction on the acquisition of quantitative science behaviors. *Journal of Research in Science Teaching,* 5, 174–182.

Krisnick, J. & Alwin, D. (1989). Aging and susceptibility to attitude change. *Journal of Personality and Social Psychology,* 57, 416–425.

Lonning, R. & DeFranco, T. (1994). Development and implementation of an integrated mathematics/science preservice elementary methods course, *School Science and Mathematics,* 94(1) 18–25.

Lehman, J. (1994). Integrating science and mathematics: Perceptions of preservice and practicing teachers, *School Science and Mathematics,* 94(2), 58–64.

Lehman, J. R. & McDonald, J. L. (1988). Teacher perceptions of the integration of mathematics and science. *School Science and Mathematics,* 88, 642–649.

McBride, F.W. & Silverman, F. L. (1991). Integrating elementary/middle school science and mathematics. *School Science and Mathematics,* 91, 285–292.

Moore, E. (1903). On the foundations of mathematics. *Science,* 17, 401–416.

National Assessment of Educational Progress. (1995). Washington, D.C.: U.S. Publications.

NCTE Newsletter of Standards Initiatives for NCTE Members. Content standards take shape, *The NCTE,* 1(2), 3–5.

Shamos, M. (1995). *The myth of scientific literacy.* New Brunswick, NJ: Rutgers University Press.

Shoenfeld, A. (1985). *Mathematical problem solving.* Orlando, FL: Academic Press.

Silver, E. (1985). "Research on Teaching Mathematical Problem Solving: Some Under-represented Themes". In *Teaching and Learning Mathematical Problem Solving: Multiple Research Perspectives.* E. Silver (Ed.), Lawrence Erlbaum Associates.

Steen, L. (1990). Numeracy, *Daedalus,* 119(2), 211–231.

Wandersee, J. (1992). Exploring human growth: Using a calculator to integrate mathematics and science. *School Science and Mathematics,* 92, 96–98.

Chapter 5

EDUCATION IN THE ARTS:

COMMUNICATION, IMAGINATION, AND COLLABORATION

The artist is the antennae of a nation
— Ezra Pound

National identity has always been connected to the arts. European countries, for example, see support of the arts and much like a public utility that is worthy of significant financial support. France now has the equivalent of three billion dollars in the federal budget for the arts. Even in the most difficult of times, Germany supports art galleries, dance troupes, theatrical productions, school programs, and symphony orchestras in its larger towns and small cities (*The New York Times,* August 2, 1992). With parents, teachers, and the rest of the community so involved, it is little wonder that arts education shines in European schools. The best American orchestras, dance groups, theater, and visual arts are as good as those found anywhere. The problem is that there are fewer of them and they do not connect to a significant percentage of the general population. Commercial popular culture rules the day here and even exerts a strong influence overseas. Can a high quality arts education elevate cultural understanding in this country and contribute to the imaginative life of the nation?

National educational goals recognize the arts are central to under-standing and functioning in today's world. The standards for education in the arts suggest how the visual arts, dance, music, and theater can challenge educational passivity and play a major role in the education of children. Cooperative learning has been identified as one of the approaches that can help us move towards standards of content, achievement, and performance. The best American programs have always placed an emphasis on knowing about the arts and understanding how to use the collaborative processes associated with the visual arts, music, dance, and theater.

Although the emphasis of this chapter is on collaboration we also explore how:

159

- the arts can provide for alternative ways of knowing.
- visual art, music, dance, and drama can be integrated with other subjects to enrich the curriculum.
- the arts invite student inquiry into the "big ideas" that link several areas of knowledge.
- the arts can enhance multicultural understanding.
- cooperative learning groups enable students to engage in the arts in a way that is infrequently used in traditional classrooms.

Communicating (with the arts) is a process of sharing experience till it becomes a common possession. It modifies the disposition of all parties who partake it.

— John Dewey

School Reform, National Standards, and Arts Education

When the *Goals 2000: Educate America Act* was passed in 1994, the arts were identified as one of the core content areas in which students should show competency at grades 4, 8, and 12. Testing in the arts will make use of performance exercises to measure student ability in the visual arts, music, dance, and theater. One example might be asking students to use a computer to rearrange a piece of music. A performance assessment example in theater would be asking students to identify elements of a scene, assume characters, and act out a scene from a story. Sample question: "What would you change in the characters if you could restructure the scene and do it again?" Other items would assess the student's ability to perform, create, and critique various art forms.

Encouraged by *Goals 2000*, the U.S. Office of Education initiated the federal government's first written prescription for reversing the decline of instruction in the visual arts, dance, drama, and music. The result: *The National Standards for Education in the Arts*. It suggests, among other things, that the knowledge and practice of the arts is fundamental to the healthy development of children's minds and spirits (National Standards for Education in the Arts, 1994). It builds on many sources, including Howard Gardner's theory of multiple intelligences, to suggest how the arts can incorporate the whole range of "intelligences" to "reach students and therefore more comprehensively teach students" (*The Arts and Education Reform, Goals 2000*, 1994). The report makes it clear that there is a strong relationship between the quality of *education* and the quality of *arts* instruction. The best schools have the best arts program and in the weakest schools such programs have usually been weak or nonexistent

(Association for Supervision and Curriculum Development, Fowler, ASCD Update, 1994).

How can the new arts standards influence educational reform? To begin with, the process itself requires educators to think about priorities in arts education. Secondly, setting standards in the arts can help combat the idea that the arts are "soft" and expendable. They give a level of accountability and demonstrate that knowledge and skills in the arts matter—countering the widespread idea that the arts don't contribute to a child's "real" education. Standards also support the notion that the arts present a range of alternate paths to learning, so the uniqueness of each child can be attended to. The arts can also help connect the mind and the senses—uniting the cognitive and affective dimensions of learning. Finally, national standards serve as an advocate for arts education; acting as a lever on public awareness and a stimulus to teacher training.

The specific goals contained in the national standards were unanimously approved by representatives from the U.S. Office of Education, the National Endowment for the Arts, the National Endowment for the Humanities, and the Music Educators National Conference. Classroom teachers, artists, musicians, dancers, actors and business leaders also played an active role the process (The Report of the National Commission on Music Education, 1991).

Encounters with the arts are crucial to pursuing a curriculum that releases the young to pose their own questions and look for solutions. Examples of skills associated with learning about the arts: elementary school children should be able to understand how to use symbols in visual art, middle school students should be able to master harmony and improvisation, and older students should be able to analyze cultural influences in dramatic works. As the new national standards make clear, the arts are *not* cut-out turkeys, color-the-numbers, or connect-the-dots bunny rabbits. The arts *are* a serious discipline.

The standards say that every student should:

1. Be able to communicate in four arts disciplines—music, visual arts, theater, and dance.
2. Be able to communicate proficiently in at least one art form.
3. Be able to present basic analysis of works of art.
4. Have an informed acquaintance with exemplary works of art from a variety of world cultures and historical periods.
5. Be able to relate various types of arts knowledge and skills across

the arts disciplines. (National Standards for Education in the Arts, 1994)

Teaching the Arts in Tomorrow's Schools

The arts and all their related subtlety are being woven into the national vision of education in tomorrows schools. Subtlety, ambiguity, and intelligent decision making do not play to the strength of our adolescent culture. Yet it is in the "vague" where creative things and a great deal of important decision making happens. As William James said, "We need to restore the vague to its proper place in our mental life." It may be more comfortable for some, but if you provide too much structure for your students, they will miss the chance to learn many skills. For example, exaggerated structure may prevent students from learning the important intellectual tools of subtlety, imagination, and insight—all three are at the heart of most subject matter.

Although quality programs in the arts come in a wide variety of shapes, the report on standards suggests the following as common *keys to success:*

- The arts are integrated throughout the curriculum at all age levels.
- Regular arts classes are of comparable length to other academic disciplines and time is made for art specialists to enhance the curriculum.
- Effective teacher training and professional development in the arts.
- Artists are involved as teachers, coordinators, or as resources for arts specialists and non-arts teachers.
- Arts education is inclusive—all students study and practice the arts.
- The community, business, and local arts organizations are actively involved in helping students learn about the arts.
- Teaching and learning are regularly assessed and evaluated to determine what works best in arts education.

Under the influence of the new arts standards, the nation has taken a significant step towards ensuring the study and practice of the visual arts, music, dance, and theater. It will be left to the educational community to make it happen.

Connecting to the Community and to Other Cultures

How do the arts fit into a shared vision of American culture and schooling? Painting, dance, and music transcend language barriers and have long served the dual function of building common values and a respect for diversity. From Puerto Rican Nyorican poems to Asian music, the very attributes of the arts can give them a credibility in creating a sense of shared public space. As one of the great civilizing aspects of human nature, the arts can give human dimension to our own society as well. Artists around the world use symbols in ways that create thought and feeling—and you can't comprehend the symbolism without some education in the arts. From the media and architecture to fashion and advertising, the arts are basic to human expression and understanding the world around us. Schools can get a boost for arts education by connecting to the resources of that world. And by reaching into the schools and into the community, the arts can play a major role in providing a solid foundation for our future as a democratic society.

Experience has shown that the arts have a potential for engaging all students and connecting to a variety of curriculum areas (Eisner, 1991). Some examples: the cultural background of many mathematicians and scientists can be taught through the study of songs composed in their time and place. Ideas like the concept of zero (0) coming from Mayan culture and the development of Roman and Arabic numerals. Geometry can be studied through the graphic and visual arts. To connect music and science it might mean writing a jingle for the human skeleton or composing a song for an endangered species or explaining the circulatory system through dance performance and choreography. Students could also, for example, write some songs or poems and practice moving as the song is sung or as the poem is read. Thus, the arts can reach across learning modalities, subjects, and cultures—providing tools for inter- disciplinary dialogue and connecting the emotions with discipline in a manner that is essential to developing a full and empowering literacy and numeracy.

The arts attend to the human spirit in a manner often missed by other subjects (Getty Center for Education In the Arts, 1989). They provide a way of understanding the world and are valid in helping us tell stories and develop a critical aesthetic. The arts can also teach divergent and convergent thinking. Along with these thinking skills they show that there are many "right" answers. As in the real world, in the arts there is rarely one way to do a problem. Thus, enriching education with the arts encourages skills needed for tomorrow's workplace: vision, imagination, critical thinking, persistence, and a deeper appreciation of who we are as individuals and as a society. Far from being viewed as an expendable luxury, national goals and standards place the arts at the center keeping America competitive, creative, and civilized.

Multiple Paths to Knowledge

The national standards for teaching the arts are beginning to influence other subjects and general curriculum writing at state and local levels. The standards hold exciting promise for helping teachers reshape the arts curriculum and how it is taught. Emphasized at each grade level are communication through arts disciplines, arts performance, analysis of art works, growing awareness of exemplary works, and the ability to connect art knowledge across disciplines. These emphases, as well as the other content specific standards, are briefly highlighted in the activities that follow.

The Arts Standards and Multiple Intelligence Theory

1. *Spatial/Visual Arts* (Standard 2: communication)
   After reproductions of paintings, sculptures, or drawings are made made available to students thinking can be generated by asking questions like:
   — Which painting really speaks to you and what does it say?
   — What in your own life reminds you a little of the painting?
   — What people, places, and things does it bring to mind?
   Write down some words and phrases that explain some of your feelings about the art. This work might start out in pairs and later be shared in small groups or with the whole class. Obviously, students need enough background in art to know what to recognize and what to ignore.

2. *Music and Beginning Literacy:* (standard 2: communication)

   — Find a song that your children like that contains words with rhyme, rhythm, and repetition.
   — Link the words to print by writing the lyrics on a song chart. Lead the group in singing the song one phrase at a time, and help the children sound out words.
   — See if musical notes can be matched with syllables to build the rhythm—you can use the old bouncing ball of community singing. Encourage the creation of new lyrics by matching new words that have the right number of syllables to the rhythmic structure of the song.
   — For children in grades 2 and up, you can introduce the concept of ascending and descending melody by directing singing with up or down hand motions.

— Students can also explore the similarities between composers writing notes on a staff for singers and authors writing words for readers.

3. *Linguistic Patterns & Intrapersonal:* (Standard 1—communicate in four arts disciplines; Standard 2—communicate proficiently in at least one art form; Standard 5—Be able to relate various types of arts knowledge and skills across the arts disciplines.)

— Whether it is exhilarating or disturbing, art can be enlightening— giving us insight into humanity and self-understanding. Older students, for example, might view a videotape of Hamlet's "Alas poor Yorick" speech to gain insight into human foibles.
— Students could read the Langston Hughes poem *The Dream Keeper* and rewrite the poem using the best dream (or daydream) they have ever had. [Poems can be read in pairs—alternating the reading of lines.]

> Bring me all of your dreams,
>   You dreamers,
>   Bring me all of your
>   Heart melodies
>   That I may wrap them
>   In a blue cloud-cloth
>   Away from the too-rough fingers
>   Of the world.
>   Langston Hughes

Dreams and Creative Drama: Give students overnight to come up with a dream from any time in their life. For those few who cannot remember their dreams, a daydream will do. Students can bring in their own dream and tell it to their small cooperative group. After each student has shared a dream (or a daydream) with the small group, the group picks one dream that can involve everybody in a 60 second bit of creative drama. After some minutes of practice, each group can put their skit on for the class—the whole class guesses whose dream it is—next the "dreamer" explains the dream to the class. Remember that it is best that you do not try to interpret the dreams; that insures misinterpretations and inhibits the children.

4. *Dancing to poetry:* To create a magical atmosphere with dance and poetry, darken the classroom. Two students can use a flashlight to alternate in reading the lines of the poem. (It works just as well to have one student read loudly.) As the poem is being read, four or five students use pen lights to move to the poem. (It obviously helps if the poem lends

itself to active movement.) If it is dark and there are strobe lights available near the school stage, the flashing adds a stunning effect. If you cannot get a darkened room, you can choreograph the *dancing to poetry* with long silk scarfs or long ribbons like those used with movement during the Olympic games. Small groups need to practice their routine for 15 or 20 minutes. After the choreography has been worked out, the group performs for the entire class. So that the audience gets the full effect, you may want to run it by them twice. Three examples that worked well for us:

Song of the Trains

Clickety-clack, wheels on the track
This is the way they begin the attack
Clickety-clack, clickety-clack
clickety-clackety, clickety, clack
Clickety-clack over the crack
Faster and faster the song of the track:
Clickety-clack, clickety-clack,
clickety-clackety, clickety, clack
Riding in front, riding in back,
everyone hears the song of the track:
Clickety-clack, clickety-clack,
clickety-clack, clickety-clackety,
clickety, clack.

An untitled section of a poem by Edna St. Vincent Millay

It is not so much the tune
Although the tune is lovely, growing suddenly higher
Than you expect, and neat, and something like the nightingale dropping
And throbbing very low.
It is not so much the notes, it is the quality of the voice,
Something to do perhaps with over-tone
And under-tone, and implication
Felt, but not quite heard.

Fireworks by James Reeves

They rise like sudden fiery flowers
That burst upon the night
Then fall to earth in burning showers
Of crimson, blue, and white
Like buds too wonderful to name
Each miracle unfolds

and Catherine wheels begin to flame
Like whirling marigolds.

(Shorter poems may have to be read twice through for full effect.)

5. *Music, Dance, Performance Art, & Drama* (Standard 1—communicate in four arts disciplines; Standard 2—communicate proficiently in at least one art form; Standard 5—Be able to relate various types of arts knowledge and skills across the arts disciplines.)

Movement Activity: This experience is designed for younger students. It draws on students creative imaginations. Movement plays a major role. Play some soft music. Explain to students that you're going on an imaginary journey. Have students imagine what it is like at the end of the winter season. Ask questions about their image. What does it look like around you? What does it feel like? Now imagine that you are a seed buried under the snow. You start to sense the light. You begin to feel the warmth of the sun. You feel the hard earth around you loosening up.

You begin to stretch yourself inside the seed. The sun beats down more intensely. You like the warm feeling. After a while you hear raindrops falling above you. Pitter-patter, pitter-patter, pitter-patter. You feel scared. You notice that your seed shell is getting softer. You stretch again. This time you begin to feel more room inside the shell. You start to wiggle. You wiggle so much that the seed begins to pop open.

You recognize your roots wiggling out of the seed. The ground feels so good. It feels warm. You sense the warmness, the brightness. You feel yourself stretching and growing under the ground. You keep on stretching. It feels wonderful.

And quite suddenly you are blinded. You notice that you've developed tiny sprouts, and the sun is hitting these small sprouts. Oh no, it's raining again! It feels great. You're not at all scared. You feel yourself expanding, stretching, growing. Your tiny sprouts are sprouts no more; instead they have changed and grown into leaves. You hear them rustle in the wind. You feel them absorbing the rain drops. Other things are changing too.

You feel very alive. You keep stretching and growing. Suddenly your leaves pop open to reveal a tiny bud hiding underneath. The bud slowly starts to open. Move and show how you feel. You are now a beautiful soft yellow flower. You feel happy and proud. You dance to the wind. The sun and rain don't bother you at all. But over time you're still growing and stretching. (Have students act out the photosynthesis process, students pretend their feet are roots, they burrow their roots deep into the soil, they stretch their arms wide, pretending they have leaves to gather the sun and rain. Next, they begin simulating that they are drinking through a straw, modeling the plant drinking.) Their soft yellow flower eventually turns white and feels lighter. They've turned into seeds. The wind is blowing harder now. It sets the seeds free and blows them away. The seeds scatter. They dance, and dance, and dance and finally drop back down to earth. You'll begin your journey yet again another day. At the end of this performance, students explain their feelings, explaining how they changed, and end with an art activity like movement and drama. Encourage students to reenact some of the scenes for the class. Did anyone do it differently? Students may wish to hear it again, moving differently. Children may wish to draw a picture, paint, write a story or poem, keep a dialogue journal, make up a song, or write a play that captures the experience.

Making Interdisciplinary Connections

The new recommendations also suggest a broader curriculum—using the arts to connect such subjects as math, literature, science, physical education, and social studies (National Arts Education Associates, 1992). Connecting the arts to other subjects adds depth and excitement. Instead of being taught as a separate set of skills, arts education is taking its place as an exciting and powerful way of knowing.

The need for a cross-disciplinary approach to the curriculum is cited by teachers nationwide. The arts can serve as the glue that pulls the curriculum together. Connections between subjects are even more vital as the nation implements its national standards in for the core subjects in the curriculum. The arts are a natural way to connect different disciplines without adding to the mass of nonacademic time-burners being piled onto the school day. Without coordination and a unifying theme, the curriculum will be overloaded and important standards will fall through the cracks. Nonacademic concerns such as AIDS education, Driver's Education, and Home Economics can happen after the precious hours for the core subjects are over.

High Standards for Education in the Arts

Arts education has been in steady decline over the last decade—with cuts becoming more common than exemplary programs. Still some states—for example Minnesota and South Carolina—have developed increasingly sophisticated programs (Smith, 1990). These quality programs didn't just happen; they required broad-based and sustained support. They also required vision and leadership that didn't try to escape their dilemmas by making favorable assumptions about the future. National standards encourage other states to adopt such programs. Unless the arts are specifically included in a state's education goals and curriculum content laws, then most students and teachers will not come to recognize the integral role of the arts as a vehicle of human expression, communication, and cultural identity.

In addition to reading, writing, mathematics, science, and technology, the core curriculum now includes the arts. With their inclusion in *Goals 2000,* it is time to convert standards to a practical level (Viadero, 1993). At a time when America needs more than standardized answers in a world that increasingly demands critical thinking and creative analysis, the arts teach students divergent thinking, craftsmanship, and the notion that there are many paths for solving a problem. The new standards in arts education can be viewed as an important tool for keeping America both creative and competitive.

The arts expand our world and provide us with multiple entry points to knowledge and meaning. They challenge as many people as they soothe. They help us make better use of the world, others and self. As an important language of human communication the arts can provide insights into subtle corners of the human imagination and aspects of life missed by other subjects. The arts are much more than cute bunny rabbits, personal therapy, and frivolous entertainment. By opening our eyes and touching our humanity, they replenish our spirit and inspire us.

The new arts standards will make a transforming impact across the entire spectrum of education only when they are *implemented.* The development process was immense and positive, the implementation process must be equally powerful. Now that high standards for the arts are recognized as a mark of excellence in schooling it is time to move from rhetoric to reality.

As the national arts standards make clear, quality education in the arts elevates and gives structure to creative expression and cultural understanding. But for this federal initiative to be broadly successful, then states and local school systems will have to buy into what are voluntary standards and assessment procedures. If educational reform at the local level neglects the arts, then both our schools and our lives will be more desolate places. As Education Secretary Richard Riley said when he announced the arts standards:

... Art in all its distinct forms defines, in many ways, those qualities that are at the heart of education reform in the 1990's — creativity, perseverance, a sense of standards, and, above all, a striving for excellence.

The arts have always provided a space, a sense of opening, a loving of the question, and a unique communal resource. Today's school reform process should not push aside such a basic aspect of social consciousness and interdisciplinary knowing. If there are no arts in a school, there are fewer alternatives to exploring subjects by the spoken and written word. The arts can open some collective doors of the mind and provide new spaces for the active construction of knowledge. What a powerful tool for countering the tendency towards standardization! At the classroom level it will take the skill of collaborative teachers to move forward and use the arts to shape the interconnected exuberance of learning — keeping light from the arts at the center of the human spirit.

Using the Arts to Connect Disciplines

Children without knowledge of the arts are as ignorant as children without knowledge of literature, math, or science. The arts can provide important intellectual tools for understanding many subjects. They also build on qualities that are essential to revitalizing schooling: teamwork, analytical thinking, motivation, and self-discipline. The arts provide cultural resources that people can draw on for the rest of their lives. Without attention to the substance of the discipline and concerted action, the arts more likely to be dismissed as expendable in an era of curriculum gridlock and financial difficulties.

The arts can also help get a dialogue going between disciplines that often ignore each other. When knowledge from diverse subject matter areas are brought together, the result can be a new and valuable way of looking at the world. The arts and humanities have proved very useful tools for integrating curricular areas and helping students transcend narrow subject matter concerns (The College Board, 1985). Teachers at many levels have used intellectual tools from the fine arts as a thematic lens for examining diverse subjects. Some schools have even worked out an integrated school day, where interdisciplinary themes based on the fine arts add interest, meaning and function to collaboration. Mathematics, science, social studies, and the language arts can all be wrapped around central themes in the arts so that rich connections stimulate the mind and the senses.

The research suggests that using a thematic approach improves students' knowledge of subject matter and aids in transfer of the skills learned to other domains outside the school. An additional finding is that good units organized around themes can improve the students' abilities to apply their knowledge to new subjects (Sharan, 1990). In art, for example, language development flourishes when children are encouraged to discuss the materials they are using and reflect on the nature of their art work through writing. Whatever the combination, an important result of integrating various subjects around a theme results in an enhancement of thinking and learning skills—*the metacurriculum* (Wlodkowski & Jaynes, 1990).

Before we can deal with teaching the thinking process, children need some solid content to think about. After that, teachers need to provide continuity between activities and subjects. The thinking skills engendered by the arts can serve as a connection between subjects. In making curriculum connections, it is often helpful for teachers to see model lessons that include cross disciplinary suggestions and activities. The relationships established between subjects and the way teachers facilitate these relationships are important. When disciplines are integrated around a central concept, students can practice the skills that they have learned from many subjects. This helps students make sense out of the world (Maeroff, 1988).

The goal of a interdisciplinary curriculum is to bring together different perspectives so that diverse intellectual tools can be applied to a common theme, issue or problem. Thematic approaches can help by providing a group experience that fosters thinking and learning skills that will serve students in the larger world. By its very definition, "interdisciplinary" implies cooperation among disciplines and people. The notion that students of different abilities and backgrounds can learn from each other is a natural outgrowth of the collaborative tendency inherent in this approach. Everyone's collaborative involvement not only allows input into the planning process, but can help with self responsibility and long term commitment to learning (Fraser, 1990).

Organizing parts of the curriculum around collaborative themes means that each subject is mutually reinforcing and connected to life-long learning. Subjects from the Greek classics to radiation theory need the historical, philosophical, and aesthetic perspective afforded by interdisciplinary connections. Curriculum integration provides active linkages between areas of knowledge, consciously applies language and methods from more than one discipline to examine a central theme, issue, topic, or experience. This holistic approach focuses on themes and problems and deals with them more in depth rather than memorizing facts and covering the text from cover to cover. We cannot narrowly train people in specialist areas and expect them to be able to deal with multifaceted nature of jobs in the twenty-first century.

Thematic Strategies for Linking Subjects and Students

Themes can also direct the design of classroom activities by connecting cooperative classroom activities and providing them with a logical sequence and scope of instruction.

A set of steps for developing thematic concepts is to:

1. Determine what students know about a topic before beginning instruction. This is done by careful questioning and discussion.
2. Be sensitive to and capitalize on students' knowledge.
3. Use a variety of instructional techniques to help students achieve conceptual understanding.
4. Include all students in discussions and cooperative learning situations.

Thematic instruction values depth over breadth of coverage. The content should be chosen on how well it represents what is currently known in the field and its potential for dynamically making connections (Rogoff, 1990).

The design of thematic units brings together a full range of disciplines in the school's curriculum: language arts, science, social studies, math, art, physical education, and music. Using a broad range of discipline-based perspectives can result in units that last an hour, a day, a few weeks, or a semester. They are not intended to replace a discipline-based approach, but act as supportive structures that foster the comprehensive study of a topic. Teachers can plan their collaborative interdisciplinary work around issues and themes that emerge from their ongoing curriculum. Deliberate steps can be taken to create a meaningful and carefully orchestrated program that is more stimulating and motivating for students and teachers (Novel Unit Themes, 1990). Of course, shorter flexible units of study are easier to do than setting up a semester or year-long thematic unit.

Collaborative thematic curriculum models require a change in how teachers go about their work. It takes planning and energy to create effective integrated lessons, and more time is often needed for subject matter research because teachers frequently find themselves exploring and teaching new material. Thematic teaching also means planning lessons that use untraditional approaches, arranging for field trips, guest speakers, and special events (Tebbs, 1991). Contacting parents, staff members, and community resources who can help expand the learning environment is another factor in teacher's time and planning efforts. Long-range planning and professional development for teachers are other important elements of the process.

Sharing a Sense of Wonder

The arts have a power beyond anesthetics or making us "see." They can help us view ourselves, the environment, the future differently — even challenging our certainties about the arts themselves. In connecting the basic concerns of history, civilization, thought, and culture, the arts provide spatial, kinesthetic, and aesthetic skills that are the foundation to what it means to be an educated person. Such understandings do not occur spontaneously. They have to be taught.

The process of understanding or creating art is more than unguided play, self-expression, or a tonic for contentment. The arts can serve as tools for shattering stereotypes, changing behavior, building a sense of community, and as a vehicle for sociopolitical commentary. There is a connection between productive citizenship, academics, and the arts. For students to make these connections, it will take more than a specialist in the art class for one hour a week or an inspirational theater troupe visiting the school once a year. These brief experiences can help and inspire, but it takes more sustained work in the arts to make a real difference.

Cheating on daily arts education denies students a vital quality of life experience — expression, discovery, and an understanding of the chances for human achievement (Schubert & Willis, 1991). The arts can open up a sense of wonder and provide students with intellectual tools for engaging in a shared search. This won't occur if children are having fewer experiences with the arts at school and in their daily lives. Certainly some grasp of the discipline is needed if the arts are going to awaken students to the possibilities of thoughtfulness, collaboration, and life.

Cooperating and Reflecting On Art Activities

Reflecting is a special kind of thinking. Reflective thinking is both active and controlled. When ideas pass aimlessly through a person's mind, or someone tells a story which triggers a memory, that is not reflecting. Reflecting means focusing attention. It means weighing, considering, choosing. Suppose you want to drive home, you get the key out of your pocket, put it in the car door, and open the door. Getting into your car does not require reflection. But suppose you reached in your pocket and couldn't find the key. To get into your car requires reflection. You have to think about what you are going to do. You have to consider possibilities and imagine alternatives.

A carefully balanced combination of direct instruction, self-monitoring, and reflective thinking helps meet diverse student needs. The activity examples listed here are designed to encourage higher order thinking and provide a collaborative vehicle for arts education.

1. *Looking at the Familiar, Differently*
   Students are asked to empty their purses and pockets on a white sheet of paper and create a face using as few of the items as possible. For example, one case might be simply a pair of sunglasses, another a single earring representing a mouth, a third could be a profile created by a necklace forming a forehead, nose, and chin. It gives students a different way of looking at things. It is also an example of a teaching concept known as esthetic education.

2. *Exploring Collage Photo Art*
   Students at all levels can become producers as well as consumers of art. We used a videotape of David Hockney's work from *Art in America*. Hockney, one of today's important artists, spoke (on the videotape) about his work and explained his technique. Students

then used cameras to explore Hockney's photo collage technique in their own environment. Student groups can arrange several sets of their photos differently—telling unique stories with different compositions of the same pictures. They can even add brief captions or poems to make more connections to the language arts, social studies, or science. Photographers know the meaning of their pictures depend to a large extent on the words that go with them.

Note: teachers do need to preview any videos before they are used in the classroom because some parts may not be appropriate for elementary school children. Teachers can also select particular elements and transfer them from one VCR to another so that only the useful segments are present on the tape used in class.

3. *Painting with Water Colors and Straws*
   In this activity students simply apply a little suction to a straw which is dipped in tempera paint. Working in pains students then gently blow the paint out on a sheet of blank paper to create interesting abstract designs.

4. *Creating Paintings with Oil-Based Paints Floating on Water*
   Working in groups of three, have students put different colored oil based paints on a flat dish of water. Apply paper. Watch it soak up the paint and water. Pull it out and let it dry.

5. *Examining Similarities in Folk Lore and Literature*
   Have student groups explore myths, folk tales, legends, and fairy tales to look for similarities and differences between people, times and cultures. Construct a group list, concept map, collage, visual image, or writing that shows these group findings. Students can even take photocopies of major works, paste them down on a large piece of tag board, and paint on top of them.

6. *Understanding Images of the Past Through Oral History*
   Oral history is a systematic way to obtain from the artifacts, music, photographs and lips of living Americans a record of their participation in the political, economic, and cultural affairs of the nation. It is a process of collecting reminiscences, accounts, and interpretations of events from the recent past which are of historical significance. As small cooperative groups of students gather information from an elder who grew up in a time and manner different from theirs, the students can sketch, compile, select, and organize data. This activity works best if you have an elder for each small group. You really need five or six elders there at the same time. If you get more, just

make the student groups smaller. A student in each group can give a 60-second explanation of their visitor to the whole class just before the end of the activity. *Avoid* having one elder stand alone at the front of the class for a lecture style presentation. Other possibilities:
• bringing in veterans of World War II to explain that time period and their role in the war. Be sure to ask them to bring visuals, artifacts, and possibly newspapers from that time period. If you do this a little before Veterans Day, for example, it might even be possible to notify the media and get some press coverage. Do we sometimes hear echoes of ideas about art from the 1930s and 1940s? "And don't talk to me about 'threat to artistic freedom'! . . . one does not grant anyone the freedom to use his sordid imagination to kill the soul of a people" (Adolf Hitler at the opening of a "Degenerate Art Exhibition").
• student groups can be reformed so that each group has someone who has interviewed several elders. The new small group can construct and compare the experiences of the older Americans from different cultural, ethnic, or racial backgrounds.

The Process:

a) Prior to the interview students identify topics of interest, and do some preliminary research on the topic they're going to discuss.
b) Students identify individuals to interview, contact these individuals to arrange an interview, giving the purpose, time, and place.
c) Working in groups, students prepare some questions for the interview and review with the class the questions they have chosen.
d) Students and the teacher then prepare for the interview. Questions should be simple, relevant, and varied. Procedures for interviewing should be reviewed with the class (Let the respondent do the talking, don't interrupt a story, etc.).
e) During the interview, students take notes or record (audio or video) the data.
f) Following the interview, students transcribe their notes or recorded data to prepare material for publication or oral presentation.
g) Students then interpret and edit materials, verify dates, and obtain written release from respondent for "publication" to the whole class.

7. *The Preparation that Is Needed Before Students View Modern Art*

I paint things as I think of them, not as I see them. . . .
— Pablo Picasso

You do not want students to be surprised when they go to a museum and find that the "old masters" may have no more status than an modern artist who spattered or poured paint onto an abstract canvas. An example of a response by an unprepared fifth grader: *"I can't understand it because what's in it because it doesn't look like its from real life."* Now that can photography, videotape, and film capture realistic images painting and sculpture have moved on to a different "reality." In the twentieth century it became redundant for visual artists to simply repeat what the technology can usually do better and always do much quicker.

The response of an adult who hasn't done her homework: *The perspective is all wrong, my four-year-old son could do that!"* This is not as great an insult as you may think. Many artists consider art done by many children as having an intensity and spontaneity that breaks the traditional "rules" of composition. As Henri Matisse said, "We must see all of life as if we were children." Overemphasizing technique can stifle the imagination — these days it is best not to judge a work by nineteenth century standards of perspective and composition. Now we might look for things like evidence of originality and how the work of art helps us see today's world, the past, or the future differently. Does it open new spaces for understanding?

When we accompanied a fifth-grade class to an artist's work area at the nearby university, two children came up close to a painting that the artist in residence was doing. They asked, "What does it mean?" The artists reply, "What do you think it means?" There is rarely one "right" way to interpret a work. But it helps to have at least:

- an idea of the artist as a person and the social context within which the work was created.
- a little historical background and some understanding of the arts community today.

Artists rarely conceptualize their work in a vacuum, influences come from every direction. As they experiment with new styles and techniques they may gather in groups to talk about their ideas or work together on a project. The coming together of artists with similar aims has generated most of the modern art movements of this century. Such movements have helped create a sense of solidarity. By being part of such a group artists may be taken more seriously than working alone.

8. ***Working With a Partner in the Art Museum***

   In an art museum, students might focus on a few paintings or pieces of sculpture. Have students make up a question or two about some aspect of the art they wish to explore further—and respond to five or six questions from the list in a notebook or writing pad they take with them.

Possible Art Museum Questions for Reflection

- Compare and contrast technology and art as vehicles for viewing the past, present, or future differently.
- How is the visual put together?
- How are images used to communicate?
- How did the creator of the visual image expect the viewer to actively engage the image? Is content more important than form?
- How does your social background affect how you receive (or construct) the message?
- Visuals are authored in much the way print communication is authored. How does the author of a picture or piece of sculpture manipulate the viewer through such things as point of view, size, distortion, or lighting?
- What are the largest or smallest artistic elements of the work?
- What is the main idea, mood, feeling, or intent conveyed by the image?
- When you close your eyes and think about the visual, what pictures do you see? What sounds do you hear? Does it remind you of anything—a book, a dream, TV, something from your life?
- How successful was the visual in making use of the medium?
- How successful is the sculpture or image? Does it have validity? Is it effective? What is your response to it?
- Where did the visual maker place important ideas?
- How do combinations or organization of elements contribute to an overall mood?
- Does the image tell us about big ideas such as courage, freedom, war, etc.
- Determine the nature of the image through its style, period, school, and culture. How does it fit in with the history of art?

- What does the work say about present conflicts concerning art standards, multiculturalism, and American culture?
- Estimate the esthetic value of the sculpture, image as it relates to others.
- How did the work make you feel inside?
- Was the artistic work easy or hard to understand?
- Why do you think it was made? What would you like to change about it?

Sharing information, ideas, and insights in the arts can be done with group members within small cooperative groups. In the small group each member or partnership can share ideas and discoveries. Each group may synthesize their work and present briefly to the entire class. As the small group's "reporter" reports to the whole class the information could be recorded on a class chart. A variation would be to have one student from each group visit another team to collect and share findings—returning to their original group for a discussion.

Children frequently have the innate ability to do creative work in the arts. What's frequently missing are basic artistic understandings and the opportunity for expression and group analysis. When students do have the chance to explore the discipline and express themselves there is the excitement of producing in their own way, conveying their personal aesthetic experience through the use of figurative language (metaphors, similes, etc.) in their song lyrics, expressive movement, and symbolism in their painting. There is a world out there that students must explore with the arts if they are to be broadly educated. The challenge is to provide the necessary background and opening doors so that meaningful concepts and images will emerge.

Expanding Visions of the Arts

Human societies have always depended on the arts to give insight into truths, however painful or unpopular they may be. Today, in many countries, there is wide agreement that the arts can aid children in developing creativity, becoming good citizens, and being productive workers. The basic notion is that the person, the world, and the nation is poorer without the arts. As Argentine artist Nicolas Urburu has suggested, *A country without culture is like a person without a face.*

Americans have generally not paid much attention to the arts. Little is expected of our citizens or our leaders when it comes to knowledge about

Computer Enhanced image of M.C. Escher's "Sky and Water I."

artistic forms. This is due, in part, to not having a long tradition of prizing artistic expression beyond the cute and the comfortable. As far as the schools are concerned, the arts have often received more attention as a form of therapy than as a serious discipline. It is little wonder that if the arts are found at all, they are most often found on the fringes of our curriculum—and when a budget crunch hits, arts education is one of the first things cut.

Teachers can create a space for the arts to flourish, freeing students from the predicted and the expected. Using the arts to inquire and sense openings results in what Emily Dickinson called *a slow fire lit by the imagination.* As America moves toward the new millennium we need all the imagination we can get. Advancing the understanding, culture, art, creativity, and human values have everything to do with the life and quality of this nation.

Enlightenment, richness of knowledge, and enduring resources for thoughtfulness are diminished when artistic endeavors are diminished. From Asia to Europe, serious art education is one of the integrating features of the school curriculum and national culture. The passion, vision, and the imaginative life generated by the arts is viewed as having real significance for the quality of national culture. Similar elements of passion and vision would be very useful to American educational reform. The arts have a role to play in opening new horizons, enriching the spirit, and encouraging bold visions—helping us see what can be but isn't yet.

> *There is a case for saying that the creation of new aesthetic forms has been the most fundamentally productive of all forms of human activity. Whoever creates new artistic conventions has found methods of interchange between people about matters which were incommunicable before. The capacity to do this has been the basis of the whole of human history.*
>
> —J. Z. Young

REFERENCES

Association for Supervision and Curriculum Development. (1994). ASCD Conference Report, Fowler *ASCD Update.* Author.

Calkins, L. (1991). *Living between the lines.* Portsmouth, NH: Heineman.

The College Board. (1985). *Academic preparation in the arts: Teaching for transition from high school to college,* New York.

Cooperative Artists Institute (1986). *Teacher artist connection.* Jamaica Plain.

Dissanayake, E. (1992). *HomoAestheticus.* New York: Free Press.

Eisner, E. (1991) *The enlightened eye.* New York: Macmillan.

Fowler, C. (1992). *Understanding how the arts contribute to excellent education.* A study prepared for the NEA.

Fraser, J.T. (1990). *Of time, passion and knowledge.* Princeton, NJ: Princeton University Press.

Gardner, H. (1983). *Frames of mind.* New York: Basic Books.

Gardner, H. (1993). *Creating minds.* New York: Basic Books.

Getty Center for Education in the Arts. (1989). *Education in art: Future building.*

Kaagan, S. (1990) *Aesthetic persuasion: Pressing the cause of arts education in American schools.* A Monograph for the Getty Center for Education in the Arts.

Maeroff, G. (1988). *The empowerment of teachers.* New York: Teachers College Press.

National Art Education Associates (1992). *Elementary art programs: A guide for administrators.* Reston, VA: National Art Education Association.

National Standards for Education in the Arts (1994). *The Arts and Education Reform Goals 2000.* Washington, D.C.: U.S. Office of Education, p. 3.

Nesbitt, J. (1986). *International directory of recreation-oriented assistance.* Venice, CA: Lifeboat Press.

Novel Unit Themes. (1990). *Fly high with novel units.* P.O. Box 1461, Dept. RT, Palatine, IL 60078.

The Report of the National Commission on Music Education by the Music Educators National Conference. (1991). *Growing Up Complete: The Imperative for Music Education,* Reston, VA: MENC, March 1991.

Rogoff, B. (1990). *Apprentices in thinking: Children's guided participation in culture.* New York: Oxford University Press.

Schubert, W. & Willis, G. (1991). *Understanding curricula and teaching through the arts.* New York: SUNY Press.

Sharan, S. (1990). *Cooperative learning: Theory and research.* Westport, CT: Bergin & Garvey and Praeger Publishing.

Smith, R., (Ed.). (1990). *Discipline-based art education: Origins, Meaning and development.* Champaign, IL: University of Illinois Press.

Tebbs, T. (1991), Unpublished paper dealing with art, collaboration, and gifted education.

The New York Times, August 2, 1992.

Viadero, D. (1993). *Draft Standards for Arts Education: Knowledge Performance, and Discipline Based Learners.* Washington D.C.: U.S. Education Department, the National Endowment for the Arts, and the National Endowment for the Humanities. National Panel for the Development of Standards for Art Education.

Wlodkowski, R. & Jaynes, J. (1990). *Eager to learn.* San Francisco, CA: Jossey-Bass.

Chapter 6

COOPERATIVE LEARNING IN
THE INCLUSIVE CLASSROOM:

ACCOMMODATING STUDENTS WITH SPECIAL NEEDS
IN REGULAR CLASSROOMS

Every child is special if we create conditions in which that child can be a specialist within a speciality group.

— Joseph Renzulli

Including the whole range of students with special needs in the regular classroom has numerous supporters and opponents. The inclusion debate becomes most heated when children with severe disabilities are placed in the regular classroom. Rather than segregating children with special needs inclusive schools take the support services to the child within the regular classroom.

The tremendous diversity of special needs students makes inclusion as complicated an issue today as mainstreaming was yesterday. The children involved run the gamut from those with a slight learning disabilities to those with severe mental, emotional, or physical handicaps. Even non-English speaking students and gifted children are sometimes considered as part of the special education population. Is there a general instructional strategy that can connect a wide range of special needs students to regular classroom routines? Teachers and administrators often cite cooperative learning as one of the keys to the success of their inclusion programs (Slavin, 1990). Issues related to inclusion and cooperative learning form the basis of this chapter.

Inclusion and the Law

Education of All Handicapped Children Act (PL 94-142) has been in effect since 1975 and continues to receive wide support from teachers, parents, and legislators (Cummings & Cleborne, 1985). Among other things, it gives children with any type of disability the right to "a free and appropriate public education in the least restrictive environment."

This means working at least much of the time, with mixed-ability groups of "regular" children in "regular" classrooms. It also involves developing and adhering to an individual education plan (IEP) which specifies how much time the special needs student should spend in special and regular settings (Sternberg, Tayler & Schilt, 1986). In 1991, congress renamed Act (P.L. 94-142) to the "Individuals with Disabilities Act (P.L. 101-476 and P.L. 102-119 or IDEA) and expanded the definition of disabilities (formerly handicaps) to include autism and traumatic brain injury (Shanker, 1994).

The percentage of students with special needs has remained at about 10 percent of the school population (ages 6 to 21). There has, however, been a substantial increase in students identified as "learning disabled" (LD). Learning Disabled students now make up about half of all special education students. Out of the total population of special needs students 25 percent have speech or language impairments and the rest are mentally retarded, emotionally disturbed, or have physical disabilities. Unless they have a learning disability, gifted and talented youth are usually not included in this specialized count because they spend the bulk of their time in regular classrooms. Here we will consider cooperative learning in the context of the broad range of exceptional children.

Appropriate Learning Environments

Teachers and parents alike have long searched for ways for all exceptional students to receive an "appropriate" education in the most appropriate learning environment. Labeling and separating children has often been harmful. And so has shunting students with disabilities off into a large class with a regular classroom teacher who lacks the training or support to give these students the attention they need.

General agreement seems to exist that one goal of the Acts P.L. 101-476 and P.L. 102-119 was to encourage more social interaction between disabled and non-disabled children. And much of that interaction was seen as occurring within regular classrooms. Interpretations of the "least restrictive environment" for special needs children have been debated from the mainstreaming days of the 1980s to the inclusion days of the 1990s. The definition of "least restrictive environment" has ranged from total inclusion of all disabled students in a regular classroom to "pull out" programs where students attend special classes. These varied definitions arise primarily because the sponsors of IDEA recognize that the regular classroom cannot always provide appropriate education to all students and may even be harmful to some special needs students (Stafford, 1978).

Some educators are in opposition of full inclusion. Many are worried that disabled children may not get as much attention as they need. Examples of worthy groups in opposition to certain aspects of inclusion: advocates for the deaf community, the American Council on the Blind, the Council for Children with Behavior Disorders, the Learning Disabilities Association and the Council for Exceptional Children (Fuchs and Fuchs, 1994). From this partial list you can see that classroom teachers are not the only ones concerned about mixing disabled with nondisabled students.

Today reexamination of the definition of "least restrictive environment" for special needs students leads to two groups: one advocating full inclusion and one opposed to full inclusion. Both groups list supportive research and the practical benefits of their position. It is a little like the long scientific debate over light. Is it a wave or is it a particle? Everyone agrees that can't be both. But experimenters have proven it both ways, depending on how they set up the experiment. So the professional argument goes on.

A broad definition of an inclusive school might be a school that places all students within regular classrooms—while providing appropriate educational programs that challenge each student. School districts cannot save money by dumping students who need all kinds of special services into the regular classroom. For inclusion to work teachers must receive the support and assistance that they need to help special needs students. When they get the right support services and training, teachers can structure lessons so that all children work cooperatively in small groups, taking responsibility for helping each other master the material. This helps make the inclusive classroom a place where everyone belongs, is accepted, and is supported by peers and other members of the school community (Stainback and Stainback, 1990).

Educators generally agree that each child has the basic human right to be "successful" in school: that is, each child has the right to enjoy learning, to undertake learning tasks that challenge but that do not overwhelm, to achieve, to know and sense that they can learn, to enjoy being in school, to thrive, and to grow from the schooling experience.

To a certain extent expectations drive the achievement of students. Inclusion supporters believe that disabled students benefit academically, because students are exposed to more challenging content, inspired by the example of their nondisabled peers, and expected to perform at a higher level (Willis, 1994). Supporters also believe that inclusion helps nondisabled students learn tolerance and build a better appreciation of human differences. The basic idea is that differences can lead to enriched learning for all students. Thus disabilities and differences actually come to constitute a diversity that is valued.

Student Potential Lost

Student Potential Gained

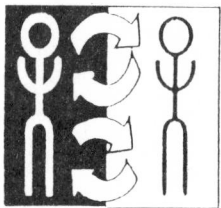

COLLABORATION & INCLUSION CAN MAKE A DIFFERENCE

Searching for Effective Strategies

The search for effective techniques for "inclusive" students who have various types of handicaps has not been an easy one, nor has it been a sufficiently successful search. Advocates for inclusion believe that inclusion helps eliminate the problems caused by labeling students. Careless or poorly assessed labeling or categorization based on ability has a long-lasting impact on the student and may result in the student not receiving the proper type of education. Today, more than half of children with disabilities are still rejected from inclusion programs and whisked off to special places for much of their education. Thus, rejection processes still operate within many schools (Maloney, 1994). School life is group life and part of what schools are about is teaching students how to live effectively in diverse groups. Yet there is a troubling dissonance between our stated values and our revealing practices. What are the obstacles that block teachers from fully and genuinely integrating students with disabilities into their classrooms?

The phrase "to accommodate the needs of students with disabilities into our classrooms" implicitly suggests a belief that the primary or original placement of the student with a disability is or should be somewhere other than in the regular classroom. The phrase additionally implies that teachers are being morally and legally obligated to now bring those students into their classrooms and to accommodate their learning needs. With higher average classroom scores on standardized tests being a prime determinant of teaching "success," it is little wonder that classroom teachers fear an influx of special students who don't do well on these assessment instruments.

Our current model of schooling gradually established the position that regular classroom teachers did not need to assume primary responsibility for students with disabilities. Special education, which developed over the last century, was thought to provide more suitable programs for children and young adults who could not succeed in the regular program as the regular program was structured. From this beginning, special education grew to become a subsystem of regular education—and later a parallel system to regular education (Flynn & McPhee). Now, as we move through the second decade of PL 94-142 and its associates, it is important for schools to try new things and help regular educators broaden their repertoire of methods so that they can reach a broader group of students.

Sometimes the child's disability has less to do with his being perceived as different than school grouping and segregation policies. When children don't adjust well to the school curriculum—and many don't—they are often labeled "handicapped" and separated from their peers. Here we look at avenues for making changes in the schooling process so that children can be grouped with their peers as much as possible. We recognize that there may be times when certain exceptional students need special settings and that quality experiences can occur across educational settings.

Moving from a traditional model to a new way of educating requires rethinking the educational process. Inclusion and strategies such as cooperative learning require restructuring of the classroom. Additionally, physically or mentally handicapped students often present practical problems for teachers. Whatever the disability, the special services currently provided to students in a separate environment must also be available when they are included in the regular classroom.

Teachers in the inclusive classroom must identify whether the special needs student can participate in a lesson in the same way as other students and determine what supports or modifications are necessary for full participation (Tashie et al., 1993). Such assessments require skills and time. The schools must ensure that the teacher has the necessary resources to make such assessments which will likely involve teacher training.

For more fifteen years schools, in cooperation with parents, have been required to develop an Individual Educational Program (IEP) for every student who has been identified as having some sort of handicap. Cooperative learning is not simply a technique that a teacher can adopt in order to "accommodate" a student with a disability within the regular classroom in order to satisfy the "least restrictive environment" requirement of an IEP. Making significant change in the classroom process is going to require that teachers undergo changes in the ways that they teach and in the ways that they view students. This means creating comfortable—yet challenging—learning environments that are rich in diversity. The goal is cooperation among all types of learners. In mixed-ability groups, the emphasis must be on proficiency rather than age or grade level as a basis for student progress.

Cooperative learning is clearly an approach that lends itself to inclusion (Wang & Birch, 1987). It requires everyone to think, learn, and teach. Within a cooperative learning classroom, there will be many and varied "differences" among students. Every student will possess differences that will lend themselves to enriching learning for all students. Sometimes these "differences" may constitute a conventionally defined "disability," sometimes it simply means the inability to do a certain life or school-related task. And sometimes it means, as with the academically talented, being capable of work well beyond the norm. Within a strong cooperative learning environment, gifted students do not have to become bored and the academically handicapped do not have to be left out.

Strategies for Change

Active collaboration requires a depth of planning, a redefinition of planning, testing, and classroom management. Perhaps most significantly, cooperative learning values differences of abilities, talents, skills, and background knowledge. Within a cooperative learning classroom, conventionally defined "disabilities" fade into the heterogeneity of expected and anticipated differences among all students. "Disabilities" and "differences" come to constitute part of the fabric of diversity that is celebrated and cherished within the cooperative learning classroom. In such an educational climate, no individual is singled out as being different. No one student presents a challenge to the teacher as to how to accommodate a student with special needs.

In an active team learning environment, students are less likely to be stereotyped by others when they realize that there are many and varied "differences" among students. It is easier for the student with special needs to fit in. Differences need not constitute a handicap as cooperative learning is a joint enterprise. Some may have a disability or special talent, but all have information, and skills to contribute to the learning of others.

The central question is, how do individual classroom teachers, already overwhelmed with tasks, find ways to adapt techniques and modify approaches to successfully accommodate one or more students with a disability within their classrooms? After all, the stress of responding to the needs of a typical classroom is demanding enough. The problem is more than adapting techniques or modifying current approaches, and getting the support of special education specialists. It involves rethinking— seeking different approaches for teaching all students that lend themselves to accommodating unique human qualities.

Research on Collaborative Learning and Inclusion

Including physically or mentally handicapped students with their normal-progress peers presents enormous practical problems for classroom teachers and often leads to social rejection for special needs students. In working with special needs children, teachers find that learning strategies that work well with non-labeled children work well with labeled students. Cooperative learning methods have been so successful in reducing ethnic barriers, it seems appropriate to apply them to special needs students, though much more time may be required for explaining, modeling, interacting, or practicing (Barry, 1994).

Research on cooperative learning with mainstreamed students has shown significant gains in academic achievement and self-esteem (Madden & Slavin, 1984). Cooperative learning also significantly reduced the degree of rejection encountered by these students and increased positive interaction and gained friendships (Slavin, Madden & Leavy, 1984).

Even emotionally disturbed students were more on task and better behaved than students not involved in collaborative groups (Janke, 1978).

Perhaps most importantly, using cooperative learning methods in inclusive classrooms benefited all students in terms of academic achievement, self-esteem, and positive interaction. Students reported being more accepted by their peers and enjoying the camaraderie of working in small groups. Many reported feeling more comfortable working in teams, and more successful in their approach to academic tasks. Cooperative supportive experiences in school were found to help withdrawn children and those with antisocial attitudes outside of school (Slavin, 1977).

With such success, why have many teachers been slow to respond? One explanation for such resistance is that cooperative learning procedures are different from the traditional competitive, stimulus-response model of teaching and learning. There is a fear of not knowing how to act, or "behave" when relating to a cooperative learning setting. Additionally, teachers have not been trained in how to organize a cooperative learning "flow" of events and materials. For teachers to successfully link collaboration and inclusion, they need models and the opportunity to experience cooperative teaching and learning in action. Familiarity with a conceptual model makes working with cooperative groups easier.

The research on effective instruction suggests that good instructional practice:

1. respects different interests, abilities, and learning styles,
2. uses active learning techniques to relate what's being learned to the student's personal environment,
3. develops collaboration and reciprocation,
4. communicates high expectations (Westberg, Archambault, Dobyns and Salvin, 1993).

Within new learning environments, collaboration can help produce instruction that enhances learning across many domains, is relevant to students' anticipated experiences, and is inclusive. In her unpublished research, Mary McArdle reports that as students show more willingness to interact and reward others there is more lasting cross-cultural friendship and more acceptance of students with disabilities.

Cooperation and Standards in the Classroom

The notion of national standards for what students learn in public schools is an important item in education reform today. Through the

Goals 2000 legislation and the requirements written into the reauthorization of the Elementary and Secondary Education Act (ESEA), this is now national policy. Judging by the new standards now emerging, the emphasis appears to be on learning content through critical thinking and problem solving strategies, rather than through rote learning or memorization of discrete facts. Underlying the more general "opportunity to learn" and "deliver" standards of *Goals 2000* legislation is the concept of students working together to gain a powerful understanding of how strands of content can be integrated and synthesized.

Unlike some earlier innovations, cooperative learning has shown real staying power and has been incorporated into *content standards* that spell out the knowledge and skills that students should have and *performance standards* that suggest actual performance levels that students should reach. Embedded in performance standards is the focus on students applying and demonstrating what they know. Cooperative learning has permeated the standards projects and teacher training from the preservice to the inservice level. As teachers learn when and how to structure instruction cooperatively, the process transforms itself from a hot new method into a routine part of instruction.

As with other parts of the curriculum, cooperative learning must be fashioned with a sensitivity to how students connect content areas and relate ideas. With students, this means working in pairs or mixed-ability small groups to help each other learn. Students learn to take more responsibility for their own learning. There is a growing consensus that active team learning can enrich the special education community—as well as helping to foster cooperative relationships among teachers, administrators, and parents. More than other innovations, cooperative learning can change school climate by encouraging cooperation, cohesion, and teamwork. Teachers who are new to the technique can learn a great deal from peers who have preceded them—even if they work with different subject matter. When it comes to curriculum design and setting standards groups that are not traditionally thought of as within curriculum boundaries have a great deal to contribute.

The following list of assumptions from the standards projects open many possibilities for cooperative learning:

1. Learning is an active, very social process. Many people need to be involved with others.
2. Learning is a very active mental process. The mind is always

working, always learning. Critical and creative thinking skills help students generalize by adding information beyond what is given.

3. The prior experience of a student is an important ingredient of any learning situation.

4. The student must be a very active, self-initiating participant in the learning process.

5. Students need to verbalize their experiences and their new learnings on their own (language and conceptual) terms. Developing metaphors and analogies can assist with extending thinking and language.

6. Students are excellent teachers. They can teach each other. They can learn as much from their peers as from teachers.

7. The "things" to be learned are not really as compartmentalized as current curriculum fields may suggest. Everything is related and interrelated. Students need to discover these relationships. The relationships that students come up with may be different than the ones that teachers have because of differences in levels of past experiences and cognitive maturity.

8. Students are tremendously curious. They have a tremendous need to learn, to become competent.

9. Students enjoy and profit tremendously from working together and thereby learning together.

10. With proper development, students can become very responsible for managing their own learning opportunities.

Coupling these assumptions, with a cooperative learning approach will lead to very different styles of teaching.

Making the Classroom Environment Inclusive and Collaborative

Group interaction and information flow are major characteristics of suggested changes in teaching/learning style. The "richer" the interpersonal interaction, the more productive the learning. As students undertake learning projects, they become joint ventures where success (or grades) is not determined by who competitively achieves the highest score on a test. Rather it is determined by how well the learning project is accomplished and how well the various members of the learning "team" have worked together.

Creating the
**Inclusive / Cooperative
Classroom**

GET THERE

ANY

WAY

YOU

CAN

The characteristics of cooperation, interaction, and diversity are vital to the thinking and developmental needs of all students, but especially for the student with more severe motor, speech, or learning problems. Exceptional students who are academically talented or gifted can also gain important understandings by being work partners and friends with a wide range of peers.

The leap from the familiar competitive, stimulus-response, production control model of schooling to a communication cooperative model can seem enormous. To consider a change of such magnitude can seem threatening and unnerving. The search for effective techniques for integrating students who have various types of handicaps has not been an easy one, nor has it been a quick and always successful search. Effective inclusion requires commitment of the part of all involved as well as adequate funding. Making a commitment to facilitate learning for all students has been a common thread among schools that successfully utilize inclusion. Schools with successful inclusion problems typically utilize a variety of "best" practices, including authentic assessment, portfolios, an emphasis on critical thinking, collaborative planning, and teamwork (O'Neil, 1994). In one form or another, collaboration also plays a key role in successful programs. There is considerable structure, motivation, and individual freedom within cooperative learning. Trusting peers and valuing diverse contributions is central to developing a collaborative framework.

Cooperative learning can be applied within any curriculum area as conventionally defined by existing curriculum guides or content area textbooks. Thus, a teacher can adapt this model quite easily without making drastic changes to the knowledge or skill objectives that are already specified for a course (McIntosh, Vaugn, Schumm, Hager and Lee (1993). The textbook does not have to be thrown out, but rather extended to include active learning procedures where student groups are involved in seeking information, clarifying concepts, working on cooperative projects, solving problems, and "finding out—rather than filling in."

Extensions of the Textbook

Special needs students often need adaptations of standard textbook materials. The following is a collaborative activity adapted from a math textbook lesson on estimation.

Math Estimation Lesson

Objectives: To have the class estimate the size, weight, circumference, and number of seeds of a class pumpkin.

Activity 1—Measuring the height of the pumpkin

Materials:

One six pound pumpkin, small cut out (1 inch) squares, Zip Lock® bag

Procedure:

1. Place the pumpkin on a table at the front of the room.
2. Make a poster with this questions and room for students' estimates:
   • "How tall are you Mr. Pumpkin?"
3. Have students lay out the squares in a line on their desks.
4. Next instruct students to line up the squares next to the pumpkin

and guess the number of squares they think will be equal to the pumpkin's height.

5. Direct students to find their name on the poster in the front of the room. Ask them to write their estimate on the poster.

6. Then have the class measure the pumpkin by counting the squares. Ask them to write in their science journal or portfolio their estimate and how many inch cut out units they used.

Activity 2—Measuring the pumpkin's weight

Materials:

One six pound pumpkin, scale, one 3 pound book

Procedure:

1. Make a poster with this questions and room for students' estimates: "How much do you weigh Mr. Pumpkin?"

2. Instruct students to hold the book to feel how much 3 pounds is.

3. Now have them hold the pumpkin. Does it weigh the same as the book, more or less? Does it weigh as much as two books? How much would that be?

4. Have students record their estimates on the class chart and in their science journals or portfolios.

5. To measure how much the pumpkin weighs put it gently on the scale and have students record the number.

Follow-up:

The teacher holds the scale and reminds the class of when they weighed themselves. Then she weighs the pumpkin and draws the scale on the board. Students read the estimate chart to see who is the closest.

Activity 3—Measuring circumference

Materials:

One six pound pumpkin, Yarn, scissors

Procedure:

1. Make a poster entitled: "What is your circumference Mr. Pumpkin", leave room for students names and estimates.

2. Using yarn and a scissors, instruct students to cut a strip of yarn to the length they think would go around Mr. Pumpkin's waist.
3. Have students measure their yarn estimate (number of inches).
4. Direct students record their estimates in their portfolios.
5. Next have students hang their string from the chart under their name marker.

Follow-up

The teacher then measures the circumference of the pumpkin. Students check the chart to compare accuracy.

Activity 4 Measuring the Number of Seeds Inside the Pumpkin

Materials:

One six pound pumpkin, index cards

Procedures:

1. Make a poster entitled "How many seeds do you have Mr. Pumpkin?" 0–50, 51–100, 101–150, 151–200, 201–250, 251–300, 301–400 leave room for students names and estimates.
2. Have students write their estimate on an index card and tape it in the right column on the chart.
3. The teacher will either cut the pumpkin and remove the seeds for the class to count or enlist a parent to help. The pumpkin can also be sent home with a note to a consenting parent to remove the seeds and return the seeds with their student back to the class.
4. When the pumpkin is cut, seeds removed and washed, the class can count the seeds and compare estimates.

Follow-up

Students may wish to draw the face they'd like to carve on the pumpkin. (Susan Terrell, San Francisco State Credential Student, and SFUSD Special Needs Teacher)

The Central Role of the Teacher

There is general agreement that American schools don't have a choice about changing. Our educational systems need massive, system-wide restructuring and educators must be intimately involved in the effort. At the school site level there must be wider participation by all faculty in developing school policy. Tinkering around the edges just won't get it done. Teachers need time and incentives for becoming involved in taking on new responsibilities, planning, collaborating with peers, and attending inservice programs to keep their skills at a high level. And new teachers need thorough orientation programs and mentors who are successful in the school environment where they are expected to teach.

Many educators are in the process of making the transition from the competitive/stimulus-response-production control model, where the teacher is somewhat of an external operator of the system, to a model of cooperation, where the teacher is a facilitator or academic choreographer. Consciously thinking about and affirming a new set of values means recognizing the importance of diversity, valuing students prior knowledge, and actively engaging student groups in the learning process.

When teachers have assimilated the cooperative learning model as an important part of their teaching repertoire, students with learning disabilities will benefit along with everyone else (Savich and Sterling, 1994/95). In some cases, depending upon the severity of the disability, there will be a different set of teacher responsibilities. Yet, within the context of cooperative teaching and learning, the demands for integrating students with diverse needs are much more easily absorbed because of the nature of the teaching/learning process. As peers take responsibility for some of the teaching power of the teacher can be multiplied (Bateman, 1993).

Collaboration With Colleagues

Inherent in the concept of the cooperative model is the notion of teacher-to-teacher collaboration. The interactive nature of the cooperative model itself enhances the possibility of working closely, collaboratively, with many other teachers and support professionals. In some schools this may mean a revamping of traditional departmental arrangements to facilitate interdisciplinary coordination.

Teachers with strengths in social science topics may find themselves planning and working with teachers whose strengths are in music or science or language. Similarly, classroom teachers may find themselves working jointly, with special education teachers. Co-teaching and cooperation between special education and regular education teachers appear to be important elements of successful inclusion programs. At Millar School in Marshalltown, Iowa, co-teaching is the norm. A recent survey at Millar showed that 80 percent of the students prefer co-taught classes because of greater adult support. A teacher at the school, Sue Merryman, says that "The kids don't even know they're in special ed. anymore" (Willis, 1994).

Making sure that teachers have collaborative opportunities is central to involving them in a larger role such as shaping their profession or changing school organizational patterns. As a team, teachers can plan and teach together to meet the equal access needs of students. They can also jointly plan enrichment activities for those exceptional students who are academically talented—breaking down the barriers known as "regular" education and "special" education. This collaboration between professionals allows the regular classroom teacher to broaden their teaching techniques—and reach a wider range of students.

A Collaborative Model for Students and Teachers

Teaching is the only profession where what you do evaporates almost as soon as it's done. It's just gone. It's fleeting memories.

—Lee Shulman

Collaboration-inclusion models place exceptional students in normal-progress classrooms where a team made up of regular classroom teachers and special educators can better serve all students. The regular classroom teacher structures the physical environment and provides broad educational goals and curricula; the special education teachers adapts methods and materials to meet the needs of low achieving learning disabled and other students with special needs (Baker, Wang and Walberg 1994/95).

The research suggests that a wide range of students in cooperative learning situations (in an inclusive setting) had significantly higher achievement gains in reading and mathematics. Students reported that they felt more satisfied and perceived their work as less difficult. In addition, teachers who worked with colleagues on collaborative projects were very positive about the support system which developed and the benefits to learning. They reported the process added to students and teachers enjoyment of learning and improved the educational experiences of both (Westberg et al., 1993). In many respects, cooperative learning is more than a method; frequently it serves as a catalyst for other changes that are needed in the educational environment.

Collaborative Activities for the Inclusive Classroom

A carefully balanced combination of inclusive instruction, self-monitoring, and active group work helps meet diverse needs. The activities suggested here are designed to encourage critical and creative thinking and provide a collaborative vehicle for active learning across the curriculum content areas.

Activity 1: Oo-bleck: The Magic Compound

Topic Area: Exploring Matter
Is Oo-bleck a solid or a liquid?

Purpose

Students will experiment with a cornstarch and water mixture trying to discover some of the properties of the magic mixture. Students will perform a variety of experiments to answer if the magic compound is a solid or a liquid.

Materials:

1 box of cornstarch
1 cup of water
1 aluminum pie tin
2 paper cups
student worksheets or science/math journal

Background Information:

To make oo-bleck mix 1 box of cornstarch with 1 cup of water. Food coloring can be added if you choose. The magic matter mixture has properties of both a solid and a liquid. Students make a prediction about the mysterious matter mixture, record their observations, and then use data to support that prediction.

Procedure:

1. Review the properties of matter. Ask the question "Today we're going to find out if this magic matter oo-bleck is a solid or a liquid?"
2. Pass out materials and allow students to "play" with the substance for a few minutes and record their observations.

3. Have students conduct the experiments with oo-bleck and record their results on their worksheets or in their science/math journal.
4. Instruct students to analyze their data, answer the question, and support their conclusion.

Data (Observation) Sheet:

1. Color
2. Texture: (What does it look and feel like?)
3. What is its shape?
4. What does it smell like?

Experiment: Do each test. Record your results.

1. The quick finger poke test
   Try to poke your finger into the oo-bleck so that the tip of your finger touches the bottom of the pan. In order to make sure that this is the quick finger poke test, try to touch the bottom of the pan in 1 second. (Like your finger is touching a hot stove!)
2. The slow finger poke test
   Try to poke your finger into the oo-bleck so that the tip of your finger touches the bottom of the pan. In order to make sure that this is the *slow* finger poke test, try to touch the bottom of the pan in 10 seconds. (Like your finger is moving in slow motion.)
3. Shape test
   Put some oo-bleck into one paper cup. Check to see if the oo-bleck takes the shape of the cup or if it stays in its first shape.
4. Pour test
   Try to pour the oo-bleck from one cup to another.
5. Bounce test
   Hold the oo-bleck about 12 inches from the desk. Drop the oo-bleck. Does it bounce?
6. Ball test
   Try to form the oo-bleck into a ball. Check to see if it holds its shape for 5 seconds.
7. Heat test
   Let the teacher know when your group gets to this point. The teacher will do this experiment for your group or your group may wish to try it with teacher supervision. Make a container out of foil. Fashion a bump on one side to clip on a clothes pin. Put a small amount of oo-bleck in the container over a votive candle.

8. Cool test (after heat test)

    Let the oo-bleck cool to room temperature.

9. Shatter test

    The teacher will do this experiment for your group or your group may choose to try it with teacher supervision. Put the oo-bleck in waxed paper on the table see if you can shatter it with the hammer.

Evaluation:

1. How did the oo-bleck act as a solid? as a liquid?
2. What are some reasons that you can think of why this material would act in this way?
3. What are some ways you might use this material?
4. Make a circle graph of the results.
5. Can you think of another test to try?

Activity 2: Create a Static Electric Horse

Objectives:

1. Students will have an opportunity to explore static electricity.
2. No previous knowledge of static electricity is necessary.
3. Students will learn through fun, hands-on experimentation, more about the concepts of static electricity, positive and negative charges.

Materials:

1 inflated balloon for each child
scissors
tag board horse patterns
construction paper
crayons and/or markers

Procedure:

1. Short introduction focusing on the horses and a mystery question: "Do you think you could make a paper horse move without touching it?" (No mention yet of static electricity concepts)
2. Teacher describes how to construct the horse:
    a. Fold the paper in half and trace the horse pattern on one side of paper. (Trace forms are passed out.)
    b. Hold both halves of paper together, cut out pattern—making

sure to leave the horse joined together at the top of its head and tail.

    c. Decorate (color) both sides of the horse.

3. Teacher describes how to "electrify" the paper horse:
    a. place horse on smooth surface.
    b. rub a balloon over your hair a few times
    c. hold balloon in front of the horse.

4. The teacher passes out the balloons.

5. Next the teacher instructs the students to get in groups of four or five sitting around the table.

6. Now students "electrify" their horses and have short races across tables.

7. After the races have ended have a class discussion on what happened between balloon and horse.

8. Ask students to describe their views. Then add the scientific explanation describing static electricity:

[The outer layer of electrons from atoms on the hair are rubbed off and cling to the atoms of the balloon, producing static electricity. When you hold the positively charged balloon close to the uncharged (negatively charged) horse, there is a strong attraction between them—and the horse races toward the balloon.]

Evaluation:

1. Instruct students to write in their journal about their experiment.
2. Some possible assignments:
    - In your own words explain the connection between the horse, the balloon, and static electricity.
    - Write a short story about your horse in the race.
    Illustrate the "Electric" horse race, provide commentary.
    - Have the group write an article for the school newspaper describing your experiment.

Postassessment:

Assessment is based on observing the children and from reading their written/illustrated journals about their experiments.

Activity 3: Discover Math Statistics

Objective:

Students will discover and use the research skills of collecting, recording and interpreting data. This data will be used in a class bar graph that the students create for their classroom.

Materials:

example of a picture graph
data collection sheets
chart paper, markers, and tape
clipboards
a picture of each kind of snake to be represented on the graph.

Procedure:

1. Introduction of the activity
2. Show the example picture graph.
3. Discuss the graph until the students are able to interpret it and understand how it is used. Check for this understanding by asking the students questions about the graph such as "more, less, how many and the least." Students will gain practice in making comparative and quantitative statements in response to the questions.
4. Pass out the data collection sheets and explain that it will be used to collect information so that it can be shown on the graph. Model with another student how to ask the question and record the answer on the data collection sheet.
5. For a few minutes have students try collecting sample data on their own by asking questions and recording the answer.
6. Next have students communicate this process to the teacher. As the students tell the teacher the process, the teacher writes the steps on chart paper to be displayed for the students to refer to.

Exploring:

1. Students in small groups now practice asking questions and recording the answers. This will involve speaking, reading, and listening to other members in the group.
2. For students who are finished have them write on the back of their data sheets two sentences about the data they collected using the mathematical language modeled for them during the introduction.
3. When all students are finished, discuss the data their group collected. Ask questions that facilitated the formation of their sentences using mathematical language that makes comparisons and communicates information about quantity.
4. Teachers should check for understanding during the exploring

stage by observing the strategies and procedures the students are using to collect and record their data.

Intervention:

1. If students seem confused, are showing frustration, or are not on task, the teacher should:
   a. restate how to collect data and record the information.
   b. remind students to look at the chart paper that lists the steps of how to ask and record information on the data collection sheets.
   c. have a student tell the group how to ask and record.
2. If students are not getting along:
   a. help them to find the students they still need to ask and collect data from.
   b. if needed, help the students communicate by mediating the interviewing process using the steps on the chart paper.

Summarizing:

1. On chart paper, record each students predictions of which snake they think will be the most popular among their classmates, friends, and family and why they think that.
2. Ask the students what they did to collect their data. Discuss with them what worked and what did not.
3. Ask the students how they knew who they had already asked and who they still needed to ask. Discuss the different ways in which students dealt with this issue.

Closure:

1. To ensure reliability students will check their survey data. Give students new data sheets with the names of the people they should ask (every student will have different names so that each person gets asked only once) and 2–4 blanks for names they may want to add (family and friends not in their class).
2. Tell the students to interview the people on their lists and that they have two days to do it. They can do it during recess, lunch, after school, or during free time in the classroom.
3. Explain that the class will make a graph with the information they have collected on their data sheets, so it is important that they ask all of the people on their list so that we have enough information to graph.

Activity 4: Beginning Measurement

(This is lesson 2 of a unit on snakes and measurement.)

Objectives:

1. Students will learn that a ruler is one foot or 12 inches long.
2. Groups will use rulers and string to measure out the lengths of different snakes.
3. Students will sit at a table with their group while the teacher is explaining.
4. After the teacher has explained about measurement using a ruler, students will get up to do the actual measuring.

This lesson relates to a previous lesson in which the students looked in books to find the actual lengths of snakes of their choosing. Before they looked up the actual lengths, they guessed how long they thought the snakes were using string. Snakes included the boa constrictor (18 feet), king cobra (18 feet), anaconda (30 feet), rattlesnake (8 feet), and python (30 feet).

Materials:

string (two different colors), books on snakes, scissors, masking tape, felt tip pens, rulers, chart paper or chalkboard, chart paper with lengths of snakes (actual and guessed)

Procedure:

1. Discuss rulers with the class. Have students review by showing that a ruler is one foot long and that one foot has 12 inches in it.
2. Have students get into pairs. Remind them of the previous lesson they did on snakes, guessed and actual. Explain that in pairs they will be measuring string to match the length of the snakes. Assign each pair two snakes to measure out using the string.
3. With a student volunteer the teacher should explain and model how one student should stand holding one end of the yarn to the floor while the other student holds the yarn and pulls it to the length they think matches the actual length of the snake they have chosen to measure.
4. Instruct both students in the pair to lay down the rulers next to the string and label it with the length of the snake and the kind of snake written on the masking tape. The pair does this again for the other snake they have been assigned.

5. Dismiss pairs of students to get materials they need (scissors, string, rulers, tape, and a pen) and begin measuring.

6. If the pair finishes measuring and labeling each of their snakes actual lengths, tell them to begin measuring the guessed lengths from the previous lesson.

Guided Practice:

Teacher walks around observing the pairs working together. He/She should provide help when needed and encourages the students as they measure.

Closure:

The teacher should ask students if they liked doing the activity, what they liked or did not like, to receive feedback about teaching methods. Have students share something they feel they learned from the activity.

Independent Practice:

This can be arranged for by organizing new activities for the students to choose from. For example, students can use the string of the actual length of an anaconda to see how many times an anaconda could wrap itself around a student's waist. Another example is comparing the of the estimated length to the string of actual length and then calculating the difference. Students could record their findings in a journal in order to incorporate writing. Journals are also a good method of assessment.

Activity 5: Rain Forest Interdependence

This inclusive science activity is designed for all students, but it is an ideal lesson to use for Limited English Proficient (LEP) learners. It encourages the students to come together and establish themselves as groups; speaking and writing is not mandatory! The only adaptation required in this activity is a simple color coding of the identifying cards which will enable the student to visualize what other students (plants and animals) he or she is connected with, rather than just reading the card. Additional adaptations might include: pictures of the plant or animal on the cards that show the actual relationship, or more color coding, by matching the color of the yarn to the color of the cards. The student will be able to see his or her group members by the colors, pictures, and yarns, and understand the interrelationships, without having to read the card.

This is a valuable lesson; not only for LEP students, but also for students with other language deficiencies and all students within the classroom. The exceptional student will not be singled out, and all the students can benefit by the simple color classification. The color coding and pictures serve to reinforce the written relationships, and the students will receive graphic, physical examples of the purpose of the activity—to show interdependence. The activity will also help increase social inter-action within the classroom, and might help break down the barrier caused by the difference in language.

The evaluation and conclusion to this activity will be for students to discuss and then write their reaction to, or interpretation of, what occurred when the connections were broken. This will be an opportunity for the student and his or her classmates to artistically describe the lesson.

Purpose:

This activity will introduce the concept of interdependence to the students. All the plant and animal life will be connected and the students will be able to see and understand how everything in the rain forest depends on each other for survival.

Objectives:

1. Students will follow directions, participate in all activities and work cooperatively with their classmates.
2. Students will discuss, as a class their feelings about this activity.
3. Students will draw a picture of the interdependence of the rain forest.
4. Students will utilize some of the information that has been gained in the previous lessons.

Materials:

Plant and animal cards pasted on 3 x 5 index cards
Pictures of rain forest plants and animals
Yarn (3 yard pieces) for 3 pieces per student
Paper and other art supplies

Preparation:

1. Teachers, Aides or student helpers will cut and paste pictures of plant and animal cards onto 3x5 cards for each student.

2. Pictures or books of rain forest plants and animals should be available for reference if needed.
3. Move the desks to the edges of the classroom, so that the students can move around.

Procedure:

1. Distribute one card to each student.
2. Pass out several long pieces of yarn to each student.
3. Each student will read their card and then find the person or people who are related to theirs.
4. When a match or relationship is made, the students then attach themselves with a long piece of yarn (tie around wrist). More than two students can be connected. Example: Kapok tree will be attached to parrots, insects, etc.
5. If a student wants more information, direct them to the pictures and other reference material.

Evaluation:

1. The class will discuss, while still connected, how does it feel to depend on the other organisms?
2. Instruct students to guess what part of the rain forest their plant or animal lives in: canopy, under story, or forest floor?
3. Have students reflect on these questions:
   • What plant or animal did you represent?
   • What do you depend on for food or shelter?
   • How does it feel to have so many connections?
   • What did you learn from this activity?
   • Would you like to live in a rain forest? Why?
4. The teacher may then cut several pieces of the yarn that are attached to the Kopok tree and ask the class:
   • What would happen if the Kopok tree is cut down?
   • What other animals would be affected?
5. After discussing the effects of destroying part of a delicate ecosystem students may generate other ideas.

The Future of Collaborative-Inclusive Learning

The academic, motivational and social aspects of cooperative learning become more powerful with practice. As students recognize that with some of their work it's *sink or swim together* and they become quite interdependent. By balancing academic challenge with a supportive social group, everyone can do a better job with difficult or stressful assignments. As cooperative teams develop strong personal relationships, individual accountability, and a shared sense of purpose, they also become better at contributing to larger learning communities. In the inclusive classroom, the popularity of cooperative learning comes from how its different styles all seem to lend assistance to teachers striving to reach a wider range of students more effectively.

Inclusion brings students to the edge of many possibilities, sharing visions and enhancing individual learning. By actively engaging special needs students in the collaborative process, teachers have been able to integrate the teaching of social skills and critical thinking with academic content. With the support of teachers and a solid research base, cooperative learning is becoming widely used in the inclusive classroom. The result is destined to make a real difference in U.S. education.

Making a space for diversity in the presence of others involves caring and community. Going beyond labels, we need a commitment to tap the multiple realities of human experience.... such an education for freedom takes into account our political and social realities as well as the human condition itself.

—Maxine Greene

REFERENCES

Baker, E. T. (1994). Meta-Analytic evidence for non-inclusive educational practices: Does educational research support current practice for special needs students? Doctoral Dissertation, Temple University, Philadelphia.

Baker, E. T., Wang, M. C., & Walberg, H. J. (December 1994/January 1995). The effects of inclusion of learning. *Educational Leadership* 52: 33–35.

Barry, A. L. (Dec. 1994/Jan. 1995). Easing into inclusion classrooms. *Educational Leadership.* 52:4–6.

Bateman, B. (1993). Learning disabilities: The changing landscape. *Journal of Learning Disabilities.* 25(1)29–36.

Cummings, R. W. & Cleborne, D. M. (1985). *Parenting the learning disabled: A realistic approach.* Springfield, IL: Charles C Thomas.

Flynn, G. & Kowalczyk-McPhee, B. A School System in Transition. (unpublished manuscript) (no date).

Fuchs, D. & Fuchs, L. S. (Dec. 1994/Jan. 1995). Sometimes separate is better. *Educational Leadership* 52:22–26.

Janke, R. (1978). The teams-games-tournament (TGT) method and the behavioral adjustment and academic achievement of emotionally impaired adolescents.

Paper presented at annual convention of American Educational Research Association, Toronto.

Making the transition: A curriculum and materials for educators who work with beginning teachers. (1995). PAC–TE/PSEA. 38.

McIntosh, R., Vaughn, S., Schumm, J., Hagger, D., & Lee, O. (1993). Observations of students with learning disabilities in general education classrooms. *Exceptional Children*, 60(3): 249–261.

O'Neil, J. (Dec. 1994/Jan. 1995). A call for placement options. *Educational Leadership*. 50(2) 7–11.

Renzulli, J. S. (December 1994/January 1995). Teachers as talent scouts *Educational Leadership*. 52: 75–81.

Savitch, J., & Sterling, (Dec. 1994/Jan. 1995). Paving a path through untracked territory. *Educational Leadership*. 52: 18–21.

Schlesinger, A. M., Jr. (1992). *The disuniting of America.* New York: Norton.

Slavin, R. E. (1977). A student team approach to teaching adolescents with special emotional and behavioral needs. *Psychology in the Schools*, 14(1), 77–84.

Slavin, R. E., Madden, N.E. & Leavy, M. B. (1984). Effects of team assisted individualization on the mathematics achievement of academically handicapped and non handicapped students. *Journal of Educational Psychology*, 76, 813–19.

Stafford, R. (1978). Education for the handicapped: A senator's perspective. *Vermont Law Review*. 3:71–76.

Stainback, W. & Stainback, S. (1990). *Support networks for inclusive schooling.* Baltimore: Brooks.

Sternberg, L., Taylor, R. & Schilt, J. (1976). *So you're not a special educator.* Springfield, IL, Charles C Thomas.

Tashie, C., Shapiro-Barnard, S., Schuh, M., Jorgensen, C., Dillon, A., Dixon, B., & Nisbet, J. (1993). *From special to regular: From ordinary to extraordinary.* NH: Institute on Disability/UAP, University of New Hampshire.

Wang, M. C. & Birch, J. W. (Eds.) (1987). *Handbook of Special Education Research and Practice*, Vol. 1, London: Pergamon.

Westberg, K., Archambault, S., Dobyns, & Salvin, T. (1993). The classroom practices observational study. *Journal for the Education of the Gifted.* 16(2): 120–146.

Willis, S. (October, 1994). Making schools more inclusive. *Association for Supervision and Curriculum Development Curriculum Update.*

Special thanks to the Research Assistants:

Melissa Jack	Andy Mahoney
Kathleen Weber	Mary Fisher
Jen Potts	Sara Donohue
Anthony Grisillo	Donna Hohn
Sue McGuire	Karen Senior
Joyce Gamble	

Chapter 7

EDUCATIONAL MEDIA AND
COOPERATIVE GROUPS:

COLLABORATING WITH TECHNOLOGY
AND EACH OTHER

Education and its technological tools are ... a regulation of the process of coming to share in the social consciousness.

— John Dewey

In this chapter, we examine how the cooperative interaction possibilities of educational technology can overcome the solitary nature of electronic media. We recognize the fact that even the most intelligent use of television, computers, multimedia, and the information highway will not reform American education or improve instruction on its own. The key is good software and how the content of technology-assisted lessons connect to classroom interaction and the fluid nature of today's knowledge.

The role of educational technology is changing how subjects are taught by changing the instructional environment and providing opportunities for students to create new knowledge for themselves. With the *Internet*, for example, it is easy for students to share ideas with people around the world and it is hard for authorities to stop them. At its best, networking technologies can serve as a vehicle for giving students access to data, collaborative simulations, and visual models of fundamental processes. At its worst, it wastes a great deal of time and gives students access to the adult concerns.

We now live in a multimedia age where the technologies of computers, television, telephone, cable, and satellite communications are converging. New communications tools are transforming our social and educational environments before we have a chance to think carefully about *why* we want to use the technology. The impact is global. The sudden worldwide explosion of interest in the *Internet*, for example, has some countries worried about the dominance of the English language and American popular culture in cyberspace.

The digital technology at the heart of computers is moving into television sets, VCR's, and systems that link the telephone to the television. Digital devices manipulate data as electronic pulses represented by the 1's and 0's of computer code. Increasingly they are converting text, pictures, sound, and video into a form that can be recorded, played back, transmitted, and received. Like everyone else, teachers are consumers of technology and they need to be able to judge critically the quality and

usefulness of the electronic possibilities springing up around them. This requires continuing high-tech inservice training and attention to the education of new teachers.

Students and teachers need minimal competencies in other to use classroom computers as tools. In one technologically savvy sixth-grade classroom we visited, small groups and pairs of students were involved with software evaluation, spreadsheet application with *Claris Works,* e-mail merge letters, interactive writing with *Prompt Writer,* making posters with Broderbund's *Printshop,* multimedia-based reports with *Hyperstudio,* and navigating the Internet with *Mosaic.* The homework question of the week: "What is the role of media in our society?" Not many of us could juggle all this and integrate the result into the curriculum. This chapter should help teachers less familiar with technology consider some of the general issues and make the appropriate match between the problems they face and potential technological support.

Shaping Technology Before It Shapes Us

Computers are the most powerful recent example of a technology being promoted in our schools before teachers have a clear understanding of what might be accomplished with it. Since the early 1980s, the schools have been caught between aggressive marketing hype and promising possibilities. Inservice training and software evaluation were neglected— even though the key to success turned out to be the quality of the software and the way teachers integrated technological tools into their classrooms.

The computer can be used as a power tool for visually exploring models, experiencing simulations, and graphically solving problems. But what are some technological negatives that we should keep in mind as we read the chapter? To begin with, people often uncritically accept the parameters of computer programs—even when the simulated environment is very wrong. Multimedia compounds the problem of uncritical consumers. Second, technology can have a distancing and solipsistic effect on youngsters who grow up with television, computers, and video games. Sven Berkerts goes so far as to suggest that as electronic media pushes print aside, we are experiencing "the progressive atrophy of all that defines us as creatures of the spirit." In "The Gutenberg Elegies," he suggests that we are on the verge of losing more than we know. For example, it may be easier to attend to multimedia than it is to read print, but simply being motivated by a CD–ROM program doesn't mean that students are learning something important.

In today's media-fed society, images can engage public attention with small controversies and trivial banalities. This same media-connected world can also provide students with the possibility for controlling and charting the course of their education and their culture. Electronic information can be gathered and even constructed by anyone with a computer, a modem, or a camcorder. The best of the new technology can move you out of a passive realm and into cooperative interaction with others.

New ways of relating to electronic information requires a break from habit. Thousands of years ago it was the written word. Next, it was the printing press. Today, it is multimedia computing — the coming together of computers, video, sound, and animation, and telecommunications. Computers are both evolutionary and revolutionary. At their best, they help you do important things better, while conjuring up new possibilities for critical thinking, collaboration, and creativity. In the struggle for school reform, we need all the help we can get. Multimedia computing adds a new dimension to learning by communicating meaning with vivid motion video, animation, and quality sound. Some multimedia "workstations" even have built-in video cameras so that users can hold video teleconferences with people in distant locations and construct their own video compositions.

By motivating students through the excitement of discovery, technology can assist the imaginative spirit of inquiry and make lessons sparkle. For example, if you want to use multimedia to get the latest news about geography, technology, or anything else, there is a recently developed news service called "What on Earth." It delivers news stories from around the world in a program that includes video, text, sound, graphics, and digital photographs. It also combines elements of interactivity, multimedia, and distance learning. The result is that children can click a mouse and hear the correct pronunciation of foreign words, get explanations, and play educational games that help them understand the content. *What on Earth* costs about as much as a newspaper subscription and is a joint venture of Reuters New-Media and the giant Telecommunications cable TV company. They supply a gadget to translate the cable signals into a language the computer can read. Back issues are available on CD–ROM.

There is a major expansion of the kinds of services and courses that are being provided through distance learning, satellites, and networks like the Internet. Some of these efforts supplement classroom activities and others are aimed at others who are seeking alternatives to classroom attendance. New systems are much less passive and allow distant teachers to illustrate course material with sound, high-quality graphics, animation, full-motion video, and interactive problem solving and simulation.

Technological Horizons

As technological and human horizons change, a sort of flexible drive and intent is required for innovation and progress. Computers and their media associates can add power and help us kick against educational boundaries. The vivid images of multimedia can stimulate students as they move quickly through mountains of information, pulling out important concepts and following topics of interest. The process changes students' relationship to information by allowing them to personally shift the relationship of elements across time and space. By using computer platforms with new multimedia possibilities, learners can follow a topic between subjects, reading something here, and viewing a video segment there. This changes how computers are used and how information is structured, giving students more control of the technology and more responsibility for their own learning.

Training the mind to notice things goes a long way towards making unpredictable advances happen. Rx for thinking in the future: following curiosity, leaving doors open, using technological tools, and making room for good luck to happen. Keeping up with advances in the field helps because each new finding can open up fresh questions and possibilities. It is often difficult to detect the subtle happenstance and how we make room in our own lives for positive accidents to happen. To break the habits that get in the way of creative thinking and collaborative change means continuously learning and being open to new experiences. Anything that changes perspective, from travel, to technology, to human teaching, can help generate new ideas. The motivation is also there because it is usually more fun to do things where the unexpected may turn up than sticking with the easily predictable. Playfulness and experimentation can often open up to creative possibilities, increasing the capacity to fashion ideas or products in a novel fashion. Creatively playing with various ideas, some of which may seem silly at the time, may result in getting lucky with one or two of them.

The yeast of knowledge, openness, and enterprise raises the need for a multiplicity of learning media and technological tools. Educators need time, space, support, and professional development to make all the changes required. In spite of the dangers, it is our belief that teachers can use technology to support and strengthen the best in student learning. Just as schools can teach students to recognize how technology can undermine social values, human goals, and national intention, they can also harness these powerful technological tools so that they might strengthen and support the best in human endeavors.

Using Multimedia Technology to Open Doors for Learning

To be valuable, educational technology must contribute to the improvement of education. Technological tools should be designed to help open doors to reality and provide a setting for reflection—making important points that might otherwise go unnoticed. For example, computers can use mathematical rules to simulate and synthesize life-like behavior of cells growing and dividing. The CD–ROM storage medium used for such programs has expanded to the point where there are now many thousands of titles for home and school use. Like computer programs in general, there are several boring or irrelevant multimedia titles for every informative science simulation or museum tour.

The term "multimedia" usually refers to computer programs that use the CD–ROM medium to build-in large amounts of text, excellent graphics, video clips, and stereo sound. Print, sound, and images can all be stored on small silvery disks. Most desktop PC's now come with built-in CD–ROM drives—for those that do not, you can plug an external drive into the back of your computer. The multimedia possibilities are a big reason why we now have as many computers being sold to homes as to businesses.

Video and CD–ROM disks have room for many video clips, graphics, and text. Most importantly, they have a random access feature that allows the user to quickly move to the part of the program that they wish to view. For example, it is possible to set the computer to the section of the video you wish to view, play that portion, and bring up print describing the imagery. If you want to play it again, or switch to another part of the disk, you can do it with a few strokes on the computer keyboard.

Progress in school reform will be limited if teachers are forced to use traditional instructional delivery tools or models. "Ask and tell," "tell and ask," are limited patterns—with or without the computer. The interactive design of new multimedia programs are profiting from findings regarding cognitive development, and collaborative learning. Computer-based activities can have problem-centered structures that wrap learning experiences around problems in new ways. You can visually enter the body as a blood cell or explore another planet. As budding experimenters students can use computer tools to visually explore empirical claims and examine all kinds of evidence that allows them to support or critique important findings.

As new technologies and related products start to fulfill their promise, students will become active participants in knowledge construction across a variety of disciplines—providing a technological gateway to learning in the twenty-first century. As state-of-the-art pedagogy is connected with state-of-the-art technological tools, it will change the way knowledge is constructed, stored, and learned.

Sampling of Multimedia: CD-ROM and Videodisc Packages

Multimedia Dictionary for Children
The Macmillan Dictionary for Children—Multimedia Edition
CD–ROM version
Maxwell Electronic Publishing, Cambridge, MA.

Interactive NOVA: The Race to Save the Planet
Animal Pathfinders
Miracle of Life

Scholastic Software, New York, NY

Computer Visions: The Electronic Instructional Media System for Teaching Computer Literacy
South Western Publishing Company
(800) 824-5179

Science 2000 Thematic approach to science study
Decision Dev. corp.
San Ramon, CA
(800) 800-4332

The Great Solar System Rescue (simulation)
Tom Synder Productions
Cambridge, MA
(800) 342-0236
Hardware needed: Laserdisc player and monitor, 2MB Mac Interface cable

Multimedia Grolier Encyclopedia
Now available on CD–ROM
Grolier Electronic Publishing Inc., 95 Madison Ave., 11th floor, New York, NY 10016.

National Air and Space Museum Archives (CAV)
The three videodiscs contain still photographs of rockets, airplanes, and important events and people in the history of aviation and space exploration. Smithsonian Institution, Customer Services, P.O. Box 4866, Harriden Station, Baltimore, MD 21211

National Gallery of Art (CAV).
One side of the disc contains a narrative history of the National Gallery of Art collection, the other includes a tour of the gallery plus 1,645 color slides of art work in chronological order. A print index orders the frames by author and title. Videodisc Publishing Inc., 381 Park Ave. S., Suite 1601, New York, NY 10016

Science Discovery: Image and Activity Bank
This videodisc has thousands of images, film clips, and graphics for elementary school students (K–6). It is from the same company that brought out "Bio Sci II Elementary" and they supply a teacher's guide and lessons. Available from: Videodiscovery, 1700 Westlake Ave. N. Suite 600, Seattle, WA 98109 (1-800-548-3472)

PREHISTORIA is a multimedia program, for a Macintosh with CD–ROM drive, that allows students to do things like become a "Time Tracker" and interact with animals that lived in many eras. It works best at grades 5 through 7. The museum part of the program includes movie clips, screen sequences, maps, and diagrams. A science teacher could use this program to construct a science environment—with real museum visits and laboratory work. Available from: Grolier Electronic Publishing, Inc., Sherman Tpke., Danbury, CT 06816

Studies confirm that the power and permanency of what we learn is greater when visually-based mental models are used in conjunction with the printed word. Inferences drawn from visual models can lead to more profound thinking (Dorr, 1986). Children learn to rely on their perceptual (visual) learning even if their conceptual knowledge contradicts it. Even when it runs contrary to verbal explanations or personal experience, the video screen can provide potent visual experiences that push viewers to accept what is presented.

Extracting Meaning from Television

The advocacy group *Children Now* released an analysis of 1995 programming that found that in the virtual (unreal) world of television, children rarely have real-world problems. They usually live carefree lives of affluence, have obscure family ties, and have neither pleasant learning experiences nor homework. If school is shown at all, it is as a backdrop. In addition, physical aggression usually pays off better than showing affection or meeting responsibility. Can we do anything about the adults who produce this stuff?

One way to help students become more intelligent video consumers is to learn to "read" and "write" with the beast itself. Children can become adept at extracting meaning from the conventions of video production—zooms, pans, tilts, fade outs and flashbacks. But distinguishing fact from fiction is more difficult. What we perceive falls within the framework of concept formation. Like print, visual imagery from a TV screen can be mentally processed at different levels of complexity. The ability to understand what's being presented is becoming more central to learning and to our society.

Piaget showed how certain notions of time, space or morality are beyond children's grasp before certain developmental levels are reached.

Research on TV viewing suggests that it is not vocabulary limitations alone which impede children from grasping some adult content (Dede, 1985). Children lack fundamental integrative capacities to "chunk" (group) certain kinds of information into meaningful groups which are obvious to adults. Thus children who need help in developing strategies for tuning out irrelevancies may be especially vulnerable to unwanted adult content (McKibben, 1992).

Most of the time children construct meaning for television content without even thinking about it. They attend to stimuli, and extract meaning from subtle messages. The underlying message of most TV programming is that viewers should consume as much as possible while changing as little as possible. How well television content is understood varies according to similarities between viewers and content, viewers' needs and interests, and the age of the viewer. Sorting through the themes of mental conservatism and material addition requires carefully developed thinking skills.

Meaning is constructed by each participant at several levels. For better or worse, broadcast television has provided us with a common culture. When viewers share a common culture they must also share a similar set of tools and processes for interpreting these signals (construction of meaning, information processing, interpretation, and evaluation). Generalized "world knowledge" is important in learning how to process and use televised information.

The greater the experiential background, the greater the understanding. The ability to make subtle judgments about video imagery is a developmental outcome that proceeds from stage to stage with an accumulation of viewing experience. Thus different age groups reveal varying levels of comprehension when they view TV programs. Eight year olds, for example, retain a relatively small proportion of central actions, events, or settings of typical programs. Even when they retain explicit content, younger children fail to infer interscene connections. Improvement in comprehension occurs with maturity. But substantial understanding of the medium requires training for parents, teachers, and children. Training for parents may involve how to interact with their children, how to critique, analyze, and discuss what is viewed, and how to model good viewing habits.

Lessons structured around the TV medium can assist students in becoming intelligent video consumers *and* help them evaluate the multimedia medium that relies so heavily on video clips. Many public television stations are now offering special workshops for teachers in how to use educational television programs effectively in their classrooms. Some ideas include: selecting short segments from programs, designing carefully crafted questions, after viewing getting students to talk together about what they watched, turning the sound off, replaying the tape again, encouraging students to come up with 2 or 3 things they found out from the short clip, and sharing that information with others. Have students work together to look for and identify propaganda techniques, act them out, make up some skits (ads) of their own. Evaluation of television viewing is also an important comprehension skill. Encourage student groups to analyze and rate what they view.

What's understood while viewing depends on the interplay of images and social conditions. Physical stimuli, human psychology, and information processing schemes taught by his culture helps each person make sense of the world. In this respect, reacting to TV and its content is no different from any other experience in life. The cathode ray tube (or video screen) can be as valid a source of information as what is learned on the street or in school. It is just as possible to internalize ideas from electronic visual imagery as it is from conversation, print, or personal experience.

Cooperative reflective thought and imaginative active play are an important part of the growth process of a child. Contrary to popular belief, children must do some active work to watch TV, make sense of its contents, and utilize its message. Evaluative activities include judging and assigning worth, assessing what is admired, and deciding what positive and negative impressions should be assigned to the content. In this sense, children are active participants in determining television's meaning.

Traditional television is vulnerable to more invigorating interactive electronic competition. Children will often pass up passive television viewing, for example, when they can use a computer or game controller together with friends to interact with the medium. Many children, for example, are already familiar with *Where in the World Is Carmen Sandiego.* They learn geography by electronically rushing around the world— trying to catch up with Carmen. When the computer-controlled version goes up against the linear PBS television program of the same name, the interactive version usually wins hands down because of higher levels of personal involvement. Like many other titles, Broderland software has brought several versions of this program out on CD–ROM. For example: *Where in the World Is Carmen Sandiego, Junior Detective Edition,* is intended for ages 5 to 8 and costs around $50. Carmen is a stylish crook, with henchmen like Manny Mistakes, whom the player chases around the world. The player can only catch them by matching up geographical clues that are scattered along the way. *Carmen Sandiego* programs for upper grade students follow a similar pattern. Another example of a detective program (for children 8 and older) is *Eagle Eye Mysteries in London,* by Electronic Arts software for about $40. This CD–ROM title helps students develop deductive reasoning skills by mixing in clues from the poetry of T.S. Eliot and the British Museum. There are encyclopedia type summaries of real castles and cultural icons (in full motion video) often pop onto the screen for a chat.

People learn best if they take a collaborative active role in their own learning. Relying upon a host of cognitive inputs, individuals select and interpret the raw data of experience to produce a personal understanding of reality. Ultimately, it is up to each person to determine what he or she pays attention to and what he or she ignores. How elements are organized — and how meaning is attached to any concept — is an individual act that can be influenced by a number of external agents. The thinking that must be done to make sense of perceptions ultimately transforms the "real world" into different things for different people.

Developing Thinking Tools for Assessing Media Messages

Parents, teachers, and other adults can significantly affect what information children gather from television. A student's social, cultural, educational, and family context influences what messages they take from the medium, how they use television, and how "literate" they are as viewers (Bryant & Anderson, 1983). To become critical viewers who literate about media messages students should be able to:

- understand the grammar and syntax of television, as expressed in different program forms.
- analyze the pervasive appeals of television advertising.
- compare similar presentations or those with similar presentations or those with similar purposes in different media.
- identify values in language, characterization, conflict resolution, and sound/visual images.
- identify elements in dramatic presentations associated with the concepts of plot, storyline, theme, characterizations, motivation, program formats, and production values.

- utilize strategies for the management of duration of viewing and program choices.

Parents and teachers can engage in activities that affect children's interest in televised messages—and help them learn how to process video information. Good modeling behavior, explaining content, and showing how the program content relates to student interests are just a few examples of how adults can provide positive viewing motivation. Adults can also exhibit an informed response, point out misleading TV messages, and take care not to build curiosity for undesirable programs.

The viewing habits of families play a large role in determining how children approach the medium. The length of time parents spend watching television, the kinds of programs viewed, and the reactions of parents and siblings toward programming messages all have a large influence on the child (McLeod et al., 1982). If adults read and there are books, magazines, and newspapers around the house, children will pay more attention to print. Influencing what children view on television may be done with: rules about what may or may not be watched, interactions with children during viewing, and the modeling of certain content choices.

Whether co-viewing or not, the viewing choices of adults in a child's life (parents, teachers, etc.) set an example for children. If parents are heavy watchers of public television or news programming, then children are more likely to respond favorably to this content. Influencing the settings in which children watch TV is also a factor. Turning the TV set off during meals, for example, sets a family priority. Families can also seek a more open and equal approach to choosing television shows—interacting before, during, and after the program. Parents can also organize formal or informal activities outside the house that provide alternatives to TV viewing.

It is increasingly clear that the education of children is a shared responsibility. Parents need connections with what's going on in the schools. But it is *teachers* who will be the ones called upon to make the educational connections entwining varieties of print and visual media with language arts, reading, mathematics, science or art. Teachers can even use the TV medium as they encourage students to become intelligent video consumers.

Activities That Can Help Students Make Sense of Television

1. *Help Students Critically View What They Watch.*
   Decoding visual stimuli and learning from visual images requires practice. Seeing an image does not automatically ensure learning from it. Students must be guided in decoding and looking critically at what they view. One technique is to have students "read" the image on various levels. Students identify individual elements and classify them into various categories, then relate the whole to their own experiences, drawing inferences and creating new conceptualizations from what they have learned. Encourage students to look at the plot and story line. Identify the message of the program. What symbols (camera techniques, motion sequences, setting, lighting, etc.) does the program use to make its message? What does the director do to arouse audience emotion and participation in the story? What metaphors and symbols are used?

2. *Compare Print and Video Messages.*
   Have students follow a current event on the evening news (taped segment on a VCR) and compare it to the same event written in a major newspaper. A question for discussion may be: How do the major newspapers influence what appears on a national network's news program? Encourage comparisons between both media. What are the strengths and weaknesses of each? What are the reasons behind the different presentations of a similar event?

3. *Evaluate TV Viewing Habits.*
   After compiling a list of their favorite TV programs, assign students to analyze the reasons for their popularity; examine the messages these programs send to their audience. Do the same for favorite books, magazines, newspapers, films, songs, and computer programs. Look for similarities and differences between the media.

4. *Use Video for Instruction.*
   Using a VCR, make frequent use of 3-to-5 minute video segments to illustrate different points. This is often better than showing long videotapes or a film on a video cassette. For example, teachers can show a five-minute segment from a video cassette movie to illustrate how one scene uses foreshadowing or music to set up the next scene.

5. *Analyze Advertising Messages.*
   Advertisements provide a wealth of examples for illustrating media messages. Move students progressively from advertisements in print

to television commercials, allowing them to locate features (such as packaging, color and images) that influence consumers and often distort reality. Analyze and discuss commercials in children's TV programs: How many minutes of TV ads appear in an hour? How have toy manufacturers exploited the medium? What is the broadcaster's role? What should be done about it?

6. *Create a Scrapbook of Media Clippings*
   Have students keep a scrapbook of newspaper and magazine clippings on television and its associates. Paraphrase, draw a picture, or map out a personal interpretation of the articles. Share these with other students.

7. *Create New Images From the Old.*
   Have students take rather mundane photographs and multiply the image, or combine it with others, in a way that makes them interesting. Through the act of observing, it is possible to build a common body of experiences, humor, feeling, and originality. And through collaborative efforts, students can expand on ideas and make the group process come alive.

8. *Use Debate for Critical Thought.*
   Debating is a communications model that can serve as a lively facilitator for concept building. Taking a current and relevant topic, and formally debating it, can serve as an important speech/language extension. For example, the class can discuss how mass media can support political tyranny, public conformity, or the technological enslavement of society. The discussion can serve as a blend of social studies, science, and humanities study. You can also build the process of writing or videotaping from the brainstorming stage to the final production.

9. *Include Newspapers, Magazines, Literature, and Electro-Media (like brief television news clips) in Daily Class Activities*
   Use of the media and literature can enliven classroom discussion of current conflicts and dilemmas. Neither squeamish nor politically correct, these sources of information provide readers with something to think and talk about. And they can present the key conflicts and dilemmas of our time in a way that allows students to enter the discussion. These stimulating sources of information can help the teacher structure lessons that go beyond facts to stimulate reading, critical thinking, and thoughtful discussion. By not concealing adult disagreements everyone can take responsibility for promoting under-

standing—engaging others in moral reflection and providing a coherence and focus that helps turn controversies into advantageous educational experiences.

New Media Symbol Systems Change the Character of Learning

Print and the video screen (or film) take different approaches to communicating meaning. Print relies upon the reader's ability to interpret abstract symbols. The video screen is more direct. In both cases, thinking and learning are based on internal symbolic representations and the mental interpretation of those symbols. The impact of either medium can be amplified by the other.

We live in a complex society dependent on rapid communication and information access. Lifelike visual symbol systems are comprised, in part, of story structure, pace, sound track, color, and conceptual difficulty. Computers, distant databases, television, and their associates are rapidly becoming our dominant cultural tools for selecting, gathering, storing, and conveying knowledge in representational forms (Bagdikian, 1987).

Because electronic symbol systems play such a central role in modern communication, they cannot be ignored. It is important that students begin to develop the skills necessary for interpreting and processing all kinds of video screen messages. Symbolically different presentations of media vary as to the mental skills of processing they require. Each individual learns to use a media's symbolic forms for purposes of internal representation (Bianculli, 1992). To even begin to read a child needs to understand thought-symbol relationships. To move beneath the surface of video imagery requires some of the same understandings. It takes skill to break free from an effortless wash of images and electronically-induced visual quicksand.

Unlike direct experience, print or visual representation is always coded within a symbol system. Learning to understand that system cultivates the mental skills necessary for gathering and assimilating internal representations. Whether 25+ hours a week at home (TV) or 5 hours a week at school (computers), the video screen is changing the texture of learning.

Each communications medium makes use of its own distinctive technology for gathering, encoding, sorting, and conveying its contents associated with different situations. The technological mode of a medium affects the interaction with its users—just as the method for transmitting content affects the knowledge acquired. Learning seems to be affected more by *what* is delivered than by the delivery system itself. In other words, the quality of the programming and the level of interactivity are the keys. But different media are more than alternative routes to the same end. Studies suggest that specific media attributes call on different sets of mental skills and, by doing so, cater to different learning styles (Solomon, 1986).

Processing must always take place and this process always requires skill. The closer the match between the way information is presented and the way it can be mentally represented, the easier it is to learn. Better communication means easier processing and more transfer. Recent research suggests that voluntary attention and the formation of ideas can be facilitated by electronic media—with concepts becoming part of the child's repertoire (Brown, 1988). New educational choices are being laid open by electronic technologies. Understanding and employing these technological forces requires a critical perspective that interprets new literacies from a unique and critical perspective. We would do well to remember that while certain educational principles remained constant, each step along the way—from speech to handwritten manuscripts to print—required major changes in teaching and learning.

Understanding and Creating Electronic Messages

Understanding the conventions of visual electronic media can help cultivate mental "tools of thought." In any medium, this allows the viewer new ways of handling and exploring the world. The ability to interpret the action and messages on a video display terminal requires going beyond the surface to understanding the deep structure of the medium. Understanding the practical and philosophical nuances of a medium moves its consumers in the direction of mastery.

Seeing an image does not automatically ensure learning from it. The levels of knowledge and skill that children bring with them to the viewing situation determine the areas of knowledge and skill development acquired. Just as with reading print, decoding visual stimuli and learning from visual images require practice. Students can be guided in decoding and looking critically at what they view. One technique is to have students "read" the image on various levels. Students identify individual elements, classify them into various categories, and then relate the whole to their own experiences. They can then draw inferences and create new conceptualizations from what they have learned. Many students can now videotape their own scenes with a camcorder, edit their work, and use the family VCR for playback. These new "video pencils" can transform the landscape of student visual creations. They can also have a major impact on our society as once "invisible" events get put on the air.

Planning, visualizing, and developing a production allows students to critically sort out and use electronic media to relay meaning. Young multimedia or video producers should be encouraged to open their eyes to the world and visually experience what's out there. By realizing in the medium, students learn to redefine space and time. They also learn to use media attributes such as structure, sound, lighting, color, pacing, and imaging. Lightweight camcorders have made video photography much easier, and programs like *Hyperstudio* have done the same thing for multimedia production. By "writing" in such a medium, students can gain a powerful framework for evaluating, controlling, and creating in electronic media.

Inventing Methods for Understanding Symbol Systems of the Future

Since the field of education seems to be entering a unique period of introspection, self-doubt, and great expectations, theoretical guidelines are needed as much as specific methods. To give teachers the freedom to reach educational goals means knowing what those goals are. It is dangerous to function in a vacuum because rituals can spring up that are worse than those drained away. As electronic learning devices flood our schools and homes, we need to be sure that findings are linked to practice. A close connection between these two domains requires defining educational needs in a more theoretical and practical way. If the two are not integrated, then one will get in the way of the other.

A wide range of intellectual tools can help students understand social and physical reality. Technology can be an ally in the learning process; or it can be an instrument to subvert human integrity. To avoid the latter, adults and children need to have control over the technology they are using. The research suggests that for students to create in the print medium requires that they read good literature, know how to search out information, write for a real reader, tap their personal experiences, and cooperatively edit their material. Learning about electronic communications technology can follow a similar pattern.

Reaching students requires opening students' eyes to things they might not have thought of on their own. This means tapping into real experience, fantasies, and personal visions, with technological tools serving as capable collaborators. The combination of thoughtful strategies and the enabling features of video tools can achieve more lasting cognitive change and improved performance (Riel, 1989). With this mind-eye approach, previously obscure concepts can become comprehendible, with greater depth, at an earlier age.

Print, writing, and hand drawn pictures (the oldest technological media) have been the cognitive tools that western culture has traditionally chosen to teach children. Good theoretical and practical techniques developed for understanding how a traditional communications medium interacts with human learning will be helpful in understanding the new media—even after we have gone beyond the current technological horizons in education. As with print, computers and video merge, children and young adults can develop explicit metacognitive strategies as they search for data, solve problems, and graphically simulate their way through multiple levels of abstraction.

The Internet and Access to the World of Ideas

Telecommunications technology in and of itself isn't the solution to our educational problems. However, it is a helpful element that can help us reclaim the sense of possibility in education. The Internet, that international network of networks, has become so popular that some technologically savvy businesses are beginning to exploit its openness. Although it can be frustrating to use at first, computers, modems, and telephone lines gives teachers and students access to a wealth of information. What about the costs? Many of the services and much of the software is free (or inexpensive) and many American states and Canadian provinces allow schools to gain access through a local telephone call. If the inexpensive direct approach doesn't work, the Internet is also available through commercial subscription services like America Online and CompuServe. Smaller networking companies charge a monthly fee of under $20—plus a small set-up fee. Two examples here are Netcom and CRL Network Services.

Getting there still takes lots of memory space, a fairly good modem, and an Internet connection. Perhaps the best news is that there are new interface options that someone other than a computer wiz can figure out. Students can use software, like *Mosaic* or *Netscape*, to retrieve images and text from information sources arranged as "World-Wide Web" pages by clicking the mouse on highlighted words or phrases.

While Mosaic originally unlocked the Web for ordinary users, it is not the only key to the Internet. "Netscape Navigator" is one of the more popular browser tools that make the Internet accessible. Such "browsers" now are often part of the all-in-one Internet starter kits that are taking the pain out of the process. As Web browsers are finding their way into applications programs, the necessary software for connecting into the Internet will come already installed in many computers.

The Internet is an example of how a virtual community can connect telecommunicators around the world. When you add in commercial on-line services like CompuServe and America Online, the number of people taking advantage of these possibilities is doubling every year. Prodigy Services got a recent lift in the on-line information industry recently by installing special software that helps their subscribers make easy connection to the Internet's *World Wide Web.* The competition is already hot on their heels for an even better interface. Educators are increasingly looking to the cyberspace reached by data highways as they strive to make their classrooms more interactive, collaborative, and student-centered.

As we put together the technological components that provide access to a truly individualized set of learning experiences, it is important to develop a modern philosophy of teaching, learning, and social equity.

While new educational communications technology has the potential to make society more equal, it has the opposite effect if access is limited to those with the money for equipment. As we enter a world of computers, camcorders, interactive TV, satellite technology and databases, the schools are usually behind the curve and find themselves trying to catch up with the more technologically sophisticated.

Electronically connecting the human mind to global information resources will result in a shift in human consciousness similar to the change that occurred when a society moved from an oral to a written culture. The challenge is to make sure that this information is available for all in a twenty-first century version of the public library. The technology could give us the ability to impact upon the tone and priorities gathering information and learning in a democratic society. Of course, every technology has the potential for both freedom and domination. Who can argue with easy access to vast troves of information? With the Internet,

for example, opportunities could be lost in a land rush generated by corporations. Like other technological advances, this one can mirror back to us all sides of the human condition.

There is no doubt about the fact that the world is reengineering itself with many technological processes. The convergence of communication technologies may be one of the codes to transforming the learning process and making people more creative, resourceful, and innovative in the things they do. While learning to use what's available today, we need to start building a social and educational infrastructure that can travel the knowledge highways of the future. Experts may disagree about the ultimate consequences of innovation in electronic learning. But the development of basic skills, habits of the mind, wisdom, and traits of character will be increasingly affected—one way or another—by the technology.

The Computer as a Tool and Tutor

When school microcomputers first appeared in the early 1980s, most instructional work consisted of learning programming languages or using drill and practice software as a kind of an electronic worksheet. By the mid 1980s, we started to see some educational software which used the unique characteristics of the medium to enhance students' learning. Today, we see many simulations and computer-based, problem-solving experiments that provide students with experimental learnings which are unavailable otherwise. Of course, real objects and chemicals must be used; however, you need a computer simulation to deal with an explosion at an atomic power plant or to visually explore the inner workings of DNA.

At their best, software programs encourage students to create models and reflect on the fundamental nature of the discipline being studied. Students benefit when they are given control over system parameters so they can explore their effects. It is even more helpful when children can choose the roots for information gathering and analysis. The curriculum materials that are most effective and most popular are those that provide for social interaction and problem solving. Capitalizing on computer-controlled interactive activities can reach the child through many senses.

Many of the new multimedia programs embed information in visual narratives to create context and interaction that gives meaning to facts. Some also use windowing techniques which place one or more images on the screen while the action takes place elsewhere. With many of these programs, a viewer can even zoom in on an item or pull away, turn the item, or flip it to get a closer view. When a telecommunications modem is added to the mix, students can communicate with libraries, schools, and peers across the country. Such joint problem solving in science and mathematics is similar to how real scientists work with distant peers.

Classroom Teachers and Educational Technology

There were only about 30,000 microcomputers in the schools in 1980. Today, there are well over five million. Most schools now have at least some computers and several VCRs. In its annual report on technology in U.S. public schools, Quality Education Data (QED) (Denver, CO) also reports that the number of Macintosh computers in K–12 schools has doubled over the last three years. With the phenomenal growth of both hardware and software, there is a greater than ever need for teachers to be able to combine their knowledge of effective instruction with the effective use of computer technology. Professional knowledge about children, learning, curricula, and schools goes hand-in-hand with the competencies needed to use computers to advantage. Armed with new ideas and technological tools, teachers can meet the challenges of school reform head on.

Blaming teachers for the failure of computer-based technology to radically change education is a mistake. The successful use of computers in the classroom will *not* solve our more serious educational problems. But if teachers aren't able to use the medium the schools less able to cope with these problems. It's relatively easy to buy computer equipment— and even get children interested. The difficult thing is to engage teachers and principals. Teachers need to be able to use computers to solve problems and communicate—giving and receiving information. Becoming competent and confident users of educational technology means main- taining a professional development effort to insure that there will be some success.

In the world outside of school, computers are seen as real tools for real people. A similar view would be appropriate for schools. Teachers may have to make some changes in how they teach, but computers will never be electronic teachers or administrators of learning. Schools of the future need more adults than ever: teachers' aides, parents, older students, and more. The technology can be a facilitator of thought and learning. Computer programs can be a unique and useful supplement; allowing teachers to enhance what they are already doing—and do some new things. Nowadays computers are proving indispensable in just about any intellectually significant enterprise.

Teachers seem to agree that having students work on computers in pairs is often better than working alone. Sharing with peers is crucial to any literacy learning process; solitary confinement with a teaching machine isn't. It is also important to teach students about the technological revolution of which electronic media are a part.

Teachers frequently complain that school districts are notorious for bringing in hardware—and avoiding staff development. To help teachers become more uncomfortable with technology means providing assistance—and letting them take a computer home. A cross-section of the teachers we interviewed in three schools wanted to:

1. know how to use a computer, CD–ROM and videodisc players.
2. know how to hook up a modem for distance learning and the Internet.
3. attend a conference or professional development workshop on the topic.
4. have some sources—like books and professional journals available.
5. have guidelines so that they could fit the technology into their day-to-day curriculum.

Most teachers in our survey were interested in training. This was especially true if the district pays for it, release time is provided, and the location is convenient. Teachers, in general, are ready, willing, and eager to learn new skills. Many express an interest in attending high-tech conferences and are willing to share the cost. When schools make a commitment, preparing their staff for the future, money can be scrounged from various categories and professional development can be given the highest priority.

Trained people *are* more important than machines. Most large companies in the private sector recognize this and spend anywhere from 10 to 20 percent of their annual salary budget on training. The more successful the enterprise, the more likely they are to put a great deal of effort into training their personnel. It is time to stop blaming teachers for their technological inadequacies and build a significant level of professional development into the school budgets.

Using computers should, like using any other media, be directed by knowledgeable teachers aimed at achieving some instructional purpose. This goes well beyond having a few computer programs in a learning center at the back of the room where a student goes when everything else is done. Like any good learning material, computer software needs to be enhanced and extended by the instructor. A computer program with the best instructional design is no better than the classroom teacher who integrates it into the curriculum. Most teachers would not think of assigning a chapter from the history or science book without some kind of follow-up activity. They should feel the same way about computer lessons. Every other subject incorporates some kind of teacher intervention. There is no reason why students should be left to fend for themselves when the computer enters the process.

Reviewing Software Is a Little Like Reviewing Books

In an informal survey of public school children, we found that those most familiar with computers were also most excited about educational computing. Familiarity with good programs seemed to breed positive attitudes toward evaluating software, modifying existing programs, and incorporating computer-based instruction into their instructional plans. Having them in the regular classroom, rather than all in a lab, breeds familiarity.

The teachers in our survey who indicated that they were familiar with educational computing felt that it was possible for microcomputer courseware to stand side by side with books as important instructional tools. Like books, programs were viewed as good, bad, and indifferent. It takes training to be able to tell the difference.

Given the tools, children are capable of more penetrating evaluative thinking and intensive inquiry than has been allowed for in school. The program must make sense to the child. Having students work together on software evaluation can be turned to an excellent learning experience. Remember, even the most technologically-advanced teacher won't have time to review all the programs that come down the pike. We suggest giving a new program to a couple of students, have them figure it out, teach it to two others—and then show the teacher how it works. Allowing students to have a hand in helping construct elements of the learning process can assist the teacher and help build a learning community.

Curriculum is a cooperative and interactive venture between students and teachers. On both an individual and social level, those directly involved with the process must be taken seriously. Working together, they can decide what benefits are gained from particular software programs. After all, the software user is in the best position to decide if the program is taking people out of the process—or whether learners are in control of the computers. Good software programs let students learn together at their own pace—visualizing, talking together, and explaining abstract concepts so that they can relate them to real-life situations.

A checklist for choosing software:

Software Checklist

1. What skill is the program trying to teach?
2. Is this a skill that fits into curriculum objectives?
3. What examples does the program use to teach these skills?
4. What kinds of teaching techniques are used?
5. What prerequisite skills do students need to use this piece of software?
6. Where does this piece of software fit into the learning sequence for this topic?
7. What directions need to be given to students before using the software?
8. What activities would serve as a follow-up to this software program?
9. How will students' performance be evaluated?
10. What other materials would enhance the skills developed by this software program?

Do the students like it? We suggest that teachers reserve their final opinion about software until they see it used by the student.

A Sampling of Programs to Review

The future of educational technology is good pedagogy and high-quality content. In evaluating software it is important to have a narrative that students can interact with; otherwise, you just have a group of facts. For *multimedia* to work as a unique medium, you also need an easy-to-use program, compelling imagery, and enough depth to draw students into the content.

• *Life Story* is a CD–ROM program designed by Apple's Multimedia lab, LucasArts Learning, and the Smithsonian Institution. This one is for middle school students on up. Annotated film clips, scientific dramas, biographies, and text ties together people and science. The discovery of DNA is one example of how this program gives students a better sense of what science is and how it is practiced. It uses strong story lines made to encourage learning in an exploratory, creative and non-linear fashion. Available from Sunburst Communications, 800-321-7511.

• If you can add the power of video to your computer with a videodisc player, then *Interactive NOVA: Earth* is a good earth science program to evaluate. It provides a unique prospective by taking an approach called "Earth System Science" that was pioneered by NASA. Available from Scholastic: 1-800-325-6149.

• *Science 2000* is an interesting multimedia science program that has integrated thematic content aimed at the middle school level. It lets you go beyond the technology and into some hands-on, interactive investigation with real materials and real problems. Available from D.C. Heath 1-800-235-3565.

• *MathKeys* is a straightforward computer program from MECC and Houghton Mifflin. This program helps elementary school students (K–6) use their Macintosh to explore, question, observe, and connect manipulatives with symbolic notation. This software is designed to support and encourage students as they build new math ideas. The program builds on NCTM standards to strengthen almost any local mathematical curriculum. 1-800-758-6762.

• *Classroom Newspaper Workshop* (MAC* CD–ROM* Grades 3–7) is a complete newspaper writing unit that makes every student a reporter and every classroom a newsroom. It has built-in assessment tools and teachers can get lesson plans and training from advisors. This one is a *project.* It can extend over a couple of months and takes students through generating ideas, conducting interviews, story writing, editing, design, and publication. Available from Tom Snyder Productions: 1-800-342-0236. To emphasize science and math you can get the students to look for science/math concepts in the paper and use the once-a-week science section of the newspaper. Many other papers have a special day for a section on science stories. *The New York Times,* for example, has a large science, math, and technology section every Tuesday.

Children can learn to critique both software and the quality of programming much as they learned to critique the dominant media of yesteryear—books. One of the first tenants of book review criticism is to critique what is usually taken for granted. Another is that a critic must have at least a little affection for the media being critiqued. Why not have students do "book reports" on computer software? Students can quickly check to see if the flow of a program makes sense. They can also sift through some of the software evaluations and advertisements in magazines and journals. Next, they can try out the software as they think a successful or unsuccessful student might. What happens when mistakes are made? How are the graphics? Do you think you can learn anything from this? Is it exciting? The bottom line is: Do you like it?

Without question, teachers and students are the ones who experience the consequences of making good or bad choices in software selection. And they are the ones who most quickly learn the consequences of poor choices.

Software Evaluation—for the Teacher and the Student

The same criteria that are applied to other instructional materials can be applied to evaluating educational computing courseware. The following list is an example:

1. Does the program meet the age and attention demands of your students?
2. Does the program serve as a good model of reality or as a jumping off point for examining important science/math understandings?
3. Does the program hold the student's interest?
4. Does the program develop, supplement, or enhance curricular skills?
5. Does the program require adult supervision or instruction?
6. Children need to actively control what the program does. To what extent does the program allow this?
7. Can the courseware be modified to meet individual learning requirements?
8. Can it be adjusted to the learning styles of the user?
9. Does the program have animated graphics which enliven the lesson?
10. Does it meet instructional objectives and is it educationally sound?
11. Does the program involve higher level thinking and problem-solving?

It is important to remember that a major danger in the use of computers comes from their power over the imagination and their ability to persuade and teach. If people uncritically accept what is built into the computer program, they may be accepting a flawed model of reality.

Student Evaluation Checklist

Name of student evaluator(s) _____

Name of software program _____

Publisher _____ Subject _____

1. How long did the program take? _____ minutes
2. How close do you think this program is like the real world? What are the differences?

3. Did you need to ask for help when using this program? _____
4. What skills do you think this program tried to teach? _____
___

    Please circle the word that best answers the question.
5. Was the program fun to use? yes no somewhat not very
6. Were the directions clear? yes no somewhat not very
7. Was the program easy to use? yes no somewhat not very
8. Were the graphics (pictures) good? yes no somewhat not very
9. Did the program get you really involved? yes no somewhat not very
10. Were you able to make choices in the program? yes no
11. What mistakes did you make? _____
12. What happened when you made a mistake? _____
13. What was the most interesting part of the program? _____
___

14. What did you like least? _____
15. What's a good tip to give a friend who's getting started with this program? _____
___

Extended activities:
- Make up a quiz about the program and give the questions to other students in the class who have used the program.
- Create your own soundtrack for part of the program.
- Make up a student guide for the program. Use your own directions and illustrations.
- Write or dramatize a TV interview with one of the characters in the program.
- Interview other students who have used the program and write their responses.
- Write a review of the program for a magazine.
- Call for information about tapping into *Prodigy* (an electronic subscription service) 800-776-3449. Some of the best educational software can come to you over the telephone line ("Reading Magic Library" and "Where in the World is Carmen Sandiego" are just two examples).

    We are experiencing a fundamental change in our relationship to information, the world, and each other. If we make electronic Faustian bargains in the name of efficiency or personal laziness, print literacy and our essential human spirit will lose. The power of our memories gets applied to print differently as we descend into an inner space of meaning and wisdom. We use our imaginations to create and collaborate with the author as we read. There is no suggestion here that we dismiss the electronic revolution, only that much that makes us human will be diminished if the meaning and power that comes from reading the printed word fades from our national consciousness.

    Reaching for a higher plane seems more common in literature than in film or television. There is a real shortage of articulate role models. Hollywood and the TV industry often reflect an uneasiness with technological sophistication and make intelligence a villain. Just when the schools seem in drastic need of repair, we get a rash of movies and TV series that present being very stupid as very chic. In "videoland," a lack of erudition is usually enough to equate a character with inner goodness. Intelligence puts a character under suspicion on television and on the movie screen. This anti-intellectualism comes most powerfully to the fore when rational thinking seems to fail society.

Technological immodesty has always been larger in the United States than in other countries. Those involved with technology have a bad habit of promising more than they can deliver. There is a lot that we can do with the TV set off and without computers. And there is a lot, like using real paints and chemicals, that we should do without them. Still, the unrelenting advance of the technology-intensive future opens more possibilities than it closes. In the hands of well prepared teachers, technology-assisted lessons can be a powerful tool for collaboration and involving students in active learning. The human imagination can be enhanced by computer-based instruction in a manner that makes actual experience more meaningful. On occasion, the experience can even transcend print or actual experience as an analytical tool. The technology can amplify learning and a wide range of carefully thought-out interactive networks can add a great deal to what teachers are trying to do.

The human mind can create communication possibilities beyond either what it intends or what it can foresee. *What* is communicated is far more important than the technological vehicle we use. When it comes to the schools, the technology itself is not as interesting as what we can contribute to the schools with it.

Using Converging Technologies to Stimulate Creative Collaboration

The convergence of broadcast television, cable, computer, telephone, videogames, educational software, and publishing offers opportunities to entertain for profit, to inform, and to educate. The explosion of technological advances can enslave our youth with mindless video games (in an attempt to stave off boredom) or empower to learn and to think in new, interactive and interesting ways. Even leisure time should be held to a higher standard than "killing time." It should concern itself with replenishing the spirit—for example: a discussion of ideas, attending a fine arts event, watching and discussing good films or theater, listening to music, or hiking. According to the Centers for Disease Control and Prevention (in Atlanta) nearly twice as many students were not active in the 1990s (as compared to the mid-1980s). The same study found correlations between economic class, television watching time, weight gain, and a lack of exercise. The void left when the homework is finished and the chores done is often filled with lowest common denominator: television. The result is a lot of unhealthy fat children and young adults. Why not raise expectations and use the communications tools at hand to enhance healthy cooperative physical recreation, the enjoyment of the arts, and lifelong learning. Isn't it possible to structure media systems so that they enable students to become active, intelligent, and informed citizens?

On the eve of the twenty-first century there is a race in the communications industry to merge two-way telecommunications, computers, and television in order to offer new digital entertainment and information services. Satellite dishes the size of a large pizza are already competitive with the cable TV industry and the new interactive TV services are being provided by regional telephone companies. The process will redefine the nation's watching and thinking habits. Fiber optics, digital transmission, and a trove of multimedia choices will change not only *what* Americans experience but *how* they experience it. A major focus: How to provide more choice and how to make the interactive experience just as new and exciting as when television and computers first came out.

To help students develop clear technological writing skills, we have had them try their hand at rewriting some of the technological directions they come across—occasionally sending the result to the hardware or software manufacturer. When it comes to regular classroom writing assignments, computers can be a great aid for helping children learn to write well across the disciplines. They can even add a multimedia dimension to traditional writing. At the prewriting stage, students can gather information and stimulate possibilities; during writing phase a sharing social context can affect their awareness of how their work communicates with others; and during the revision phase they learn to collaborate, revise, and edit their early drafts. Motivation is also enhanced and the final sharing ("publication") effort is bound to be more professional looking.

From theme park attractions to simulated surgery in virtual operating rooms, the technology is moving through its infancy and into early childhood. Within the multisensory world of virtual reality, people can see, hear, and touch objects. Some of the applications being developed involve what has been called "telepresence," which gives the operator the sensation of putting his/her hands and eyes in a remote location.

One could, for example, send a robot to "Mars" or the bottom of the ocean, control the action, see what it sees, and feel what it feels.

Creating New Media Realities

In today's world, children grow up interacting with electronic media as much as they do interacting with print or people. Does being engaged by electronic media mean that children are making good use of leisure time or learning anything meaningful? Whether it is computer games or television, the programming is often violent, repetitious, and mindless. It can distract students from more important literacy and physical exercise activities.

The future may be bumpy, but it doesn't have to be gloomy. Some innovative schools are using computer-based technology to examine basic educational principles and possibilities for change. But it is important to note that it is informed educators who are driving the change rather than the technology itself. Whether or not there is definitive evidence of the educational benefits of multimedia or just how academic computing can improve learning are not the only issues. Since the technology pervades our society, students must be familiar with it. And new communication technologies can be used to help students understand imagery, solve problems creatively, and apply these solutions to real-life situations. It takes some effort, but the *engaging* can be made more *meaningful.*

As technology progresses, the difference between the real and the unreal become blurred. Even using the Internet tends to blur words and deeds—devaluing the significance of physical reality. Another example: *virtual reality,* where electronically sensitized gloves, goggles, and body movement allow characters to merge and give people the feeling that they are interacting with electronic characters and environments. As computer-based technology causes us to learn to communicate in different ways, it creates new media realities.

The 1990s are ushering in a brave new world of technology in which television and its computer-controlled associates are being designed for interacting, problem solving, learning, shopping, ordering movies, exploring digital environments, and "surfing" the Internet. Many U.S. households and some schools already have their choice of services. If educational concerns are given the attention they deserve, the nation's information pipelines will make it possible to take part in educational simulations that closely mimic reality. In addition, students can electronically explore time and space—while collaborating with people around the world.

Harmonizing the present and the future means more than reinventing the schools. It means attending to support mechanisms. To successfully sail through the crosscurrents of our transitional age requires the development of habits of the heart and habits of the intellect. People are more important than machines. Parents, teachers, and programming are the foundations on which these things can be built. In schools, the technology can help lead the way to a reexamination of what to teach and how to teach it—while ending the isolation of teacher and student.

To avoid creating a technological underclass in schools, more than 40 states have set up organizations to provide technological support for their public schools. Recognizing the fact that the impact of technology on the schools grows as teachers come to understand it, some states have provided teachers with a computer to use at home. This beats being embarrassed by students who know more about the technology than most adults. Well financed school districts have followed the lead of many corporations and provided teachers with a series of two-day workshops in pleasant surroundings—rather than the usual after-school crunch.

When television first gained a central place in the American consciousness,. the sociologist, Leo Bogart, wrote that it was a "neutral instrument in human hands. It is and does what people want." The same thing might be said about today's multimedia technologies and the "information superhighway." Rapid changes in information technology are resulting in less and less of a difference between the television screen, the computer screen, and telephone-linked networks. The mass media is becoming part of a new and larger canvas—a more personalized two-way street that is altering how we learn, work, play, and live. Today's technological and marketplace changes in communications are sweeping and profound. If the schools do not participate in shaping new media, then they are bound to be shaped by it.

Although technology has become an efficient power tool for instruction, good things don't automatically happen. The internet is just one example of how multimedia computers can help us weave a new community—or waste a great deal of time. As technological potential and hazard intrude on our schools, teachers need high-tech inservice training to deal with the explosion of electronic possibility. When it comes to using educational technology wisely, we would do well to remember that just about everything that happens in the classroom must be filtered through the mind of the teacher.

As teachers look for ways to engage students with the technology, they must ask themselves, "What is the problem to which this can be applied?" It is a Faustian bargain, something important is given and something important taken away. The quality of the technological content, the connection to important subject matter, and a recognition of the characteristics of effective instruction are central factors in determining instructional success. Many educational computer programs, for example, emphasize individualized learning (a plus) in isolation (a minus). Designers of electronic learning programs have to recognize the power of collaboration. School is, after all, a place where students should work together in groups.

It's language that makes us human
Literacy that makes us civilized
Technology that makes us powerful
And it's being in community
with others that makes us free

REFERENCES

Anderson, R. (Ed.) (1992). *Computers in American schools: An overview.* Minneapolis: University of Minnesota Department of Sociology, 1993.

Bagdikian, B. H. (1987). *The media monopoly.* Boston: Beacon Press.

Bianculli, D. (1992). Taking television seriously. New York: Continuum.

Birkerts, S. (1995). *The Gutenburg elegies: The fate of reading in an electronic age.* New York: Faber and Faber.

Brown, A. L. *Metacognitive skills and reading.* White Plains, NY: Longman.

Bryant, J. & Anderson, D. R. (Eds.) (1988). *Children's understanding of television: Research on attention and comprehension.* San Diego, CA: Academic Press.

Cuban, L. (1994). Neoprogressive visions and organizational realities. In *visions for the use of computers in classroom instruction: Symposium and response.* Cambridge, MA: Harvard Educational Review Reprint.

Dede, C. J. (1985). Assessing the potential of educational information utilities. *Library hi tech,* 3(4), 115–119.

Dorr, A. (1986). *Television and children.* London: Sage.

Educational telecommunications: The state-by-state Analysis. Henzel Associates, 1201 E. Fayette St., Syracuse, NY 13210.

Gallas, K. (1994). *The languages of learning: How children talk, write, dance, draw, and sing their understanding of the world.* New York: Teachers College Press.

Kroker, A. & Weinstein, M. (1995). *Data trash: The theory of the virtual class.* New York: St. Martin's Press.

McKibben, B. (1992). *The age of missing information.* New York: Random House.

McLeod, J. M. (1982). *Television and behavior: Ten years of scientific progress.* (Vol. 2, Department of Health and Human Services). Washington, DC: U.S. Government Printing Office.

National Education Goals Panel. (1994). *The national education goals report 1993: Building a nation of learners.* Washington, DC.

Pea, R. (1992). Distributed multimedia learning environments: Why and how. *Interactive Learning Environments,* 2(2), 73–109.

Riel, M. (1989). The impact of computers in classrooms. *Journal of Research on Computing in Education,* 22, pp. 180–190.

Solomon, C. (1986). *Computer environments for children: A reflection on theories of learning and education.* Cambridge, MA: MIT Press.

Stoll, C. (1995). *Silicon snake oil: Second thoughts on the information highway.* New York, NY: Doubleday.

Zillman, D. (Ed.). (1992). *Media, children, and the family: Social, scientific, psychodynamic, and clinical perspectives.* Hillsdale, NJ: Erlbaum.

Chapter 8

ASSESSING COOPERATIVE GROUP LEARNING

I believe that we should get away altogether from tests and correlations among tests and look instead at more naturalistic sources of information about how peoples around the world develop skills important to their way of life.

— Howard Gardner

This chapter presents some new methods of group assessment and examines a variety of assessment alternatives. The goal is to come up with more authentic assessment tools. The emphasis is on portfolio assessment and the related concept of performance assessment. Some procedures have already been developed by others and some have to be created or adapted by the district and the school. Although projects, open-ended questions, holistic scoring, and other evaluative procedures are included, this chapter limits itself to those assessment procedures that relate to cooperative learning and have the potential for playing a positive role in learning.

Educators are beginning to look at assessment in a number of new and exciting ways. Designing good assessment tasks requires thinking through the curriculum and coming up with activities that demonstrate what students know. Many teachers have a vision of what they think should be happening in their classes. It goes something like this: students work in small groups or independently doing investigations or accomplishing tasks using tools such as manipulative materials (blocks, beakers, clay, rulers, chemicals, musical instruments, calculators, computers), assorted textbooks, and other references. As students consult with each other and with the teacher, they keep journals and other written reports of their work (Stenmark, 1989). Occasionally, the entire class gathers for a discussion or for a presentation. Traditional testing methods do not do a good job of supporting such an approach.

Assessment is a broader task than testing because it involves collecting a wider range of information that must be put together to draw meaning from what was observed or measured. Of course, the first use of assessment is within the classroom, to provide information to the teacher for making instructional decisions. Teachers have always depended on their own observations and the examination of student work to help in curriculum design and instructional decision-making.

In the world outside of school people are valued for the tasks or projects they do, their ability to work with others, and their responses to difficult problems or situations. To prepare students for future success, both the curriculum and related assessment methods must encourage this kind of performance (Stenmark, 1989). Many groups of educators are exploring and creating exciting new possibilities for what has come to be called authentic assessment. This implies that students are doing worthwhile meaningful tasks.

Authentic assessment means evaluating by asking for behaviors you want to produce. For assessment to be authentic, the form and the criteria for success must be public knowledge. Students need to know what is expected and on what criteria their product will be evaluated. Success should be evaluated in ways that make sense to them. It allows students to show off what they do well. Authentic assessment should search out students' strengths and encourage integration of knowledge and skills learned from many different sources. It encourages pride and may include self and peer evaluation. Assessment of products that students produce may include portfolios, writing, investigations, projects, class presentations and verbal responses to open-ended questions. Whether it is small group class presentations, journal writing, storytelling, observation or portfolios, alternative assessment procedures pick up many things that children fail to show on pencil-and-paper tests.

Assessing Teamwork

Learning requires communication with self, peers, and knowledgeable authorities. It also requires effort and meaningful assessment. A lesson from twentieth century physics is that *the world cannot ultimately be objectified.* The same is true of people. Still, whether in science or education, we need to know where we're going, how we're going to get there, and how far we have progressed. To move on school reform we have to know the content standards at various levels of schooling. Once we know where we are going, teachers need the freedom and the tools to get there. As far as cooperative learning is concerned, this means coming up with a quality assessment system for individuals and for groups.

Sample assessment questions for individuals:

HEMISPHERICITY

LEFT/Analytic   RIGHT/Global

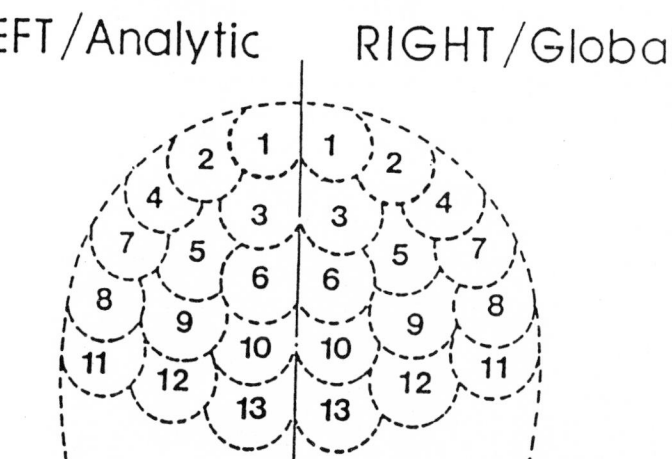

Pick a color for each number and fill it in on one side.

LEFT (Analytic)	RIGHT (Global)
1 Verbal	1. Visual, tactual, kinesthetic
2. Responds to word meaning	2. Responds to word pitch, feeling
3. Recalls facts, dates	3. Recalls images, patterns
4. Sequential	4. Random
5. Processes information linearly	5. Processes information in chunks
6. Responds to logical appeal	6. Responds to emotional appeal
7. Trusts logical appeal	7. Trusts intuition
8. Looks tidy, organized	8. Looks disorganized
9. Plans ahead	9. Spontaneous
10. Punctual	10. Less punctual
11. Reflective	11. Impulsive
12. Recalls people's names	12. Recalls people's faces
13. Speaks with few gestures	13. Gestures when speaking

- What did other members of your group learn from you?
- What and how did you learn from teammates?

Sample assessment questions for groups:

- What did the group learn about solving a problem as a team?
- How much did members of your group come to see themselves as being part of a team?
- What did you learn from the group?
- What should members of your cooperative group do to be more effective in the future?

Standardized multiple choice tests are not all that helpful in answering complex and multifaced problems facing American education. In fact, they can even be counterproductive by brow-beating schools with enormous pressure to raise test scores—often deadening critical thinking and aesthetic appreciation. Performance assessment, including portfolios, are more authentic and help us get closer to what we really want schools to be doing. Portfolios help teachers and students become actively involved in evaluating and providing examples of their own learning. This allows them to create, evaluate, and act upon material that is valued by themselves and others. Higher level thinking goes beyond simply recognizing that a mistake was made to imagining *why*, getting feedback from others, and finding practical ways to do something about it.

The Portfolio as a Conversation Tool

Portfolios have long been associated with artists and photographers as a means of displaying collected samples of representative work. What is new is the interest in using these performance assessment techniques across the curriculum. Portfolios have been used for a number of years by various reading and writing projects (Graves, 1983). Harvard University has had a successful arts program in place for years which uses portfolios for instruction and evaluation (Mitchell, 1989). In addition, the National Assessment of Educational Progress has recently suggested using portfolios to assess students' writing and reading abilities. Increasingly, colleges and universities are asking students to submit portfolios as part of their entrance requirements (Farr, 1990). Some schools are even starting to use teaching portfolios to assess faculty and assist with their professional development.

Portfolios can help document the probing questions that are being asked, identify thinking, and help connect to real-world understandings. They can also help measure elements of the thinking process: working independently, collaborating in small groups, discussing ideas, keeping journals, brainstorming, and listening. Students clarify their thinking through such "conversations," while building knowledge, skills, and values. As learners express their ideas and reveal examples of their thinking, teachers can gain insights into how to design instruction to match students' needs. As teachers become knowledgeable about assessing the change in students, they may also become more knowledgeable in directing the change process in themselves and in their schools (Graves & Sunstein, 1992).

Portfolios may be viewed as containers of evidence, demonstrating a student's skills and dispositions. As such, it can be described as a powerful conversation tool. The contents of this conversation will vary depending on its purpose. A portfolio is more than a "folder" of students' work. It is a deliberate, specific collection of student accomplishment. The focus is on what a student can do, not on mistakes.

Portfolios can also be used in the classroom to bring students together, to discuss ideas, and provide evidence of understanding and accomplishments. By taking a good look at their work and the work of peers, students develop a sense of different ways of looking at their own work. This kind of reflection can also provide insights into ways of thinking, understanding, and potential directions for the future (Farr, 1990). Far from squelching inspiration like many fill-in the bubble tests, portfolio assessment is more likely to promote creativity and self-reflection. The procedure encourages students to work collaboratively to analyze, clarify, evaluate, and explore their own thinking. A portfolio type of assessment also invites students to invent, organize, predict, represent, visualize, and genuinely reflect on what they are learning. In addition, the connection between instruction, learning, and assessment is strengthened by linking the teacher and student in a very personal and meaningful way.

Critics correctly contend that portfolios can get in the way of standardized comparisons and that they may not be as easily quantifiable as traditional exams. It is also true that they are more time-consuming and expensive. Filling-in the bubbles *is* easier. In spite of these negatives, many educators now believe that it is more than worth the effort to use performance and portfolio assessment to get a more realistic measure of what students know and can do.

Choosing Evidence for a Portfolio

The evidence chosen for a portfolio can be used as a tool for gaining a more powerful understanding of student achievement, knowledge, and attitudes. At the same time it can be used to help the person represented become aware of his or her own learning history. Although gaining popularity in art, language, and reading classes, the concept of portfolio assessment has yet to span the entire curriculum. For some subject matter areas, teachers are just beginning to look at the possibility of using these processes to collect, organize, reflect on, and display selected work samples.

A portfolio is not a one-time collection of examples, but rather a means of bringing together representative material over time. The purpose is to gain a more accurate understanding of students' work, development, and growth. There are many possibilities, but some portfolios contain:

- samples of students' written compositions
- journal entries, reactions to their work, personal reflections, feelings
- attempts at solving problems, ideas about group projects, investigations
- art, audio and video tapes, photographs, or other creative expressions
- selected samples of specific content presented over time
- computer readouts, disks
- student logs, collected data entries
- group recordings and assignments
- rough drafts and polished products

(We suggest a brief caption on each item.)

To help the person reading the portfolio to clarify the contents, it is useful to include a table of contents (or index) and some background information about the individual who constructed the portfolio. A cover letter by the author, dates on all items, and a description of the assignment or task are other ways of assisting the reader. The contents of a portfolio can be added to, deleted, improved, revised, edited, or even discarded over time. Each element can represent a different form of expression and means of representing the world.

Collect, Select, and Reflect

How do you explain portfolios to parents? To begin with, you can explain the rationale behind portfolios to everyone—parents, students,

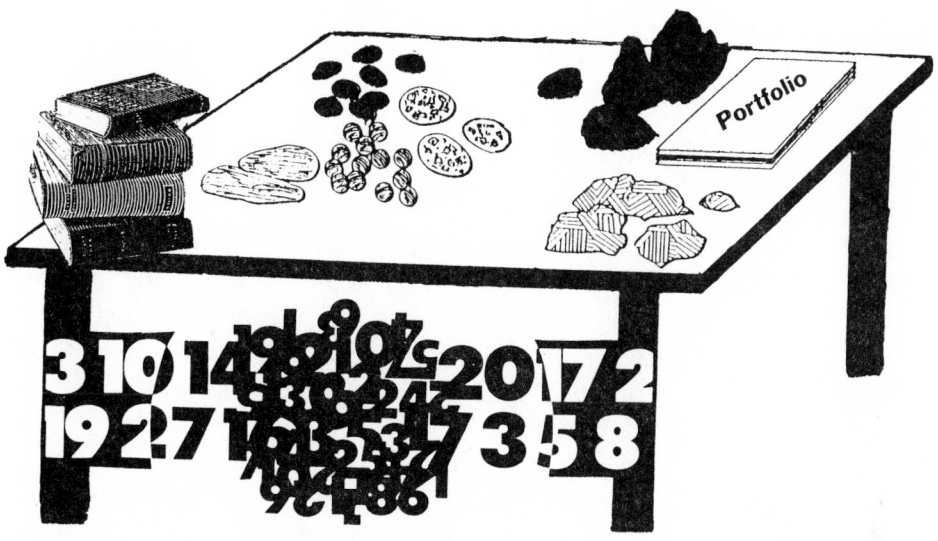

principals—*before* you start using them. After explaining the process to everyone involved you can have students label a file folder (with name) and designate a file drawer. Everyone should know that this is not to be a collection of test scores. It is also important to develop a year-long plan for using the portfolio, including things like dates, times, and places for individual conferences with students, parents, and supervisors (principals).

You need to be ready to discuss student progress and explain why portfolio assessment is an asset. Some educators maintain that students should keep almost all their work in the portfolio, while others design a portfolio with carefully selected items. There is no formula or "right way." The *purpose* behind the portfolio should determine the design. The range and depth can be determined by the teacher, the student, the group, or the nature of the content. For example, teachers could ask students to choose two examples from several categories. These might include:

- *a sample that reflects a problem that was difficult for your group*
- *work that shows where you started to figure it out*
- *evidence that you learned something new*
- *a piece of work that shows how your group reached a solution*
- *a sample of your group work where you need to keep searching for ideas*
- *two things your group is proud of*
- *two things your group would like to forget*

The portfolio type of assessment can go hand in hand with developing intellectual autonomy in an accepting cooperative environment. Having students select what they want to represent their work can be a powerful educational experience in its own right. Portfolio contents can reveal a surprising depth of thinking and provide personal insights that touch students' personal and academic lives. Performance assessment and portfolios can be used to assess analyzing, predicting, estimating, problem-solving, and other reasoning type skills. Once these challenging questions are part of the formal evaluation process, the teaching of such group skills will be considered more than an evaluation frill or something for gifted students. In this sense portfolios can be used to legitimize what good teachers want to do anyway.

The information accumulated in an assessment portfolio assists teachers in diagnosing learners' strengths and weaknesses. It can also be used as a tool for gaining a more powerful understanding of student achievement, knowledge, and attitudes. In the process, the person represented becomes aware of their own learning history and becomes directly involved in assessing their progress. Thus the barrier between the learner *and the assessment of the learner* starts to crumble. The next step in broadening the portfolio evaluation process involves using it as a conferencing tool with children, parents, and supervisors. The process itself is a powerful educational experience (Quinta & McKenna, 1991).

The Purpose and Design of a Portfolio

Portfolios sketch a picture of students' understanding. The intent is to recapture the past so that the future is shaped more effectively.

Careful attention should be given to:

- what is being assessed
- the design of the portfolio
- the appropriateness of the contents to what is being assessed
- the audience for which it is intended

The purpose behind the portfolio should determine its design. The range and the depth can be determined by the teacher, the student, or the nature of the portfolio's contents. Students may choose the contents based on specific categories. Involving students in the selection process gets them directly participating in their own learning and their own evaluation—thus promoting intellectual autonomy and self-respect.

Learners, teachers, and parents can gain a better understanding of the "student" in and out of school, because portfolio contents can reveal a surprising depth of thinking and provide insights into personal issues. Collecting, organizing, and reflecting on their school experience and that of their peers allow students to communicate who they are and how they view themselves in relation to others. Portfolios may include such things as:

- group assignments and team ideas
- teacher comments and assessments
- student writings
- student reflections, journal entries, reactions, and feelings
- collected data entries, logs, and research
- problems, investigations
- individual and group projects
- creative expressions (art, audio and video tapes, photographs)
- rough drafts and polished products (Mumme, 1990).

How are portfolios evaluated?

Some suggested criteria for evaluating student portfolios:

1. *Evidence of critical and creative thinking.* Does the student's work show that he or she has:
   - organized and displayed data? This means going beyond statistical data to include other items the student group worked on in the problem/project. (For example, the data could be a statistical graphing assignment based on student survey data.)
   - conjectured, explored, analyzed, looked for patterns, etc.
   - made use of the intellectual tools of analog and inquiry
   - used concrete materials (and/or drawings or sketches) as an aid in interpreting and analyzing problems/issues (video excerpts, computers, graphics, calculators, etc.)
   - searched out information, explored, and critically examined research data.

2. *Quality of activities and investigations.* Will the student's activities or investigations help him or her develop an understanding of significant science and mathematics concepts? Do the activities cut across several curriculum areas?

3. *Variety of approaches and investigations.* Does your set of portfolios provide evidence that students used a variety of approaches? Do portfolios include a variety of resources and provide research to support opinions and differing approaches to solving a problem? Do the portfolios include different activities or investigations?

4. *Demonstrate understanding and skill in situations that parallel prior classroom experience.* The portfolio should provide evidence that students know why they are using certain procedures, what they are looking for, and what the data mean.

5. *Assessment should be integrative* and oriented toward critical thinking and solving problems, not simply recall based. Some other integrative assessments which can be added to the portfolio include:
   • observational notes by the teacher
   • student self-assessments
   • progress notes written by the teacher and student often these are written collaboratively

Some teachers rank a portfolio for purpose, voice, organization, and grammar, ranking each item with "rarely," "sometimes," "frequently," or "extensively."

Portfolios provide a chance to look at what and how students are learning while paying attention to students' group ideas and thinking processes. This can help both teachers and parents. As children express ideas and reveal their thinking, teachers gain insights into how to design instruction to match students' demonstrated needs.

Practical Questions That Are Frequently Asked

What type of physical container would hold representative pieces?

• For older students a three-ring binder is most frequently used for items such as: oral history interviews, copies of historical documents, photos of community service activities, worksheets, and class notes. Handouts can be 3-hole punched and added, along with journal entries, written comments, quizzes, and other documents. Students may wish to purchase 3-ring separators with folder compartments to stick in maps, magazines, software disks, etc. More elaborate kinds of 3-ring notebook containers may include plastic casings in which pictures, articles, posters, etc. have been added. In group assignments, each student is responsible for keeping their own portfolio.

• An artist's folder (portfolio container) is useful for gathering things like videocassettes and three-dimensional kinds of projects. The cardboard folder has a string closure to prevent things falling out. They are fairly inexpensive and come in a variety of sizes from 3 × 5 inches for index cards to 3 ft. × 3 ft. for larger projects. Photographs can be taken of large projects and videotapes made of others.

- Elementary teachers often use large boxes. Students place their written work in folders by subject area and the folder is put in a decorated box with the student's name. Other kinds of items are also included in the box (copies of artifacts, relief map, etc.). The items may change month by month, but the boxes are kept for the year. Selected "treasures" remain. Boxes are stacked for easy access and neatness.
- *A combination of containers may be the best approach depending on the contents and nature of the assessment.*

Who uses portfolios?

Portfolio assessment is not just for younger students. Portfolios can be used with students from kindergarten through graduate school.

The demand is increasing for authentic assessment alternatives to multiple choice testing. Portfolios are often mentioned as one means of providing genuine, practical, performance-based assessment which can aid in assessing students' ability to *apply* facts, concepts, knowledge, and higher-order thinking skills. Portfolios can help provide an ongoing conversation about processes relating to teaching and learning. They can also help us attend to subjects that don't lend themselves to traditional testing methods—like the arts (Mitchell, 1989). Portfolios also assist in exploring what is going on *in* and *between* subjects. These samples, drawn from different times and contexts, can serve as an ongoing means of getting people talking and learning across disciplines, so important for critical and creative thinking.

Portfolios are proving useful in linking assessment with instruction allowing students and teachers to reflect on their movement through the curricular process (Mumme, 1990). They also provide a chance to look at what and how students are learning while paying attention to students' ideas and thinking processes. We do not suggest that the "pure" objectivity of more traditional testing has no place in the classroom. Rather we must respect its limits and search for more connected measures of intellectual growth. Coupled with other performance measures, portfolios can make an important contribution to educational reform and serve as a stimulus for new paradigms in learning.

Portfolios provide a chance to look at what and how students are learning while paying attention to students' ideas and thinking processes. This can help both teachers and parents. As children express ideas and reveal their thinking, teachers gain insights into how to design instruction to match students' demonstrated needs.

How Projects Can Expand Portfolio Assessment

Students need to become actively involved in evaluating their own learning. Constructing portfolio projects can promote an attitude of efficacy, wonder, and curiosity that stirs an appetite for lifelong learning. As students learn to work cooperatively in small groups, writing about and discussing their ideas, keeping journals, brainstorming, sharing, and constructing projects, they expand their knowledge, horizons, and possibilities. Through such collaboration, in a caring community, students construct meaning as they document and build their knowledge of themselves and the world.

Assessment should not simply measure decontextualized skills, but show how a learned skill can be applied in a new context—in and out of school. It is more important to demonstrate actual *understandings* than it is to do well in a rote ritualized performance. After graduation, many of us spend more time working on things that resemble *projects* than we do answering true/false questions or filling in the blanks on a test. About the only time we spend on anything like a multiple choice test is when we go to get a driver's license. Projects help students stretch their knowledge and show that they can really use what they have learned. Projects can also be assessed for school and for the outside world. It is good to ask questions while reviewing projects. The following list may be helpful.

How to Assess Projects:

1. *How was the project conceptualized?*
2. *What techniques were used?*
3. *Is it accurate?* (There must be individual accountability.)
4. *How has the presenter collaborated with others?*

(If you work together with people on a project, it's a "plus" . . . and it's something you should describe honestly.)

5. *How is the project presented?*

(Woody Allen has said that 80% of any job is showing up . . . here 80% of the job is the presentation.)

Using Process-Folios to Track and Transform Thinking

A process-folio is a cognitive map of your pivotal decisions as you work on a project. It should cover the key points and times when ideas or concepts were added. A process-folio might also include illustrations, graphs, drafts, and critiques by peers and experts. Finally you have the

end product (project) and a map exploring what you might do next.
The greatest thing in this world is not so much where we are, but in what direction we
are going.

—Oliver Wendell Holmes

A process-folio can call attention to items of related professional development processes in a unique way. This assessment technique allows important background thinking and conceptualizing to become concrete and easier to pay attention to. The contents of a process-folio might be snapshots of professional projects and their development over time. An art student, for example, might show the initial sketches for a painting, the middle stage, and the final product. This would help demonstrate whether or not the student can carry out a project over a significant period of time—while documenting what they have learned and explaining where they might go with a concept.

A process-folio can help individuals track their own growth as they develop a project and *make the essence of thinking visible.* Being aware of the thinking and decision-making process is an important step in the transformation of thinking. If teachers and students can do this—while taking on more responsibility for their own learning—they are more likely to untangle the mysteries of learning and deep understanding (Schrag, 1988).

Embedded Assessment Through Investigations

One of the best ways to assure the connection between instruction and assessment is to embed assessment into instruction. When students become involved in practical involved work, assessment can become natural and invisible. Assessment activities or questions can be presented to the students without their being aware of a difference between assessment and other classroom work.

Instruction and assessment practices go hand in hand. Assessment gives direction to teaching and teaching guides assessment. Assessment helps teachers understand what students are learning; it becomes a method of inquiry. By observing students' interactions with objects, asking questions, and giving suggestions, teachers are collecting data about students. Inquiry begins with asking questions and listening. Questions that focus on science and mathematics processes and learning emphasize what students are doing in their investigations. A teacher might ask students to describe relationships such as "Explain how you know . . . ?" or "Why . . . ?"

PORTFOLIOS

Avoid being trapped under an avalanche of minutia

By using data collected through observing, asking questions, and listening, teachers will be able to detect students' levels of understanding. This close interaction with students allows teachers to gain almost immediate feedback on their students' performance. Mirroring instruction and assessment through inquiry can make learning not only more exciting for students but also for teachers.

Group investigations may be related to many subject areas, such as social studies and art, or they may be explorations of purely single content questions (like science, reading, or math). Although the most typical form of assessment is collection of student writings, diagrams, tables, or maps, there are also opportunities for observation or videotaping of student performance.

In reviewing students' group work, look for whether students can:

- identify and define a problem and what they already know
- make a plan, creating, modifying, and interpreting data
- collect needed information
- organize the information
- discuss, review, revise, and explain results
- persist, looking for more information if needed
- produce a quality product or report

The opportunities for instruction are endless. Here is a brief list of investigations that would allow for inclusion of assessment.

A few possible investigations:

- maps
- traffic patterns near school
- collecting and analyzing litter
- population and availability of resources
- sound waves and music
- use of tools
- sports statistics
- measurement of parts of body
- diet, exercise, and health
- plant growth

Open-ended Questions

An open-ended question is one in which the students are given a situation and asked to communicate (in most cases to write) a response. It may range from simply asking a student group to clarify their thinking, writing directions, making generalizations, and so on. Questions may be more or less "open" depending on how many restrictions or directions are included. Open-ended questions help match assessment to good classroom questioning strategies. Here are several examples from mathematics:

name	age						
David		******************					
Nicki	***********						
Ron			*********************************				
	1	2	3	4	5	6	7

1. Look at this graph. Explain what the graph might mean?
2. Nancy wants to paint one wall of her room. The wall is 8 meters wide and 3 meters wide. It takes one can of paint to cover 12 square meters, and the paint is sold at two cans for $9. What else will Nancy need to consider? Make a group plan for this painting job.
3. The air in Plain City is warm and contains a great deal of water vapor. During the night, the temperature drops to 20 degrees C. What would a person likely find outdoors in the morning? Give a rationale for your group's thinking.

There is a wealth of information to be gained from this kind of assessment. The variety of acceptable thinking reflected in student responses goes far beyond what may be imagined. Misconceptions can be detected. We learn whether students as a group can:

- recognize the essential points of the problem involved.
- organize and interpret information
- work together
- report results in words, diagrams, charts, or graphs
- write for a given audience
- make generalizations
- understand basic concepts
- clarify and express their own thinking

For a classroom teacher to read all of the papers generated by frequent writing might seem burdensome. Teachers who have had their students write, however, say that the results are worth it because they learn more about student understandings and about the gaps in their knowledge. Students have a chance to show more of what they know, with a wider range of problem approaches.

Holistic Scoring and Rubric Scoring

A random sample of papers can reveal what the class as a whole understands. One of the simplest yet most effective ways to grade student writing is to use a holistic scoring method. For example, papers may first be sorted into stacks that might be labeled "acceptable," "missed the point," "has some special quality." To look for students' thinking rather than small bits of knowledge, each stack can then be divided again into two levels each. This method minimizes the need for structuring questions to draw forth predetermined responses.

A "rubric" or a description of the requirements for varying degrees of success in responding to an open-ended question may be predefined; it should allow for the uncommon responses that are often seen in investigative work by students.

For each open-ended question, a rubric should be created to reflect the specific important elements of that group problem. This general rubric is included to give examples of the kinds of factors to be considered (Stenmark, 1989).

Demonstrated Competence

Exemplary Response . . . . . . Rating = 6

Group gives a complete response with a clear, coherent, and unambiguous explanation; shows understanding; identifies all the important elements; presents strong supportive argument.

Competent Response . . . . . . Rating = 5

Group gives a fairly complete responses with reasonably clear explanations, presents solid supporting arguments.

Satisfactory Response

Minor Flaws, But Satisfactory . . . . . . Rating = 4

Group completes the problem satisfactorily, explanations may be confused, argumentation may be unclear, uses ideas effectively.

Serious Flaws, But Nearly Satisfactory . . . . . . Rating = 3

Group begins the problem appropriately, but may fail to address significant parts of the problem. Response may reflect an inappropriate strategy for solving the problem.

Inadequate Response

Group Begins, But Fails to Complete the Problem . . . . . . Rating = 2

Group explanation is not understandable, shows no understanding of the problem situation.

Group Unable to Begin Effectively . . . . . . Rating = 1

The words the group uses do not reflect the problem, the group makes no attempt at a solution and fails to indicate which information is appropriate to the problem.

No Attempt . . . . . . Rating = 0

Performance Assessment

Performance assessment involves students in the evaluation of their own work. Educators no longer view assessment as an end point to learning. Assessment becomes an integral part of teaching. As teachers design evaluations they develop an understanding of what needs to be taught, reflect upon and plan the best methodologies for teaching.

Luckily, performance assessment is not new or difficult. Basically, it is something that good teachers have always done—the process of questioning and observing cooperative learning students to evaluate their progress and then modifying instruction based on these observations. Through performance assessment, teachers are encouraged to:

- incorporate assessment into the learning and teaching process;
- use their own judgment when evaluating learning;
- establish criteria to assure reliability;
- describe the skills, attributes, and qualities to be developed;
- focus on important concepts and problem-solving skills, rather than memorization of facts;
- design group tasks to provide opportunities for students to perform, create, or produce a satisfying product;
- involve students in the evaluation of their work.

The object of performance assessment is to look at how students are working as well as at the completed task or product. An observer or interviewer may stay with the group or make periodic visits. Activities may be videotaped, tape recorded, or recorded in writing by an outside adult, the teacher, or the students. Looking at student performance gives teachers information about students' abilities to reason and raise questions. This type of group assessment focuses on finding out what students know and building experiences around that information. This involves student groups working together gathering information and supporting their data. Often teachers construct a chart at the beginning of a unit showing:

- what students already know
- what they want to find out
- how data was collected as evidence.

At the beginning of each unit of study, teachers measure students' understanding and establish learning objectives by also writing them on the chart "What our class wants to find out." Next, the teacher introduces hands-on activities. Through firsthand experience, students discuss and develop their own meanings. Throughout the unit, teachers and students refer to the chart to find out how thinking and questions have changed, and what new questions have arisen. At the end of the unit, students complete the chart stating what they have learned as supported by the gathered data. This knowledge is then incorporated into group writings entitled, "What our group learned." Student groups meet as a class to discuss their findings, compare and review concepts learned, and check to see if they met all the objectives. This gives the teacher insights into how well students are concentrating, how they communicate, how well they work together, organizing and presenting information.

Integrating Instruction and Assessment

When teacher observation is focused, it is as accurate as any formal test. By making inferences about individual and group performance the connection between instruction and assessment becomes more coherent. Do the individuals consistently work with others, try to assist others, become actively involved in the problem? Focused observation also zeros in on students' ideas. Are they able to explain their ideas, support their arguments, give evidence, consider the ideas of their peers? How do students verbalize in the group? Do the students talk for self-clarification, are they good listeners? Cooperation also enters into the attuned observer. How did the group divide the tasks, agree on a plan, provide support for each member?

When assessing understanding, the teacher is trying to get a picture of the student's own thinking rather than whether the student can provide the "correct" answer. It is important to find out how students are making sense of their work. Interviewing students (assessment questioning) can be brief and informal as in many typical classroom interactions between teacher and students. The logistics of time, people, and curriculum mean planning is necessary for interviews. The interviewer must find a level of understanding at which the student is comfortable. It is generally better to start asking broad general questions rather than specific narrow ones. Follow-up questions should gradually become more specific as the teacher tries to center in on what makes sense to the students.

There is general agreement that cooperative group activity can support learning. But in spite of the attention given to individual accountability, collaborative work can make the measurement of individual work more difficult. The key to having new methods of assessment work well is the informed involvement of teachers. To integrate instruction and assessment effectively means relying on the professional judgment of teachers and giving them the leeway to track progress over time. It helps when teachers have an informal peer review process where they can share approaches and compare how they connect assessment with subject matter standards. As teachers share portfolio and related performance assessment techniques with colleagues, it can change how they think about teaching and how they structure lessons for their students.

In the end these directions are not as complex as they appear. They call on us all to act. In doing so, we make assessment a more powerful educational tool and return credibility to school practice. Most importantly, we improve the quality of student learning.

— Vito Perrone

"Would you please tell me which way I ought to go from here?"

"That depends a good deal on where you want to get to." said the Cat.

"I don't much care where," said Alice.

"Then it doesn't matter which way you go," said the Cat.

"So long as I get somewhere," Alice added.

"Oh, you're sure sure to do that," said the Cat, "if you only walk long enough."

Alice in Wonderland

REFERENCES

Farr, R. (1990). Trends, setting directions for language arts portfolios, *Educational Leadership, 48*(3), 103.

Gardner, H. (1987). Beyond IQ: Education and human development. *Harvard Educational Review* 57, 2: 187–93.

Graves, D. (1983). *Writing: Teachers and children at work.* Portsmouth, NH: Heinemann.

Graves, D. & Sunstein, B. (Eds.). (1992). *Portfolio diversity in action.* Portsmouth, NH: Heinemann.

Mitchell, R. (1989). Portfolio newsletter of *Arts PROPEL.* Cambridge, MA: Harvard University Press.

Mitchell, R. (1991). *Testing for learning: How new approaches to evaluation can improve American schools.* New York: The Free Press.

Mumme, J. (1990). *Portfolio assessment in mathematics.* California Mathematics Project, University of California, Santa Barbara.

Perrone, V. (1991). *Expanding student assessment.* Alexandria, VA: Association for Supervision and Curriculum Development.

Schrag, F. (1988). *Thinking in school and society.* New York: Routledge.

Stenmark, J. (1987). *Assessment alternatives in mathematics.* Berkeley, CA: University of California (EQUALS).

AUTHOR INDEX

SUBJECT INDEX